I0820171

Southern Living®

2025 Annual Recipes

SLOW-COOKER BARBECUE SPARERIBS (PAGE 187)

BLUEBERRY-GINGER OLIVE OIL CAKE (PAGE 109)

CHERRY-PISTACHIO OLIVE OIL CAKE (PAGE 109)

FRIED SQUASH WITH CREAMY HERB DIPPING SAUCE (PAGE 159)

TRIX NO-CHURN
ICE CREAM
(PAGE 21)

LOWCOUNTRY PERLOO WITH SHORT RIBS, SHRIMP, AND OYSTERS (PAGE 208)

CAJUN TURKEY
(PAGE 243)

Recipes at the Ready

Dear Friends,

In the March issue of this year's *Southern Living*, I wrote about how my definition of self-care includes having at least part of a weeknight dinner prepped and ready to go. In this case, it was a big-batch recipe for Easy Slow-Cooker Pulled Pork (page 50) that can be enjoyed as-is with a side dish or turned into three different meals: a pork and rice bowl, a Cuban sandwich, or a quick ragù for pasta.

If you're also always on the hunt for easy dinner options, we have plenty of meals that come together quickly but don't compromise on flavor. Stir up a 30-minute pasta such as Bacon Lover's Cacio e Pepe (page 52) or Southern-Style Baked Tortellini (page 56). Or try our Blackened-Shrimp Tacos with Shortcut Slaw (page 104).

Our food team works hard to create recipes that give you bang for your buck. Not only should the dishes in the pages of our magazine look and taste great, we want them to turn out perfectly every time and inspire you to put your own spin on things. Our Piece of Cake column features one easy dessert idea like Lemon Buttermilk Cake (page 83) or Croissant Bread Pudding (page 35) that you can change up several ways with different flavor profiles or stir-ins.

Like any region of the country, we love to celebrate seasonal produce and dream up new ways to enjoy fresh fruits and vegetables. In spring, explore the colorful possibilities of carrots with Fast and Fancy Carrot Ribbon Salad (page 48) or Pepper Jelly-Glazed Carrots (page 48). Enjoy the late summer sweet-corn season with Mexican Street Corn Pasta Salad (page 147). And when cooler weather arrives, warm up with a hearty bowl of Lowcountry Perloo with Short Ribs, Shrimp, and Oysters (page 208).

Southerners are a social bunch, so you'll also find recipes for gatherings of all kinds. Celebrate Easter with an elegant menu featuring lamb chops, salmon, or hot honey chicken paired with bright and fresh side dishes. Or invite everyone over to watch the big game with Sausage Kolaches (page 193) and spicy, cheesy Touchdown Dip (page 196).

Whether you're looking for a simple soup or pasta for a cozy night in, or a decadent dessert that's designed to impress, you'll find exactly what you need—when you need it—in these pages. Happy cooking!

Lisa Cericola
Deputy Food Editor
Southern Living magazine

Contents

Top-Rated Recipes

We cook, we taste, we refine, we rate—and at the end of each year, our Test Kitchen shares the highest-rated recipes from each issue exclusively with *Southern Living Annual Recipes* readers.

January–February

- **Smoked Cream Cheese with Pepper Jelly** (page 15) Smoking a block of cream cheese and glazing it with sweet and spicy pepper jelly adds a whole new dimension to this traditional appetizer.
- **Cinnamon Toast Crunch Pie** (page 20) Cereal in a pie? Yep, we did it. A nostalgic breakfast-food favorite is the heart of this simple no-bake custard pie with a cinnamon-toast crust.
- **Reverse-Seared Steaks** (page 30) Gently cooking a steak in the oven then searing it in a super-hot skillet creates a delicious caramelized crust and yields a tender, juicy, restaurant-worthy steak every time.
- **Sweet Potato Skillet Biscuits** (page 32) Mashed sweet potato adds moistness, flavor, and a golden hue to these pecan-studded, powdered sugar icing-glazed biscuits spiked with a pinch of cayenne. They're perfect on their own with a cup of coffee—or served alongside bacon and eggs for a hearty stick-to-your-ribs breakfast.
- **Charcuterie Sheet Pan Pizza** (page 36) We piled briny olives, fancy cheeses, and tasty cured meats—even buttery, crunchy Marcona almonds—onto purchased pizza dough for a new spin on two party favorites.
- **Parmesan-Ranch Chicken Wings** (page 38) We firmly believe that everything tastes better served with ranch, and these wings are no exception. But instead of dipping them in dressing, we added savory ranch seasoning to the buttery, garlicky tossin' sauce.

March

- **Fast and Fancy Carrot Ribbon Salad** (page 48) The name says it all! This colorful side is fast and easy but packs a visual punch. Use colorful rainbow carrots for a real wow factor.

CHARCUTERIE SHEET PAN PIZZA

- **Easy Slow-Cooker Pulled Pork** (page 50) Get a jump start on your weekly meal planning with this super-simple recipe that can be made on a Sunday while you're doing other things. It keeps in the fridge all week and is great on its own or in a rice bowl, sandwich, or pasta sauce.
- **Bacon Lover's Cacio e Pepe** (page 52) Cacio e pepe means "cheese and pepper" in Italian, and this dish has generous amounts of both. We took it up a notch by adding bacon for a Southern twist on a classic Roman-style pasta.
- **Pimm's Cup Punch** (page 57) This classic and refreshing gin punch originated in Britain but made its way to New Orleans. We love it with a bunch of colorful garnishes that also add flavor: orange slices, cucumber, strawberries, and mint.
- **Dutch Oven Cinnamon-Raisin Bread** (page 61) This no-intimidation, no-knead yeast bread is baked in a Dutch oven, creating a beautifully browned and crisp crust. It's so satisfying to pull a hot loaf of fresh bread from the oven—and even better to enjoy a warm slice slathered with butter. (This one's also a natural for breakfast, toasted.)

April

- **Blueberry-Croissant Breakfast Bake** (page 67) Flaky, buttery croissants layered with sweet blueberries in a rich egg-and-cream cheese custard are baked to golden perfection in this warm, comforting dish that blends a touch of elegance with homestyle sweetness in every irresistible bite.
- **Southern Shrimp Cocktail** (page 69) Louisiana seafood is a Southern standby. Enjoy succulent chilled Gulf-Coast shrimp paired with a classic

LEMON BUTTERMILK CAKE

Horseradish Rémoulade and/or a Vietnamese-Style Cocktail Sauce spiked with fish sauce, lime, and chile paste.

- **Stuffed Pork Loin with Bacon and Greens** (page 79) Perfect for any special occasion, this mustard-glazed pork loin stuffed with bacon, mustard greens, sun-dried tomatoes, and breadcrumbs is guaranteed to be the star of the show.
- **Margaret Bragg's Fried Chicken** (page 80) When legendary writer Rick Bragg was 6, his grandmother, Ava, made him fried chicken Saturday mornings when his mother was at work. This version with a light, barely-there crust comes from his mother, Margaret. It's as close to that chicken of his childhood as you can get.
- **Lemon Buttermilk Cake** (page 83) Every bite of this moist, citrus-infused, cream cheese frosting-topped cake is a taste of sunshine. It's a simple one-pan treat that's perfect for any occasion.

May

- **Mini Pimiento Cheese Balls** (page 88) This retro appetizer is making a comeback—this time not in one big ball but in several smaller ones that can be rolled in a variety of coatings.
- **Strawberry-Lemon Pound Cake** (page 96) Freeze-dried strawberries are the secret ingredient in this pretty-in-pink cake. They provide intense strawberry flavor to both the cake and glaze, and a crunchy topping too!
- **Farm Stand Pasta Salad** (page 104) Tote this fresh-herb-and-veggie-packed salad to the first picnic potluck of the season and you're sure to bring home an empty bowl.
- **Picnic Dip** (page 110) Stir together a few convenience products to make this savory summer staple. Serve with chips and crunchy crudités.

June–July

- **Honey-Glazed Grilled Nectarines** (page 114) These in-season stone-fruit beauties are simple—and simply stunning. Serve warm with a scoop of vanilla ice cream for the perfect summer dessert.
- **Creamed-Corn Hush Puppies** (page 123) These tiny treats are creamy on the inside and delightfully crispy on the outside. Creamed corn (and Southern charm) are the secret ingredients.
- **Peach Pound Cake** (page 131) It's peach season, y'all! Don't let it pass without making this buttery pound cake made moist with sour cream.
- **No-Bake Chocolate Pie** (page 133) Stay cool with this rich, chocolatey 5-ingredient ganache-filled pie.
- **Grilled Deviled Eggs** (page 137) Even a brief stint on the grill infuses these classic potluck favorites with a hint of smoky flavor. A pickled onion garnish makes a nice contrast to the creamy richness of the filling.

August

- **Mexican Street Corn Pasta Salad** (page 147) This sweet and savory side has all of the smashing flavors of elotes—or Mexican street corn—in a scoopable salad.
- **Pepperoni Pizza with Basil Oil** (page 155) Slices of ripe, juicy summer tomato and a drizzle of aromatic herb oil shine in this crisp-crusted cast-iron pizza.
- **Heirloom Tomato-and-Mozzarella Salad** (page 158) Use a variety of different-color tomatoes to create a gorgeous, eye-catching salad platter. A drizzle of bright-green Basil Oil adds contrast and flavor.
- **Chocolate Chip Ice-Cream Sandwiches** (page 161) Homemade chocolate chip cookies take this freezer-ready summer treat over the top. Try the Birthday Cake Ice-Cream Sandwiches and Butter-Pecan Ice-Cream Sandwiches variations too.

September

- **Coconut-Pecan Breakfast Cookies** (page 169) Breakfast on the go has never tasted so good. Try the Peanut Butter Breakfast Cookies and Apple-Spice Breakfast Cookies options too.
- **Ultimate Caramel Frosting** (page 182) Our version of the South's most finicky frosting is laid out step-by-step for success every time.
- **Sausage Kolaches** (page 193) This Czech pastry ups the ante on pigs in a blanket—given a Southern twist with Conecuh sausage.
- **Pumpkin Spice Texas Sheet Cake** (page 198) Welcome the arrival of fall with this moist, sweetly spiced, fudge icing-topped twist on a Texas classic. Our seasonal spin just might be better than the original.

HEIRLOOM TOMATO-AND-MOZZARELLA SALAD

SOUTHERN SEVEN-LAYER DIP

October

- **Stuffed Delicata Squash** (page 203) A side of stuffed squash is a snap when it's sweet, nutty-flavored, tender-skinned delicata that doesn't require peeling.
- **Herby Cloverleaf Rolls** (page 211) A secret ingredient (OK, it's beer) gives these rolls that start with a hot roll mix yeasty, homemade flavor.
- **Southern Seven-Layer Dip** (page 221) You'll love every luscious layer of this popular party dip. We added a few special ingredients to make it our own so it really stands apart from the other layered dips.
- **Beer-Braised Pot Roast** (page 226) You only need 20 minutes of prep time and your slow cooker does the rest. We love this served over a bed of mashed potatoes, but it's also great with noodles or bread.
- **Brown Butter-Chocolate Chunk Skillet Cookie** (page 233) Baking this big, beautiful, shareable cookie in a cast-iron skillet gives it a crunchy exterior and a soft, chewy interior. When the occasion calls for a simple dessert, look no further!

November

- **Sweet Potato Gnocchi** (page 237) These tender pasta pillows made with sweet potatoes and ricotta are tossed in a sage-infused browned butter for serving. It's a classic fall recipe and easy to double if you're feeding a crowd.
- **Quiche Lorraine** (page 241) This timeless recipe is perfect for brunch, lunch, or any occasion that calls for something elegant and classic.
- **Cajun Turkey** (page 243) Nothing beats leftovers from a Cajun-spiced turkey. Use every last bite (and bone!) for a rich and flavorful stock for soup or gumbo.
- **Texas Cornbread Dressing** (page 252) This recipe was dubbed "the ultimate" dressing by our Test Kitchen staff back in 1975, and it still holds true to this day.
- **Cranberry-Key Lime Pie** (page 264) Up your pie game this Thanksgiving! Enjoy a slice of sunshine with every bite of this gorgeous dessert that combines two classic flavors.

December

- **"The Cake"** (page 275) This cherished family recipe for an apple-and-spice cake has a secret ingredient (we love secrets, especially at Christmastime!): mayonnaise—and not just any mayonnaise. It must be Hellmann's. It doesn't flavor the cake, but gives it an amazingly tender, moist crumb.
- **Southern-Style Beef Wellington** (page 285) This supremely elegant and classic dish is perfect for a holiday feast. Our take has a distinctively Southern twist: a layer of garlicky mustard greens in and amongst the beef, prosciutto, and pastry. Outstanding!
- **Classic Truffles** (page 306) We love a traditional truffle—and we've got that covered here—but we've also thrown in a dozen variations, including Mexican Hot Chocolate, Milk Punch (that uses white chocolate chips instead of dark), and Pistachio Chai. Make one kind or a pick-a-mix box as a gift.
- **Lowcountry Breakfast Casserole** (page 316) With a buttermilk-scallion biscuit base, an Old Bay-spiced gravy, sausage, potatoes, shrimp, and crab, this outstanding dish from chef Carla Hall is no ordinary strata. Rich and very special, it's perfect for a Christmas-morning brunch.

January–February

BOUNTY

Radiant Radicchio

This colorful cold-weather vegetable brings bold, peppery flavor to the table.

White Bean-and-Radicchio Soup

ACTIVE 20 MIN. - TOTAL 30 MIN.

SERVES 6

Cook 4 oz. diced **pancetta** in a Dutch oven over medium, stirring often, until crisp, about 7 minutes. Transfer to a plate; reserve drippings in Dutch oven. Add 2 Tbsp. **extra-virgin olive oil;** 1¼ cups chopped **yellow onion;** and 1 cup peeled, sliced **carrots** to Dutch oven. Cook, stirring occasionally, until softened, about 5 minutes. Stir in 1½ Tbsp. minced **garlic,** 2 tsp. chopped **fresh rosemary,** and ½ tsp. **crushed red pepper;** cook, stirring constantly, until fragrant, 1 to 2 minutes. Stir in 4 cups **chicken broth,** ½ tsp. **kosher salt,** and ¼ tsp. **black pepper;** bring to a boil over medium-high. Reduce heat to medium-low, and simmer until starting to thicken slightly, about 5 minutes. Stir in 2 (15-oz.) cans **cannellini beans** (drained and rinsed) and 3 cups coarsely chopped **radicchio,** and return to a boil over medium-high. Reduce heat to medium-low, and simmer until tender, about 5 minutes. Ladle into bowls, and drizzle evenly with ¼ cup **prepared pesto;** sprinkle with shaved **Parmesan cheese** and reserved pancetta. Serve soup with **lemon wedges.**

SNACK TIME

Block Party

A family-favorite appetizer gets a smokin' upgrade.

Smoked Cream Cheese with Pepper Jelly

ACTIVE 20 MIN. - TOTAL 2 HOURS, 40 MIN.

SERVES 8

- 1 tsp. light brown sugar
- 3/4 tsp. garlic powder
- 3/4 tsp. paprika
- 1/2 tsp. dry mustard
- 1/2 tsp. crushed red pepper
- 1/4 tsp. black pepper
- 2 tsp. olive oil, divided
- 1 (8-oz.) pkg. cream cheese
- 1 Tbsp. red pepper jelly (such as Stonewall Kitchen)
- 1 tsp. chopped fresh chives
- Assorted crackers

1. Prepare a smoker according to the manufacturer's instructions, bringing internal temperature to 215°F to 225°F. Maintain the temperature inside smoker until the smoke is burning cleanly, 15 to 20 minutes.

2. Meanwhile, stir together brown sugar, garlic powder, paprika, dry mustard, crushed red pepper, and black pepper in a small bowl. Brush the bottom of an 8-inch cast-iron skillet with 1 teaspoon oil. Brush remaining 1 teaspoon oil over block of cream cheese. Coat cream cheese in spice mixture.

3. Using a knife, score the cream cheese in a ½-inch-deep crosshatch pattern. Place in prepared skillet, scored side up.

4. Place skillet on grates of smoker, and close lid. Smoke, undisturbed, maintaining temperature at 225°F, until cream cheese is golden, about 2 hours. Let cool slightly, about 5 minutes.

5. Microwave pepper jelly in a small microwavable bowl on HIGH until loosened, about 10 seconds. Drizzle over cream cheese; sprinkle with chives. Serve warm with crackers.

Cereal-ously Sweet

Beloved breakfast staples star in fun and colorful desserts.

CINNAMON TOAST CRUNCH PIE (PAGE 20)

FROOT LOOPS
CONFETTI BUNDT
(PAGE 20)

COCOA PUFFS BARS (PAGE 20)

FRUITY PEBBLES COOKIES (PAGE 20)

Cinnamon Toast Crunch Pie

(Photo, page 16)

ACTIVE 30 MIN. - TOTAL 50 MIN., PLUS 4 HOURS CHILLING

SERVES 8

- 3 cups whole milk
- 3 cups finely crushed Cinnamon Toast Crunch cereal (from about 5 cups cereal), divided, plus more for garnish
- 2 Tbsp. light brown sugar
- 1/2 tsp. ground cinnamon
- 1/2 cup butter, melted
- 1/2 cup granulated sugar
- 1 (3-inch) cinnamon stick
- 4 large egg yolks
- 1/4 cup cornstarch
- 3 Tbsp. cold butter, cubed
- 1 tsp. vanilla extract
- 1 cup whipped cream

1. Stir together milk and 1 cup crushed cereal in a large bowl. Let stand at room temperature 30 minutes.
2. Meanwhile, stir together brown sugar, ground cinnamon, and remaining 2 cups crushed cereal in a large bowl. Stir in melted butter, and toss evenly to coat. Press mixture into bottom and up sides of a 9-inch pie plate coated with cooking spray. Freeze until crust is firm, about 15 minutes.
3. Strain cereal-milk mixture into a medium saucepan; discard solids. Add granulated sugar and cinnamon stick to saucepan; cook over medium, stirring occasionally, until mixture simmers and sugar has dissolved, about 2 minutes. Meanwhile, whisk together egg yolks and cornstarch in a large heatproof bowl until smooth.
4. Using a ladle, gradually pour about 1 cup of the hot milk mixture into the egg yolk mixture, whisking constantly. Pour mixture back into saucepan. Cook over medium, whisking constantly, until mixture begins to boil. Continue cooking, whisking constantly, until consistency resembles thick pudding, about 30 seconds. Remove from heat, and stir in cold butter and vanilla extract. Strain into prepared piecrust; discard solids. Cover with plastic wrap pressed directly onto surface of pie. Chill until set, about 4 hours.
5. Top pie with whipped cream and additional cereal before serving.

Froot Loops Confetti Bundt

(Photo, page 17)

ACTIVE 20 MIN. - TOTAL 2 HOURS, 45 MIN., PLUS 1 HOUR COOLING

SERVES 12

BUNDT

- Baking spray
- 2 1/2 cups all-purpose flour
- 1/4 tsp. baking soda
- 2 1/2 cups granulated sugar
- 1 1/4 cups butter, at room temperature
- 2 tsp. grated lemon zest (from 1 lemon)
- 5 large eggs, at room temperature
- 2 tsp. vanilla extract
- 3/4 cup plain whole-milk strained (Greek-style) yogurt, at room temperature
- 1 1/4 cups coarsely crushed Froot Loops cereal (from about 2 cups cereal)

GLAZE

- 1/4 cup whole milk
- 1/4 cup Froot Loops cereal, plus more for garnish
- 2 1/2 cups sifted powdered sugar
- 1 tsp. vanilla extract

1. Prepare the Bundt: Preheat oven to 325°F. Coat a 10- to 12-cup Bundt pan with baking spray. Whisk together flour and baking soda in a medium bowl. Set aside.
2. Beat sugar, butter, and zest in a large bowl with an electric mixer on medium speed until light and fluffy, about 3 minutes. Add eggs, 1 at a time, followed by vanilla, beating until just combined, about 10 seconds per addition.
3. Reduce mixer speed to low. Beat flour mixture into egg mixture alternately with yogurt, beating until just combined after each addition, about 1 minute total. Using a spatula, fold in crushed cereal.
4. Pour batter into prepared pan. Bake in preheated oven until a wooden pick inserted into center of cake comes out clean, 1 hour to 1 hour and 5 minutes. Remove from oven, and let cool in pan 20 minutes. Invert cake onto a wire rack; let cool completely, about 1 hour.
5. Prepare the Glaze: Stir together milk and cereal in a medium bowl; let stand 30 minutes. Pour through a fine mesh strainer into a separate medium bowl, and discard solids. Gradually whisk in powdered sugar and vanilla until smooth.
6. Pour Glaze over Bundt. Garnish with additional cereal. Let set for 30 minutes before serving.

Fruity Pebbles Cookies

(Photo, page 19)

ACTIVE 30 MIN. - TOTAL 1 HOUR, 20 MIN.

MAKES 30 COOKIES

- 1 1/2 cups granulated sugar
- 1 cup butter, at room temperature
- 2 large eggs, at room temperature
- 1 tsp. vanilla extract
- 1/2 tsp. baking soda
- 3 cups all-purpose flour
- 1 cup Fruity Pebbles cereal, plus more for rolling dough

1. Preheat oven to 325°F with racks in upper third and lower third positions. Line 3 large baking sheets with parchment paper, and set aside. Beat granulated sugar and butter in a large bowl with an electric mixer on medium speed until light and fluffy, about 3 minutes. Add eggs, 1 at a time, beating until just incorporated after each addition, stopping to scrape down sides of bowl as needed. Beat in vanilla and baking soda until incorporated. Beat in flour until just combined. Using a spatula, fold in cereal.
2. Using a 2-tablespoon cookie scoop, portion dough into 30 balls. Place some additional cereal in a shallow bowl; roll each ball in cereal to coat. Arrange about 1 inch apart on prepared baking sheets; lightly pat to flatten slightly.
3. Place 2 of the baking sheets in preheated oven, and bake until bottoms are light golden brown, 13 to 15 minutes, rotating baking sheets between top and bottom racks halfway through baking. Remove from oven. Let cookies cool on baking sheets 5 minutes. Repeat procedure with remaining dough; let cool. Store in an airtight container at room temperature up to 5 days.

Cocoa Puffs Bars

(Photo, page 18)

ACTIVE 20 MIN. - TOTAL 50 MIN.

MAKES 16 BARS

- 1/2 cup butter
- 1 (10-oz.) pkg. miniature marshmallows
- 1/2 cup semisweet chocolate chips
- 6 cups Cocoa Puffs cereal (from 1 [12-oz.] pkg.)
- 1/2 tsp. flaky sea salt (optional)

1. Coat an 8-inch square baking pan with cooking spray; line pan with parchment paper, leaving a 2-inch overhang on all sides. Coat parchment with cooking spray. Set aside.
2. Melt butter in a large pot over medium-high. Continue to cook melted butter until browned, 5 to 6 minutes. Add miniature marshmallows; cook, stirring constantly, until almost entirely melted, about 1 minute. Remove from heat. Using a rubber spatula, fold in chocolate chips; stir mixture until smooth, about 1 minute. Fold in cereal until evenly coated.
3. Pour cereal mixture into prepared pan. Lightly coat a sheet of parchment paper with cooking spray, and place, greased side down, on top of cereal mixture. Press lightly to compact the cereal mixture into an even layer. Remove and discard top piece of parchment. If desired, sprinkle top of cereal mixture with flaky sea salt.
4. Let stand until firm, about 30 minutes. Remove from pan using parchment as handles. Using a serrated knife, slice into 16 bars. Store in an airtight container at room temperature up to 5 days.

Trix No-Churn Ice Cream

(Photo, page 4)

ACTIVE 10 MIN. · TOTAL 10 MIN., PLUS 6 HOURS FREEZING

SERVES 8

- **1 (14-oz.) can sweetened condensed milk**
- **1 tsp. vanilla extract**
- **½ tsp. kosher salt**
- **2 cups cold heavy whipping cream**
- **2 cups Trix cereal, divided**

1. Stir together condensed milk, vanilla extract, and kosher salt in a large bowl, and set aside.
2. Place heavy whipping cream in a large bowl, and beat with an electric mixer on low speed until thick and foamy, about 1 minute. Increase mixer speed to medium-high, and beat until stiff peaks form, about 15 seconds.
3. Using a spatula, fold whipped cream into condensed milk mixture in 3 additions. Fold in 1½ cups of the cereal. Pour mixture into an ungreased 9 x 5-inch loaf pan. Sprinkle top with remaining ½ cup cereal. Cover and freeze until firm, at least 6 hours or up to 12 hours. Cover tightly with plastic wrap, and store in freezer up to 3 months.

GET THE SCOOP!
Swap an equal amount of your favorite cereal for the Trix to create new ice cream flavors. Here are three to get you started.

Soups for the Soul

Cookbook author Yvette Zuniga Jemison's "Mex-Tex" recipes will warm you to the bone.

IF THE TERM "TEX-MEX" conjures up images of platters of sizzling fajitas at your favorite cantina, you're not alone. But South Texas–born food writer and photographer Yvette Zuniga Jemison (shown above) says there's a bigger story behind those familiar menu items. "There are huge, heated discussions about Tex-Mex and Mexican foods not being the same," she says. "True Tex-Mex cuisine comes from people of Mexican descent using American products and incorporating them with old-world Mexican techniques. We should be calling it Mex-Tex."

Growing up in the border town of Pharr, Texas, Jemison was raised to appreciate making meals as a collaborative, communal practice. "I was always in the kitchen with my grandmothers and mother," she says. "Cooking has always been part of our lives. It's not, 'Are you going to cook or not?' Everyone's involved in some way." In addition to sharing recipes via her award-winning cookbook, *My South Texas Kitchen*, she teaches classes to introduce people to dishes such as *sopa de fideo* (soup with short, vermicelli-style noodles) and *albóndigas de camarón* (tender shrimp meatballs simmered in a thick, tomato-based stew). "I love seeing the excitement when they discover something so new and different," Jemison says.

Frijoles de la Olla

"This South Texas staple can be prepared in various cooking vessels, from an olla de barro *(clay pot), like the ones that my grandmothers used, to the slow cooker my mother has," says Jemison, who prefers a pressure cooker because it's faster.*

ACTIVE 45 MIN. - TOTAL 2 HOURS, 15 MIN.

SERVES 8

- 4 bacon slices, chopped
- 1 yellow onion, sliced
- 1 lb. dried pinto beans, rinsed
- 2 Tbsp. olive oil
- 2 Tbsp. chili powder
- 1 Tbsp. minced garlic
- 2 tsp. kosher salt
- 1 tsp. ground cumin
- 1 tsp. black pepper
- 1 cup chopped fresh cilantro, divided
- Avocado slices, pico de gallo, and radish slices

1. Select SAUTÉ setting on a programmable pressure multicooker, such as Instant Pot (times, instructions, and settings may vary among brands or models). Let preheat 2 minutes. Add bacon; cook, stirring occasionally, until fat is rendered, about 10 minutes. Add onion; cook, stirring occasionally, until softened, about 6 minutes. Press CANCEL.

2. Add 6 cups water, beans, olive oil, chili powder, garlic, salt, cumin, pepper, and half of the cilantro to cooker; stir to combine.

3. Cover cooker with lid; lock in place. Turn steam release handle to SEALING position. Select HIGH setting for 1 hour and 15 minutes. Let pressure release naturally for 30 minutes. Carefully turn steam release handle to VENTING position, and let steam fully escape (the float valve will drop).

4. Remove lid from cooker, and stir in remaining cilantro. Serve topped with avocado slices, pico de gallo, and radish slices.

Sopa de Lentejas

(Photo, page 24)

Folks across the globe lean on lentils to add heartiness to soups and stews. Here, the combination of bacon, cumin, and chili powder perks up the earthy legumes with smoky, savory flavor.

ACTIVE 30 MIN. - TOTAL 1 HOUR, 15 MIN.

SERVES 8

- 1½ lb. bacon, chopped (4 cups)
- 2 cups chopped plum tomatoes (3 large)
- 1 cup sliced green onions, plus more for garnish
- 2½ cups (16 oz.) dried brown lentils
- 2 Tbsp. chicken bouillon granules
- 2 tsp. ground cumin
- 2 Tbsp. chili powder
- 1 tsp. black pepper

1. Cook bacon in a stockpot over medium-high, stirring occasionally, until crispy, about 18 minutes. Add tomatoes and green onions; cook, stirring often, until tender, about 2 minutes. Stir in lentils, bouillon granules, cumin, chili powder, and pepper.

2. Stir in 10 cups water; bring to a boil over high. Immediately reduce heat to medium-low; cover and simmer until lentils are tender, about 25 minutes. Turn off heat; let soup stand, covered, for 15 minutes.

FRIJOLES
DE LA OLLA

SOPA DE LENTEJAS
(PAGE 22)

ALBÓNDIGAS DE CAMARÓN
(PAGE 27)

SOPA DE FIDEO

Sopa de Fideo

"The aroma of garlic and cumin in a tomato broth immediately transports me to my grandmother's kitchen," Jemison says. "This easy-to-prepare sopa is filled with beef and noodles (fideo) and is sure to warm you on a chilly day."

ACTIVE 25 MIN. - TOTAL 45 MIN.

SERVES 8

- 3 Tbsp. olive oil
- 1 (7-oz.) pkg. fideo noodles (broken, if in nests)
- 1 lb. 80/20 ground beef
- 1 russet potato, scrubbed and diced (2½ cups)
- 1 cup finely chopped yellow onion (from 1 small onion)
- ¾ cup sliced green bell pepper (from 1 small bell pepper)
- 1 (15-oz.) can tomato sauce
- ½ cup chopped fresh cilantro, plus more for garnish
- 4 garlic cloves, minced (1 Tbsp.)
- 3 Tbsp. chicken bouillon granules
- 1 tsp. ground cumin
- ½ tsp. black pepper
- 8 cups hot water

1. Heat oil in a large Dutch oven over medium-high. Add fideo noodles; cook, stirring often, until noodles are toasted, about 5 minutes. Transfer to a large bowl until ready to use.
2. Return Dutch oven to medium-high; add ground beef, and cook, stirring often, until browned, about 7 minutes. Add potato, onion, and bell pepper; cook, stirring constantly, until softened, 2 to 3 minutes.
3. Add tomato sauce, cilantro, garlic, bouillon granules, cumin, and black pepper; stir to combine. Add hot water; increase heat to high, and bring to a boil. Add toasted noodles, and return to a boil. Reduce heat to medium-low; cover and simmer, stirring occasionally, until noodles and potato are tender, about 15 minutes. Garnish with more cilantro.

Albóndigas de Camarón

(Photo, page 25)

Spanish for "shrimp meatballs," this stew has the consistency of a thick tomato soup courtesy of the sautéed tomato, onion, and celery that are pureed and combined with masa harina (dried corn flour). Unlike beef meatballs, these shrimp-based ones have a light, tender texture that complements the fortified broth.

ACTIVE 40 MIN. - TOTAL 55 MIN.

SERVES 6

ALBÓNDIGAS

- 2 green onions, cut in half crosswise
- 1 plum tomato, cut in half crosswise
- 2 garlic cloves
- 1 lb. medium-size peeled and deveined raw shrimp
- 1 large egg
- 1 tsp. chicken bouillon granules
- 1 tsp. dried oregano
- ¼ tsp. kosher salt
- ¼ tsp. black pepper
- ½ cup masa harina

SOUP

- 2 Tbsp. olive oil, plus more for oiling hands
- 3 cups chopped plum tomatoes (about 5 medium)
- 1 cup coarsely chopped white onion (from 1 small onion)
- 1 cup sliced celery (from 2 large stalks)
- ¼ cup masa harina
- 1 Tbsp. chicken bouillon granules
- 2 tsp. chili powder
- 2 tsp. dried oregano
- 1 tsp. kosher salt
- ½ tsp. black pepper
- 3 cups hot cooked rice
- Sliced green onion

1. Prepare the Albóndigas: Pulse green onions, tomato and garlic in a food processor until finely chopped but not pureed. Add shrimp to vegetables, and pulse until shrimp are finely chopped. Transfer shrimp mixture to a medium bowl; stir in egg, bouillon granules, oregano, salt, and pepper until combined. Add masa harina, and stir until a sticky dough forms.
2. Using lightly oiled hands, scoop shrimp mixture, 1 tablespoon at a time, and shape into balls; place on a small rimmed baking sheet. Cover with plastic wrap, and chill until ready to cook.
3. Prepare the Soup: Heat oil in a medium saucepan over medium-high. Add the tomatoes, onion, and celery; cook, stirring often, until tomatoes and onion are softened, about 10 minutes.
4. Transfer vegetables to food processor. Process until pureed and smooth. Return pureed vegetables to same saucepan; stir in 3 cups water, masa harina, bouillon granules, chili powder, oregano salt, and pepper. Bring Soup to a boil over medium-high; immediately reduce heat to medium-low and simmer. Carefully submerge Albóndigas into Soup. Cover saucepan, and simmer until Albóndigas are cooked through, about 15 minutes. Serve over hot cooked rice, and garnish with green onion.

Dinner for Two

The way to their heart? Any of these simple recipes.

Bronzed Redfish with Smoky Cheese Grits

ACTIVE 20 MIN. - TOTAL 20 MIN.

SERVES 2

- 6 Tbsp. unsalted butter, divided
- 1½ tsp. kosher salt, divided
- ⅔ cup uncooked yellow grits (not stone-ground)
- ⅔ cup half-and-half
- ½ cup shredded smoked Gruyère cheese (about 2 oz.)
- ¾ tsp. Cajun seasoning
- ¾ tsp. dry mustard
- ½ tsp. smoked paprika
- ½ tsp. black pepper
- 2 (5-oz.) skinless redfish fillets (1 to 1¼ inches thick)
- Finely chopped fresh chives

1. Bring 2 cups water to a boil in a medium saucepan over high. Add 1 tablespoon butter and 1 teaspoon salt. Whisk in grits, and reduce heat to medium-low. Cook, whisking often, until creamy and tender, about 5 minutes. Whisk in half-and-half, Gruyère, and 2 tablespoons butter until combined. Remove from heat; cover to keep warm.

2. Stir together Cajun seasoning, mustard, paprika, pepper, and remaining ½ teaspoon salt in a small bowl. Sprinkle evenly over both sides of fish.

3. Melt remaining 3 tablespoons butter in a medium nonstick skillet over medium. Add fish. Cook, undisturbed, until browned on one side, about 4 minutes, and then turn it. Cook, spooning melted butter over fish, until fish is slightly firm and a thermometer inserted into thickest portion registers 135°F, 3 to 4 minutes.

4. Divide warm grits between 2 shallow bowls or plates. Top each with 1 fish fillet, and spoon butter from skillet over fish, if desired. Sprinkle with chives just before serving.

Wine-Braised Chicken and Vegetables

ACTIVE 45 MIN. - TOTAL 1 HOUR, 40 MIN.

SERVES 2

- 3 thick-cut bacon slices, cut into 1-inch pieces
- 4 (8-oz.) bone-in, skin-on chicken thighs
- 1½ tsp. kosher salt, divided
- ½ tsp. black pepper
- ¼ cup bourbon
- 6 Tbsp. unsalted butter, divided
- 2 carrots, peeled and chopped (about 1 cup)
- 1 sweet onion, chopped (about 1⅔ cups)
- ½ lb. baby red potatoes, halved (about 1¼ cups)
- 2 Tbsp. all-purpose flour
- 2 cups dry white wine (such as Sauvignon Blanc or Pinot Grigio)
- 5 thyme sprigs, plus fresh thyme leaves for garnish
- 1½ cups chicken stock

1. Heat bacon in a large, deep, enamel-coated cast-iron skillet over medium. Cook, stirring occasionally, until crispy, about 8 minutes. Transfer bacon to a paper towel-lined plate. Discard drippings, or save for another use. Do not wipe skillet clean.

2. Reduce heat to medium-low. Pat chicken dry, and sprinkle with 1 teaspoon of the salt and pepper. Place chicken in skillet, skin side down. Cook, undisturbed, until skin is crispy and easily releases from pan, about 18 minutes, increasing heat to medium-high after first 10 minutes of cooking. Transfer to a plate.

3. Remove skillet from heat. Add bourbon; return to heat over medium. Cook, stirring to scrape up browned bits from bottom of pan, until bourbon is evaporated, about 1 minute. Add 3 tablespoons butter, carrots, onion, potatoes, and flour; cook, stirring constantly, 2 minutes. Add wine, thyme sprigs, and stock; bring to a boil over high. Nestle chicken into sauce, skin side up; reduce heat to medium-low. Simmer, uncovered, stirring occasionally, until chicken is cooked through and a thermometer inserted into thickest portion of chicken registers 170°F, about 30 minutes.

4. Transfer chicken to a clean plate. Increase heat to medium-high; cook, stirring often, until vegetables are tender and sauce has thickened slightly or is desired consistency, 5 to 10 minutes. Remove from heat; stir in remaining 3 tablespoons butter and ½ teaspoon salt. Remove thyme sprigs. Return chicken to pan; let stand 10 minutes. Garnish with thyme leaves and crumbled bacon.

Reverse-Seared Steaks

ACTIVE 10 MIN. - TOTAL 55 MIN.

SERVES 2

- 2 (1-lb.) beef strip steaks (about 1½ inches thick)
- 1½ tsp. kosher salt, divided
- 1 tsp. coarsely ground black pepper, divided
- 1½ Tbsp. canola oil
- ½ tsp. flaky salt, such as Maldon (optional)
- Steamed asparagus and Steakhouse Melting Potatoes (recipe right), for serving (optional)

1. Preheat oven to 250°F. Pat steaks dry with paper towels; sprinkle with ½ teaspoon each kosher salt and pepper. Place steaks on a rimmed baking sheet lined with a wire rack. Bake until a thermometer inserted into thickest portion of steaks registers 115°F for medium-rare or 125°F for medium, 30 to 40 minutes. (Temperature of steaks will rise after searing.) Remove steaks from oven, and set aside.

2. Heat oil in a large cast-iron skillet over high until hot. Sprinkle steaks with remaining 1 teaspoon kosher salt and ½ teaspoon pepper. Cook steaks, undisturbed, until deeply browned, about 1 minute per side. Using tongs, turn steaks to sear edges for a few seconds until browned. Remove from skillet; let stand 10 minutes. Cut steaks crosswise against the grain into ½-inch-thick slices; sprinkle with flaky salt, if desired. Serve with steamed asparagus and Steakhouse Melting Potatoes, if desired.

Steakhouse Melting Potatoes

ACTIVE 15 MIN. - TOTAL 45 MIN.

SERVES 2

Preheat oven to 475°F with a rimmed baking sheet on center rack. Stir together 4 **Yukon gold potatoes** (cut into ½-inch-thick slices), 3 Tbsp. melted **unsalted butter**, ½ tsp. **kosher salt**, and ½ tsp. **black pepper** in a bowl. Pour mixture onto preheated baking sheet; bake until browned on bottom, about 15 minutes. Turn potatoes, and bake until browned on both sides, about 15 minutes. Stir together ¾ cup warmed **chicken stock** and 2 Tbsp. melted **unsalted butter**; pour over potatoes, carefully tilting pan to coat. Reduce heat to 400°F; bake until stock is mostly absorbed, about 10 minutes. Garnish with finely chopped **fresh parsley**, if desired.

Shrimp Pasta with Sun-Dried Tomato Cream Sauce

ACTIVE 30 MIN. - TOTAL 40 MIN.

SERVES 2

- 6 oz. uncooked thin spaghetti
- ¼ cup chopped sun-dried tomatoes in oil, plus 3 Tbsp. oil from jar, divided
- 1 cup sliced fennel (from 1 small bulb), plus 2 tsp. fronds for garnish
- 1 Tbsp. minced garlic (from 2 garlic cloves)
- ¼ tsp. crushed red pepper
- ½ cup dry white wine
- ½ cup chicken stock
- 12 oz. large peeled and deveined raw shrimp, patted dry (tails removed)
- 1 tsp. kosher salt, plus more for pasta water
- ½ tsp. black pepper
- ⅓ cup heavy whipping cream
- 1 tsp. grated lemon zest, plus 2 Tbsp. juice (from 1 lemon), divided
- 2 Tbsp. chopped fresh basil, plus small basil leaves for garnish
- 5 Tbsp. grated Parmesan cheese, divided

1. Bring a large pot of salted water to a boil over high. Add pasta; cook until 1 minute short of al dente, about 5 minutes. Drain in a colander over a bowl, reserving 1 cup of the pasta water.
2. Meanwhile, heat sun-dried tomato oil in a large skillet over medium-high. Add fennel; cook, stirring occasionally, until lightly browned, 3 to 4 minutes. Add garlic and crushed red pepper; cook, stirring constantly, until fragrant, about 1 minute. Add wine, stock, shrimp, salt, black pepper, and sun-dried tomatoes; cook, stirring often, until shrimp are pink on both sides, about 4 minutes. Reduce heat to medium-low; add cream and lemon juice. Cook, stirring often, until slightly thickened, about 2 minutes.
3. Add pasta, ¼ cup reserved pasta water, basil, and ¼ cup Parmesan cheese; cook, stirring and tossing with tongs constantly, until pasta is coated, adding up to ⅓ cup more pasta water, as needed. Divide pasta mixture between 2 shallow bowls; top each with ½ tablespoon remaining Parmesan. Garnish with fennel fronds, basil leaves, and lemon zest just before serving.

Making Kitchen Magic

Georgia TikTok star Hannah Taylor cooks from the heart and never holds back.

WITH HER UNRULY MANE of curly hair, flour-dusted clothes, and South Georgia accent, Hannah Taylor is a hoot-and-a-half. Sharing recipes from her home with a colorful cast of family and pets in the background, LilyLouTay (as she's known on TikTok and Instagram) has captured the admiration of around 1.5 million followers from all over the world with her down-home dishes, casual measurements, and playful spirit.

"When I'm in the kitchen cooking, that's my time," she says. "In that moment, I feel like a queen. When I'm in my robe and I've got flour all over me and I'm jammin' out—that's when I feel invincible."

Taylor first made a name for herself when she baked bread from scratch and shared it on TikTok. Since then, followers have flooded her feed, praising her cakes, casseroles, pies, and buns.

"I love drawing outside the lines," she says. "Play with your food like a kid would—it don't matter if it's all over the floor. If I'm always gonna be in the kitchen, I might as well make it fun."

Sweet Potato Skillet Biscuits

As much as we love Taylor's loose hand with measuring ingredients, our Test Kitchen Professionals have provided precise instructions here for those who appreciate a little extra support when it comes to baking.

ACTIVE 15 MIN. - TOTAL 45 MIN.

MAKES 8

- 3 cups all-purpose flour
- ¼ cup packed light brown sugar
- 1 Tbsp. baking powder
- 1 Tbsp. ground cinnamon
- 1 tsp. kosher salt
- ½ tsp. baking soda
- ¼ tsp. cayenne pepper (plus an extra pinch "if ya sexy," as Taylor likes to say)
- ½ cup plus 2 Tbsp. cold unsalted butter, divided
- 1 cup cold buttermilk
- 1 cup cooled mashed sweet potatoes (from 2 sweet potatoes)
- ½ cup chopped pecans
- 1 cup powdered sugar
- 2-3 Tbsp. whole milk

1. Preheat oven to 400°F. Stir together flour, brown sugar, baking powder, cinnamon, salt, baking soda, and cayenne pepper in a large bowl until combined. Using 2 forks, cut in ½ cup of the cold butter until mixture is crumbly. Stir in buttermilk, mashed sweet potatoes, and chopped pecans until ingredients are well combined. (It'll be thick and doughy, according to Taylor.)
2. Using a half-cup measuring cup, drop biscuit dough into a large cast-iron skillet. Bake in preheated oven until lightly golden and cooked through, about 30 minutes.
3. While the biscuits bake, melt the remaining 2 tablespoons butter. Whisk it together with powdered sugar and 2 tablespoons milk in a small bowl until smooth. Whisk in remaining 1 tablespoon milk, if needed. Drizzle glaze over warm biscuits.

Breakfast for Dessert

Buttery croissants dress up classic bread pudding.

Croissant Bread Pudding

ACTIVE 30 MIN. - TOTAL 1 HOUR, 55 MIN.
SERVES 12

- 4 large eggs
- 3 cups half-and-half
- 1 cup granulated sugar
- 1/4 cup unsalted butter, melted, plus more for greasing dish
- 2 tsp. vanilla extract
- 1 tsp. ground cinnamon
- 1/2 tsp. kosher salt
- 8 plain croissants, split
- Powdered sugar
- Melted vanilla ice cream (optional), for serving

1. Whisk together eggs, half-and-half, granulated sugar, melted butter, vanilla, cinnamon, and salt in a large bowl until well combined.
2. Cut split croissants in half using a serrated knife; reserve tops. Cut croissant bottoms into 1- to 2-inch pieces to yield about 8 cups, and arrange in an even layer in a buttered 13 x 9-inch (3-quart) baking dish. Pour about half of egg mixture over croissant pieces. Dip croissant tops in remaining egg mixture until just soaked; arrange, cut sides down, in an even layer over croissant pieces in dish. Pour remaining egg mixture over top. Cover with aluminum foil, and let stand at room temperature for 30 minutes. Preheat oven to 350°F.
3. Bake, covered, for 45 minutes. Uncover and bake until top is golden brown and center is set, 10 to 15 minutes more. Dust with powdered sugar. Drizzle with melted ice cream before serving, if desired.

Chocolate Croissant Bread Pudding

Prepare recipe as directed through Step 1. In Step 2, substitute chocolate-filled croissants (cut into quarters) for the plain ones. Arrange croissant pieces in a buttered baking dish. Pour all of egg mixture over top, and sprinkle evenly with 1 cup semisweet chocolate chips. In Step 3, bake as directed; omit powdered sugar. Drizzle with melted ice cream before serving, if desired.

Almond-Raspberry Croissant Bread Pudding

In Step 1, reduce granulated sugar to 2/3 cup. In Step 2, substitute almond croissants (cut into 1- to 2-inch pieces) for the plain ones. Arrange croissant pieces in a buttered baking dish, and dollop 1 cup seedless raspberry preserves evenly over top. Pour all of egg mixture over top, and sprinkle with 1/2 cup sliced almonds. In Step 3, bake as directed; omit powdered sugar. Top with fresh raspberries; drizzle with melted ice cream before serving, if desired.

SHORTCUT SAUCE
Much easier than a custard, melted ice cream makes a delicious drizzle for bread pudding.

CROISSANT BREAD PUDDING

Let's Get Together

It's no secret that Southerners show their affection through food. This Valentine's Day, whether you're cooking for your sweetheart, family, or best friends, this fancy but not fussy spread will show them how much you care. The best part? These recipes are almost effortless—because cooks deserve some extra TLC too.

Charcuterie Sheet Pan Pizza

A big board packed with fancy cheeses, good olives, and cured meats is fun, so why not transform it into a meal? Pile it all on store-bought dough for a pizza they won't soon forget.

ACTIVE 15 MIN. - TOTAL 40 MIN.
SERVES 6

- 4 Tbsp. olive oil, divided
- All-purpose flour, for dusting surface
- 2 (1-lb.) pkg. refrigerated deli pizza dough, at room temperature
- 1 (9-oz.) pkg. fontina cheese, shredded
- ½ cup grated Parmesan cheese (from 1 [4-oz.] pkg.)
- 1½ cups mixed olives, cut in half
- ½ cup thinly sliced oil-packed sun-dried tomatoes
- 1 (3-oz.) pkg. sliced coppa (12 slices), torn
- ¼ cup chopped Marcona almonds (optional)
- Fresh rosemary, for garnish (optional)

1. Preheat oven to 425°F. Coat bottom and sides of an 18 x 13-inch rimmed baking sheet with 2 tablespoons of the olive oil. On a lightly floured surface, knead dough together into a ball. Roll and stretch the dough into a large rectangle, roughly the same size as prepared pan. Place dough in pan, stretching and pressing to fit in an even layer.

2. Press fingers into dough to create dimples all over surface; drizzle with remaining 2 tablespoons olive oil. Sprinkle with half of the fontina and Parmesan cheeses; top with olives, sliced sun-dried tomatoes, and coppa. Sprinkle with remaining cheeses.

3. Bake in preheated oven until crust is golden brown, 15 to 20 minutes. Sprinkle with Marcona almonds and rosemary, if desired. Let cool 5 minutes before slicing.

Super Easy Kale Caesar Salad

This salad is made with just a few ingredients, but it delivers big flavor. Crumbled Parmesan crisps will be your new favorite crunchy topping.

ACTIVE 15 MIN. - TOTAL 45 MIN.
SERVES 8

Whisk together ½ cup plus 1 Tbsp. **mayonnaise**, 3 Tbsp. olive brine, 1½ tsp. **grated lemon zest**, 1½ Tbsp. **fresh lemon juice**, and ¾ tsp. **black pepper** in a large bowl until smooth. Add 1 (12-oz.) pkg. **chopped kale** to dressing mixture, scrunching kale slightly before adding to the bowl; toss to coat. Cover and refrigerate at least 30 minutes or up to 1 hour. Sprinkle with half of 1 (5-oz.) pkg. crushed **Parmesan crisps** (such as ParmCrisps); toss to combine. Top with remaining crushed crisps. Season salad to taste with **kosher salt**.

Big-Batch Cosmos

Shaking up cocktails to order is a hustle. Make a pitcher of Cosmopolitans so you can enjoy yourself instead of bartending.

ACTIVE 10 MIN. - TOTAL 10 MIN., PLUS 3 HOURS FREEZING
SERVES 12

Pour 1 cup refrigerated **cranberry juice cocktail** into an ice cube tray; freeze until solid, at least 3 hours. Stir together 2 cups each **vodka** and refrigerated cranberry juice cocktail and 1½ cups each **fresh orange juice** and **orange liqueur** (such as Grand Marnier) in a large pitcher. Refrigerate until chilled, about 1 hour. Add cranberry ice cubes to pitcher before serving; garnish glasses with **orange peel twists**.

Salted-Caramel Brownies

ACTIVE 15 MIN. - TOTAL 55 MIN., PLUS 30 MIN. COOLING
SERVES 9

Line an 8-inch square baking pan with parchment paper, leaving a 2-inch overhang on all sides. Stir together 1 (18-oz.) pkg. **brownie mix** (such as Ghirardelli Double Chocolate), ⅓ cup melted **butter**, ¼ cup **hot brewed coffee**, 1 tsp. **vanilla extract**, and 1 **large egg** until well blended. Spread batter evenly in prepared pan. Roughly chop 8 **chocolate-covered sea salt caramels** (such as Sanders); sprinkle evenly over batter along with ½ tsp. **flaky sea salt**. Bake at 350°F until set, about 40 minutes. Cool in pan 30 minutes. Remove brownies from pan, and cut into squares. Drizzle with **jarred salted-caramel sauce** just before serving.

SUPER EASY
KALE CAESAR
SALAD
BIG-BATCH
COSMOS
CHARCUTERIE
SHEET PAN PIZZA

Sweet Heat

Chicken wings bring back cherished memories of my grandfather.

EVERY TUESDAY night around suppertime, I think of my grandfather. When I was growing up, Tuesdays were reserved for our dinner dates. I'd call Papa up a few days before to confirm and let him know my restaurant pick. Moultrie, Georgia, is small, so we would rotate among our usual spots. One of his favorites was Barber's Drive In, a beloved local joint that was known for their cheeseburgers, slaw, fried pies, and chicken. Their wings were deep-fried and tossed in a sweet and spicy sauce—and they were the best I've ever had. Papa loved them, and I liked watching him eat them. There was a special art to the way he would clean the meat clear off the bone, and he was sure to pick off any that I might have left behind. Taking the meat from someone else's half-eaten chicken is surely a sign of true love for the other person...or for wings. In his case, I think it was probably both. It's been years since I've enjoyed a Tuesday supper with Papa, but this recipe is my way to relive all those sweet memories. Although I've made a few tweaks, including baking them instead of frying, I know he would have approved of my version. Every time I make them—or any wing recipe, for that matter—I smile and say to myself exactly what he'd say to me, "Dang, Ivy, these sure are good."

Ivy's Hot Honey–Butter Chicken Wings

Don't skip the baking powder—it helps the skin get nice and crispy in the oven.

ACTIVE 15 MIN. - TOTAL 1 HOUR, 5 MIN.

SERVES 6

- 3½ lb. chicken wings (about 13 whole wings), cut at the joints, wing tips discarded
- 1 Tbsp. baking powder
- 4½ tsp. kosher salt, divided
- ¼ cup unsalted butter
- ¼ cup hot honey
- 2 tsp. hot sauce
- 1 small jalapeño, very thinly sliced
- ¼ cup fresh cilantro leaves (optional)

1. Preheat oven to 450°F. Pat chicken wings very dry with paper towels, and place in a large bowl. Stir together baking powder and 4 teaspoons of the salt in a small bowl, and sprinkle over chicken, tossing well to coat.
2. Line a rimmed baking sheet with parchment paper or foil, and fit a wire rack inside baking sheet. Coat rack with cooking spray. Arrange wings, with fatty sides down, on rack in a single layer.
3. Bake until crispy on one side and lightly golden, about 25 minutes. Turn wings over, and bake until well browned and crispy, about 25 minutes.
4. Bring unsalted butter, hot honey, hot sauce, and remaining ½ teaspoon kosher salt to a boil in a small saucepan over medium-high. Boil 30 seconds, stirring constantly. Remove from heat. Place wings in a large bowl. Add hot honey–butter sauce and sliced jalapeño; toss to coat wings in sauce. Transfer to a platter, and garnish with fresh cilantro leaves, if desired.

Sauce & Toss

Two more flavorful variations

Parmesan-Ranch Chicken Wings

Prepare wings as directed through Step 3. Microwave ¼ cup **unsalted butter** in a heatproof bowl on HIGH until melted, 30 to 45 seconds. Stir in 1 Tbsp. **ranch seasoning,** ½ tsp. grated **garlic,** and ¼ tsp. **kosher salt.** Place wings in a large bowl. Add ranch sauce to wings, and toss to coat. Sprinkle wings with 6 Tbsp. grated **Parmesan** and 1½ Tbsp. thinly sliced **fresh chives.**

Honey Mustard–Barbecue Chicken Wings

Prepare wings as directed through Step 3. Stir together 6 Tbsp. **Chick-fil-A Sauce,** 5½ tsp. **Dijon mustard,** and 4 tsp. **honey** in a medium bowl. Place wings in a large bowl. Add sauce to wings as desired, and toss well to coat. Garnish with **black pepper.**

IVY'S HOT HONEY–
BUTTER CHICKEN WINGS

COOKING SCHOOL

TIPS AND TRICKS FROM THE SOUTH'S MOST TRUSTED KITCHEN

The Best Steak Ever in Four Easy Steps

Learn the reverse-sear technique for restaurant-quality results.

1. SEASON
Pat steaks completely dry with paper towels. Sprinkle with kosher salt and black pepper from at least 6 inches above to season the meat evenly.

2. BAKE
Place steaks on a wire rack set inside a rimmed sheet pan; bake in a 250°F oven until a thermometer registers 115°F for medium-rare. (See chart at right if you prefer a different level of doneness.)

3. SEAR
Heat oil in a cast-iron skillet over high; season steaks with more salt and pepper. Cook, undisturbed, until deeply browned, about 1 minute. Flip and repeat. Sear sides, if desired.

4. SLICE
Let steaks rest 10 minutes to redistribute the juices. Cut each against the grain; finish with flaky salt.

How Do You Like Your Steak?

Use this chart and a meat thermometer to cook your go-to cut just the way you want it.

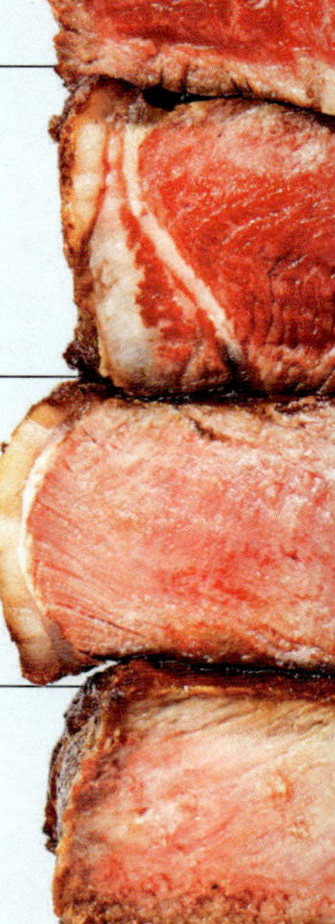

105°F–120°F

RARE
Bake at 250°F for 25 to 30 minutes; pull at 105°F. Sear to 120°F (or under).

115°F–130°F

MEDIUM-RARE
Bake at 250°F for 30 to 35 minutes; pull at 115°F. Sear to 130°F (or under).

125°F–140°F

MEDIUM
Bake at 250°F for 35 to 40 minutes; pull at 125°F. Sear to 140°F (or under).

135°F–150°F

MEDIUM-WELL
Bake at 250°F for 40 to 45 minutes; pull at 135°F. Sear to 150°F (or under).

March

BOUNTY

Green Energy

Take advantage of peak-season Swiss chard, from leaf to stem.

Chard-Wrapped Salmon

ACTIVE 35 MIN. - TOTAL 35 MIN.
SERVES 4

- 1 cup finely chopped sun-dried tomatoes in oil (from 1 [16-oz.] jar)
- 2½ Tbsp. stone-ground Dijon mustard
- 2 Tbsp. fresh lemon juice (from 1 lemon)
- 1 Tbsp. honey
- 1 tsp. kosher salt
- 1 tsp. black pepper
- ¾ tsp. crushed red pepper
- ½ tsp. garlic powder
- 4 large Swiss chard leaves, halved lengthwise and stems trimmed
- 4 (6-oz.) skinless salmon fillets
- 1 cup vegetable broth
- 3 Tbsp. unsalted butter, cut into pieces
- 1 cup cherry tomatoes, halved if large

1. Stir together chopped sun-dried tomatoes, mustard, lemon juice, honey, salt, black pepper, crushed red pepper, and garlic powder in a medium bowl; set aside.
2. Place 1 chard leaf half on a work surface. Center 1 salmon fillet lengthwise on the leaf; top with 3 tablespoons of the sun-dried tomato mixture. Fold ends of chard around salmon (tuck thinner part of fillet underneath itself, if needed). Place another leaf half on work surface. Position wrapped fillet crosswise on leaf; wrap and roll to completely enclose fillet. Repeat with remaining chard and salmon.
3. Combine broth and remaining sun-dried tomato mixture in a large skillet with lid; bring to a simmer over high. Gently place wrapped salmon fillets in skillet, seam sides down. Cover, reduce heat to medium-low, and cook until a thermometer inserted into salmon registers 135°F, 10 to 14 minutes, gently turning halfway through cook time.
4. Remove salmon from skillet; add butter to broth mixture in pan, whisking constantly, until sauce thickens, about 1 minute. Stir in cherry tomatoes, and cook until warmed through, about 1 minute. Return salmon to skillet; spoon sauce over each fillet to coat. Serve immediately.

CHARD-WRAPPED SALMON

Pickled Chard Stems

Use these quick pickles on tacos and sandwiches, or serve them on a crudités platter.

ACTIVE 10 MIN. - TOTAL 10 MIN., PLUS 2 HOURS COOLING AND 6 HOURS CHILLING
MAKES 2 (8-OZ.) JARS

Pack 2 cups (3½-inch-long) **Swiss chard stems** and ¼ cup chopped **shallot** tightly into 2 (8-oz.) heatproof glass jars. Bring ¾ cup **white vinegar,** ½ cup **water,** 1 Tbsp. **granulated sugar,** and 2 tsp. each **kosher salt** and **yellow mustard seeds** to a boil in a small saucepan over high, stirring often. Remove from heat; divide evenly between jars. Let cool, uncovered, 2 hours. Secure lids, and chill at least 6 hours before serving. Store in refrigerator up to 1 week.

PICKLED CHARD STEMS

Seriously Good Scones

Bake up three fruit-filled flavors to brighten up breakfast.

Strawberry Scones

Our Strawberry Scones are just like buttery biscuits but even better. They're tender and perfectly sweet.

ACTIVE 20 MIN. - TOTAL 1 HOUR, 20 MIN.

MAKES 6

- 1/3 cup granulated sugar
- 1 Tbsp. grated orange zest (from 1 orange)
- 2 cups all-purpose flour
- 1 Tbsp. baking powder
- 1/2 tsp. kosher salt
- 1/2 cup cold unsalted butter, cut into 1/2-inch pieces
- 1 cup fresh strawberries, chopped
- 1/2 cup cold sour cream
- 1/4 cup cold heavy whipping cream, plus more for brushing
- Turbinado sugar
- Citrus Glaze (recipe follows)

1. Preheat oven to 400°F with rack in top third position. Using your fingertips, rub together granulated sugar and zest in a large bowl until combined and fragrant. Add flour, baking powder, and kosher salt; stir to combine.

2. Cut butter into flour mixture using two forks (or pinch it in using your fingertips) until mixture is crumbly but some pea-size butter pieces remain. Toss strawberries in flour mixture to coat.

3. Whisk together sour cream and heavy whipping cream in a small bowl until smooth; gently stir into flour mixture until a loose, crumbly dough forms.

4. Turn dough out onto a lightly floured work surface. Gently flatten into a 12-inch round; fold in half. Repeat process twice to bring dough together. Shape into a 6-inch-diameter disk, about 1 inch thick. Using a knife, cut disk into 6 wedges. Arrange wedges about 1/2 inch apart on a rimmed baking sheet lined with parchment paper. Freeze, uncovered, 30 minutes.

5. Lightly brush tops of dough wedges with more heavy cream; sprinkle with turbinado sugar. Bake until golden brown and edges are crisp, about 22 minutes. Let cool on baking sheet 5 minutes. Drizzle cooled scones with Citrus Glaze.

Citrus Glaze

Whisk together 1 cup powdered sugar and 2 Tbsp. fresh lemon or orange juice until smooth.

Blueberry Scones

In Step 1, replace orange zest with 1 Tbsp. grated lemon zest (from 2 lemons). In Step 2, replace strawberries with 1 cup fresh blueberries. Proceed with recipe as directed.

Strawberry-Rhubarb Scones

Prepare recipe as directed through Step 1. In Step 2, replace 1/2 cup of the strawberries with 1/2 cup chopped fresh or thawed frozen rhubarb. Proceed with recipe as directed.

STRAWBERRY
SCONES

Carrot Gold

Make a statement with four bold, bright salads starring this versatile spring vegetable.

FAST AND FANCY CARROT RIBBON SALAD (PAGE 48)

ROASTED CARROT SALAD
W TH GOAT CHEESE
(PAGE 49)

PEPPER JELLY–GLAZED CARROTS

Pepper Jelly–Glazed Carrots

ACTIVE 20 MIN. - TOTAL 20 MIN.
SERVES 6

- 2 Tbsp. chopped roasted pistachios
- 2 Tbsp. finely chopped fresh flat-leaf parsley
- 1 Tbsp. grated lemon zest plus 1 Tbsp. fresh juice (from 1 lemon), divided
- 1 Tbsp. olive oil, divided
- ½ tsp. cumin seeds
- 1 Tbsp. tomato paste
- ¼ cup chopped pimientos (from 1 [7-oz.] jar), drained
- 2 tsp. jalapeño pepper jelly
- 1 tsp. kosher salt
- ½ tsp. smoked paprika
- ½ tsp. ground coriander
- 1½ lb. medium carrots, peeled and sliced into ½-inch-thick coins (about 4 cups)
- 1 (10-oz.) container plain hummus

1. Stir together pistachios, parsley, and lemon zest in a small bowl; set aside.
2. Heat 1 teaspoon of the olive oil in a large skillet over medium until shimmering. Add cumin seeds; cook until fragrant, 30 to 45 seconds. Stir in tomato paste; cook, stirring constantly, until tomato paste is slightly darkened in color, about 1 minute. Stir in pimientos, pepper jelly, salt, smoked paprika, and coriander. Cook, stirring often, until fragrant, about 1 minute. Stir in carrots; cook, stirring often, until carrots are tender-crisp, 4 to 5 minutes. Remove from heat.
3. Process hummus, ¼ cup water, and lemon juice in a food processor until smooth, 2 to 3 minutes, stopping to scrape down sides as needed. Spread hummus mixture evenly on a platter, and top with carrots and pistachio mixture. Drizzle with remaining 2 teaspoons oil.

Fast and Fancy Carrot Ribbon Salad

(Photo, page 46)
ACTIVE 30 MIN. - TOTAL 30 MIN.
SERVES 6

- ¼ cup plus ¾ tsp. kosher salt, divided
- Ice water
- 2 lb. rainbow carrots, peeled and trimmed
- ¼ cup thinly sliced yellow bell pepper (from 1 bell pepper)
- 1 Tbsp. extra-virgin olive oil
- ½ cup peeled and chopped yellow mango (from 1 mango)
- 3 Tbsp. fresh lime juice (from 2 limes)
- 2 Tbsp. chopped fresh mint, plus more mint leaves for garnish
- 1 Tbsp. Dijon mustard
- 1 (½-inch) piece fresh ginger, peeled
- ½ tsp. crushed red pepper, divided
- 1 avocado, chopped

1. Bring 2 quarts water and ¼ cup salt to a boil in a large pot over high. Place a large bowl halfway full of ice water near stovetop. Add carrots to boiling water; cook until slightly tender-crisp, about 3 minutes. Drain carrots; add to ice water. Let carrots stand until cool, about 5 minutes. Drain well, and pat dry using paper towels.
2. Working with 1 carrot at a time, hold carrot flat against a cutting board; peel using a vegetable peeler to create ribbons. Place carrot ribbons in a large bowl, and stir in bell pepper and olive oil; toss to combine.
3. Process mango, lime juice, chopped mint, Dijon mustard, ginger, remaining ¾ teaspoon salt, and ¼ teaspoon crushed red pepper in a blender until smooth, about 2 minutes. Add dressing to carrot mixture, stirring to coat.
4. Transfer carrot salad to a platter; top with chopped avocado, and sprinkle with remaining ¼ teaspoon crushed red pepper. Garnish with mint leaves just before serving.

CARROT-RAISIN SALAD WITH PEANUT DRESSING

Carrot-Raisin Salad with Peanut Dressing

ACTIVE 20 MIN. - TOTAL 20 MIN.
SERVES 6

- 2 Tbsp. olive oil, divided
- 1/4 cup finely chopped shallot (from 1 shallot)
- 1 garlic clove, chopped (about 1 tsp.)
- 1/2 cup unsalted roasted peanuts, divided
- 3/4 tsp. kosher salt, divided
- 1 lb. large carrots, peeled and shredded (about 3 1/2 cups)
- 1/3 cup golden raisins
- 2 Tbsp. stone-ground honey–Dijon mustard
- 2 Tbsp. grated lemon zest plus 3 Tbsp. fresh juice (from 2 lemons)
- 2 Tbsp. chopped fresh cilantro, plus more cilantro leaves for garnish
- 1 tsp. finely chopped seeded serrano chile (from 1 chile), plus more for garnish

1. Heat 1 tablespoon olive oil in a medium skillet over medium-high. Stir in shallot; cook, stirring often, until translucent, about 1 minute. Stir in garlic; cook until fragrant, 30 to 45 seconds. Transfer to a blender; set aside, and let cool. Do not wipe skillet clean.
2. Heat remaining 1 tablespoon oil in skillet over medium. Stir in 1/4 cup peanuts; cook, stirring constantly, until browned in spots, about 30 seconds. Transfer peanuts to a cutting board, and let cool 5 minutes. Roughly chop peanuts, and set aside.
3. Add 1/4 cup water, 1/4 teaspoon salt, and remaining 1/4 cup peanuts to shallot mixture in blender; process until peanut dressing is smooth, about 1 minute.
4. Stir together shredded carrots, raisins, mustard, lemon zest and juice, chopped cilantro, chile, and remaining 1/2 teaspoon salt in a large bowl. Pour 1/4 cup dressing over carrot mixture, tossing to coat. Transfer to a platter; garnish with reserved chopped peanuts and additional cilantro and chile. Drizzle with remaining 2 tablespoons dressing just before serving.

Roasted Carrot Salad with Goat Cheese

(Photo, page 47)
ACTIVE 15 MIN. - TOTAL 40 MIN.
SERVES 6

- 2 lb. rainbow baby carrots with tops
- 1/4 cup olive oil, divided, plus more for drizzling
- 1 tsp. kosher salt, divided
- 2 Tbsp. grated orange zest plus 1/4 cup fresh juice (from 1 orange)
- 2 Tbsp. chopped fresh flat-leaf parsley
- 1/4 tsp. chopped garlic (from 1 garlic clove)
- 1/4 tsp. crushed red pepper
- 4 oz. baby kale (about 4 cups)
- 4 oz. spreadable goat cheese (such as Chavrie)
- 2 Tbsp. sunflower kernels

1. Preheat oven to 425°F with racks in top third and lower third positions. Scrub and trim carrots, reserving 1/3 cup leaves from tops. Cut carrots in half lengthwise. Stir together carrots, 2 tablespoons oil, and 1/2 teaspoon salt in a large bowl; toss until coated. Place carrots, cut sides down, on 2 large rimmed baking sheets.
2. Roast until carrots are tender, about 20 minutes, rotating baking sheets from top to bottom halfway through roasting time. Remove from oven, and let cool 5 minutes.
3. While carrots roast, process reserved 1/3 cup carrot leaves, orange zest and juice, parsley, garlic, crushed red pepper, and remaining 1/2 teaspoon salt in a blender until smooth, 1 to 2 minutes. With blender running, gradually add remaining 2 tablespoons oil; process until combined, about 1 minute.
4. Stir together carrots and 2 tablespoons dressing in a bowl. Place kale on a platter, and drizzle with remaining dressing. Top with carrots. Add dollops of goat cheese, and sprinkle with sunflower kernels. Drizzle with more olive oil just before serving.

The Magic of Meal Prep

Getting a jump start on dinner is as easy as turning on your slow cooker.

FOR SOME, self-care means booking a massage or spending time with friends. For me, it's a container of seasoned pulled pork in the fridge. Don't get me wrong: I love pampering and girls' trips. But knowing that dinner is halfway done on a Tuesday does more for my mental health than a day at the spa.

The six o'clock hour on a weeknight is fast and furious. At our house, it's the window of time when the transition is made from work to home: the dog gets fed; school assignments require assistance; everyone vents about their day; clothes are changed; and, somewhere in there, dinner comes together and hits the table. This type of cooking can feel effortless or like a deranged episode of *Chopped*, depending on how the day went and what's in the refrigerator. Coming home and seeing that pork waiting to be turned into any number of simple suppers is a sweet relief.

There are people who approach meal prepping like a sport. I imagine their kitchens are filled with neatly labeled containers holding premade elements that can be mixed and matched in any number of delicious combinations. I am not that person (probably because I never played sports, but mostly because I'm not that organized), but I also know that having even one versatile component can save a lot of time and stress.

So do yourself a kindness, and make this slow-cooker pulled pork. While you can serve it as is with a side dish or two, the recipe makes 8 to 10 servings, so you'll likely have leftovers to use as building blocks for other dinners, like pasta topped with a meaty tomato sauce, a rice bowl flavored with hoisin sauce, and a Cubano so good you'll want to make it on repeat. Eating an excellent sandwich counts as self-care too.
—Lisa Cericola

Easy Slow-Cooker Pulled Pork

ACTIVE 10 MIN. - TOTAL 8 HOURS, 10 MIN., INCLUDING 8 HOURS SLOW-COOKING
SERVES 8 TO 10

- 2 large sweet onions, cut into ½-inch slices (about 6 cups)
- 1 (5- to 6-lb.) boneless pork shoulder roast
- 2 Tbsp. seasoning blend (such as Wayne O's Southern Seasoning or Kinder's All-Purpose Meat and Veggie Rub)
- 1 tsp. kosher salt
- 1 (10½-oz.) can condensed chicken broth

1. Place onions in a lightly greased 6-quart slow cooker. Rub roast with seasoning blend and salt; place roast on top of onions. Pour broth around roast. Cover and cook until meat shreds easily, 8 to 10 hours on LOW or 6 hours on HIGH.
2. Transfer roast to a cutting board; reserve onions and cooking liquid for serving or recipe variations (below). Shred pork using 2 forks; discard fat. Pork and cooking liquid may be refrigerated separately in airtight containers for up to 3 days.

Pork Rice Bowl

ACTIVE 10 MIN. - TOTAL 10 MIN.
SERVES 4

Mix 2 cups shredded **pulled pork** (recipe above) with ¼ cup **pork cooking liquid** and 3 Tbsp. **hoisin sauce.** Divide 2 cups **steamed rice** among 4 bowls; top each with ½ cup pulled-pork mixture. Serve with shredded **lettuce**, sliced **radishes**, sliced **cucumber, lime wedges**, fresh **cilantro**, and halved soft-cooked **eggs** (if desired). Drizzle with additional **hoisin sauce,** and sprinkle with **black sesame seeds.**

Cuban Sandwich

ACTIVE 10 MIN. - TOTAL 10 MIN.
SERVES 4 TO 6

Split 1 (12-oz.) **Cuban bread loaf** lengthwise. Smear cut sides of bread with ½ cup **mayonnaise** and 2 Tbsp. **yellow mustard.** Top 1 half with 2 cups **pulled pork** (recipe left) mixed with up to ¼ cup **pork cooking liquid,** ½ lb. sliced **deli ham,** 6 oz. sliced **Swiss cheese,** and 1 cup sliced **dill pickles.** Top with remaining bread half. Cut in half crosswise. Heat a large griddle over medium-high. Grease with **butter**, and add sandwich to griddle. Weigh down sandwich using a large cast-iron skillet; cook on each side until toasted, 4 to 5 minutes total.

Quick Ragù

ACTIVE 10 MIN. - TOTAL 10 MIN.
MAKES 4½ CUPS

Toast 2 Tbsp. sliced **garlic** in 2 Tbsp. **olive oil** in a large skillet over medium-high. Add ½ cup **dry white wine** and 3 cups chopped **pulled pork** (recipe above left); cook until reduced by half, about 2 minutes. Stir in 1 (24-oz.) jar **marinara sauce** and ½ cup **pork cooking liquid**; cook until heated through, about 5 minutes. Serve over cooked **pasta** with grated **Parmesan cheese** and **small fresh basil leaves.**

Coming home and seeing that pork waiting to be turned into any number of simple suppers is a sweet relief.

PORK RICE BOWL

It's Pasta Night, Y'all!

These dishes are a little bit Southern, a little bit Italian, and ready in just 30 minutes.

Little Shells with Greens and Sausage

ACTIVE 30 MIN. - TOTAL 30 MIN.
SERVES 6

- 1 (16-oz.) pkg. small pasta shells or orecchiette
- 2 Tbsp. olive oil, divided
- 1 (16-oz.) pkg. hot ground pork sausage (such as Jimmy Dean)
- 1 red onion, thinly sliced (1 cup)
- 8 cups packed stemmed and chopped mustard greens (2 bunches)
- 3 garlic cloves, finely chopped (1 Tbsp.)
- 1 tsp. fresh thyme leaves
- 1 tsp. kosher salt, plus more to taste
- 1/2 tsp. black pepper, plus more for serving
- 1 cup heavy whipping cream
- 1 cup fresh or frozen sweet peas
- 1/2 cup grated Parmesan cheese (2 oz.), plus more for serving

1. Bring a large pot of salted water to a boil over high. Add pasta; cook according to package directions for al dente. Reserve 1 cup cooking water; drain pasta.
2. While water is coming to a boil, heat 1 tablespoon oil in a large, deep skillet over medium-high. Crumble sausage into skillet; cook, stirring occasionally, until browned, about 8 minutes. Transfer sausage to a plate; reserve drippings in skillet.
3. Add onion and remaining 1 tablespoon oil to skillet; cook over medium, stirring occasionally, until softened, about 4 minutes. Add mustard greens, a handful at a time, along with garlic, thyme, salt, and pepper. Cook, stirring often, until greens are wilted, about 3 minutes. Add cream; bring to a simmer over medium. Cook, stirring occasionally, until slightly thickened and saucy, about 4 minutes.
4. Add sweet peas, Parmesan, drained pasta, sausage, and ½ cup cooking water; stir vigorously until cheese melts and pasta is coated in sauce, about 2 minutes. Add remaining ½ cup cooking water (about 2 tablespoons at a time) to keep the sauce loose and creamy. Serve immediately, sprinkled with additional salt, pepper, and Parmesan, if desired.

Tomato-Feta Penne with Pimientos

(Photo, page 55)
ACTIVE 20 MIN. - TOTAL 30 MIN.
SERVES 4

- 2 pt. cherry or grape tomatoes
- 2 (4-oz.) jars sliced pimiento peppers, drained (about 1 cup)
- 6 garlic cloves, smashed and peeled
- 5 Tbsp. olive oil, divided
- 1½ tsp. kosher salt, plus more for water
- 1/2 tsp. black pepper
- 1 (8-oz.) block feta cheese
- 1 (16-oz.) pkg. penne pasta
- 1/4 cup sliced fresh basil, plus more for garnish
- 1 tsp. grated lemon zest (from 1 lemon)
- Toasted pine nuts (optional)

1. Preheat oven to 450°F. Place tomatoes, pimientos, and garlic in a 13 x 9-inch baking dish. Drizzle with 4 tablespoons olive oil; sprinkle with salt and pepper, stirring to combine. Cut a ½-inch slice from feta; crumble and reserve for garnish. Nestle remaining feta block in center of baking dish. Drizzle with remaining 1 tablespoon oil, turning to coat feta on all sides.
2. Bake until tomatoes burst and begin to brown slightly, 20 to 25 minutes.
3. Meanwhile, bring a large pot of salted water to a boil over high. Add pasta; cook according to package directions for al dente. Reserve ½ cup cooking water; drain pasta.
4. Stir feta-and-tomato mixture together with ¼ cup reserved cooking water to form a creamy sauce. Stir in drained pasta, basil, and lemon zest until coated, adding the remaining ¼ cup cooking water (about 1 tablespoon at a time) to loosen sauce as needed. Serve topped with additional basil and reserved feta; garnish with toasted pine nuts, if using.

Bacon Lover's Cacio e Pepe

(Photo, page 54)
ACTIVE 20 MIN. - TOTAL 30 MIN.
SERVES 4

- 1 tsp. kosher salt
- 1 (16-oz.) pkg. bucatini or spaghetti
- 2 Tbsp. extra-virgin olive oil
- 2 tsp. coarsely ground black pepper, plus more for serving
- 2½ cups finely grated Pecorino Romano cheese (4 oz.), plus more for serving
- 1¼ cups finely grated Parmesan cheese (about 2 oz.)
- 1/2 cup chopped cooked bacon

1. Combine 2 quarts water and salt in a large pot; bring to a boil over high. Add pasta, gently stirring to submerge in water; cook, stirring occasionally, according to package directions for al dente.
2. While pasta is cooking, heat olive oil in a small skillet over medium-low. Add pepper; cook, stirring occasionally, until gently sizzling, about 1 minute. Transfer pepper mixture to a large bowl.
3. Reserve 1½ cups cooking water; drain pasta. Set both aside to cool slightly, about 3 minutes.
4. Stir cheeses into pepper mixture in bowl. Gradually whisk in about 1 cup of the cooking water until the cheeses are completely melted and mixture is creamy. Add drained pasta; toss vigorously to coat, adding remaining ½ cup cooking water as needed to create a glossy sauce that clings to the pasta. Serve topped with chopped bacon and additional grated Pecorino Romano and cracked black pepper.

LITTLE SHELLS WITH
GREENS AND SAUSAGE

BACON LOVER'S
CACIO E PEPE
(PAGE 52)

TOMATO-FETA PENNE WITH PIMIENTOS
(PAGE 52)

Southern-Style Baked Tortellini

ACTIVE 25 MIN. - TOTAL 30 MIN.

SERVES 6

- 4 thick-cut bacon slices, chopped
- 1 yellow onion, finely chopped (1¼ cups)
- 6 cups shredded collard greens (from 1 [1-lb.] pkg.)
- 1½ cups chicken stock
- 2½ tsp. smoked paprika, divided
- 1 (24-oz.) jar marinara sauce (3 cups)
- 2 (10-oz.) pkg. refrigerated cheese tortellini (such as Giovanni Rana)
- 1½ cups shredded smoked cheddar or mozzarella cheese (6 oz.), divided
- ¾ cup panko breadcrumbs
- ¼ cup grated Parmesan cheese (1 oz.)
- 1 Tbsp. olive oil
- 1 garlic clove, grated (about ½ tsp.)
- ¼ tsp. kosher salt

1. Preheat oven to broil with rack about 10 inches from heat source. Heat bacon in a large, deep ovenproof skillet over medium. Cook, stirring occasionally, until bacon is crisp, about 7 minutes. Add onion; cook, stirring often, until softened, about 3 minutes. Add collard greens, stock, and 2 teaspoons paprika; bring to a simmer over medium, stirring and scraping bottom of skillet. Simmer, stirring occasionally, until greens are wilted, about 4 minutes.

2. Stir in marinara, and return to a simmer over medium-high. Add tortellini; cook, stirring occasionally, until tortellini begin to plump and soften, about 4 minutes. Remove from heat; fold in 1 cup cheddar or mozzarella. Sprinkle top with remaining ½ cup cheddar or mozzarella. In a small bowl, stir together panko, Parmesan, olive oil, garlic, salt, and remaining ½ teaspoon paprika; sprinkle evenly over tortellini.

3. Broil until panko topping is golden brown, about 2 minutes.

Any-Occasion Punch

Stir up this big-batch twist on a classic British cocktail.

FUN, FIZZY, FRUITY
A Pimm's cup is often loaded with garnishes, but feel free to scale them back.

Pimm's Cup Punch

ACTIVE 20 MIN. · TOTAL 20 MIN.
SERVES 12

- 1¼ cups loosely packed fresh mint sprigs (from 1 [2-oz.] pkg.), plus more for garnish
- 1 cup fresh lemon juice (from 4 lemons)
- 3 navel oranges, thinly sliced into half-moons (about 6 cups), divided
- 1 English cucumber, thinly sliced (about 4 cups), divided
- 6 cups sliced fresh strawberries (from 2 qt.), divided
- Ice
- 2½ cups (20 oz.) Pimm's No. 1
- 5 (11.15-oz.) cans lemon-flavor sparkling water (such as Sanpellegrino or LaCroix)

1. Place mint sprigs, lemon juice, 1¼ cups of the oranges, 1¼ cups of the cucumbers, and 1¼ cups of the strawberries in a large bowl. Crush with a wooden spoon until no large chunks of fruit remain and mint is fragrant, about 2 minutes.

2. Pour fruit mixture through a fine mesh strainer over a large punch bowl filled halfway with ice; discard any solids. Stir in Pimm's and remaining oranges, cucumbers, and strawberries.

3. Top with lemon-flavor sparkling water; stir until combined. Garnish with additional mint sprigs.

History on the Half Shell

A bowl of oyster stew is a taste of Virginia's past.

IN HER ACCLAIMED 1976 cookbook, *The Taste of Country Cooking*, Edna Lewis sings a paean to the seasonal culinary glories of her home of Freetown, Virginia, which was established by the newly emancipated in the 19th century. She eloquently celebrates the people and their foodways, which were regional, seasonal, and local long before those terms became the buzzwords for an international movement.

Reading Lewis' book, you can virtually taste the pan-fried shad with roe that serves as the centerpiece of her spring breakfast menu or the summer meal of fried chicken that is dredged, not battered, and offered up along with slow-cooked green beans with pork. Fried tomatoes and Parker House rolls appear in her autumn fare, while winter was given over to pan-fried oysters and rich oyster stew. These bivalves were eaten especially at the holidays in Freetown.

Today, oysters have experienced quite a renaissance and are slurped down by connoisseurs year-round. (The old advice about not eating them in the months with no "r" has been retired.) In the early 19th century, they did not have the slightly patrician aura that they tend to have now and were a truly democratic food and a popular street snack that was consumed with gusto by all segments of society.

At that time, African American oystermen of the Maryland and Virginia coastal regions were particularly adept at cultivating them, and they established a primacy in the profession. No one was more legendary than Thomas Downing, a free Black man born on Virginia's Eastern Shore. His namesake 1825 oyster house in New York City was patronized by the elite, while the building's basement was a stop on the Underground Railroad. At his establishment, oysters turned up in chowders, were roasted with a dollop of butter, and were served in rich stews.

As fascinated as I am with the shellfish and their history, my curiosity must remain intellectual and not gustatory, as I am allergic to them. However, when I read Ms. Edna's decadent stew recipe that calls for heavy cream and butter, my mouth watered while my heart and stomach dared not follow. She proposes it as a part of her Christmas Eve supper, but the dish would be equally perfect for those March evenings when a hint of winter still lingers in the air. –Jessica B. Harris

VIRGINIA'S CULINARY MIGRATIONS: HOW FAMILIAR FOODS FOUND THEIR WAY ONTO OUR PLATES

As I was paging through *The Taste of Country Cooking*, I was struck by the number of recipes that I had grown up eating. From the thinly sliced cucumbers with white vinegar dressing to the baked ham with strawberry preserves to the holiday mincemeat pies, I was overwhelmed by the many similarities. Then I remembered that while my New Jersey–born mother was a child of the North, her mother was from Roanoke, Virginia, a place that was only about 100 miles from Freetown. Ms. Edna's recipes had connected the dots of the Great Migration from her Virginia to my mother's table in Jamaica, Queens, New York.

Edna Lewis' Oyster Stew

ACTIVE 10 MIN. - TOTAL 10 MIN.
SERVES 6 TO 8

- 1 qt. shucked oysters
- 1½ Tbsp. butter, divided
- 3 cups scalded milk (see tip below)
- 1 cup heavy cream
- ¼ tsp. cayenne pepper
- ⅛ tsp. nutmeg
- Kosher salt
- Chopped parsley

1. Drain the oysters. Melt 1 tablespoon of the butter in a large skillet over medium-high; add the oysters, and cook, turning them on both sides until they begin to curl, about 2 minutes. Pour in the scalded milk, and transfer the mixture to a saucepan.
2. Pour the cream into the same skillet, and boil rapidly until reduced by half, stirring constantly, about 3 minutes. Add the reduced cream to the oyster mixture, and heat over medium; do not boil. Add cayenne, nutmeg, and salt to taste. Just before serving, add remaining ½ tablespoon butter. Garnish stew with chopped parsley.

HOW TO SCALD MILK

To scald milk, heat cold milk in a saucepan over medium, stirring often, until a skin forms on top and bubbles appear around the edges (180°F on a thermometer). Remove from heat, and cool 10 minutes.

At the early 19th-century New York City oyster house of Thomas Downing, a free Black man, oysters turned up in chowders, roasted with a dollop of butter, and served in rich stews.

OVER EASY

Make Some Dough

Baking homemade yeast bread has never been simpler.

Dutch Oven Cinnamon-Raisin Bread

ACTIVE 35 MIN. - TOTAL 1 HOUR, 15 MIN., PLUS 2 HOURS, 30 MIN. PROOFING AND 2 HOURS COOLING
SERVES 8

- **1½ cups warm water (110°F)**
- **1 (¼-oz.) envelope active dry yeast (2¼ tsp.)**
- **3 Tbsp. light brown sugar**
- **4 cups plus 5 Tbsp. all-purpose flour, divided, plus more for sprinkling**
- **1 cup raisins**
- **1 Tbsp. ground cinnamon**
- **1½ tsp. kosher salt**
- **3 ice cubes**

1. Whisk together warm water, yeast, and brown sugar in the work bowl of a stand mixer fitted with a dough hook until combined. Let stand until foamy, about 5 minutes.
2. Add 4 cups flour, raisins, cinnamon, and kosher salt to yeast mixture. Knead on medium-low speed until a smooth dough starts to form, about 5 minutes. With mixer running, add more flour, 1 tablespoon at a time, until dough is smooth and elastic and pulls away from the sides of the bowl, about 4 minutes (you may not need all 5 tablespoons of the flour). Place dough in a large bowl coated with cooking spray, turning to coat. Cover with plastic wrap, and let rise in a warm place (75°F) until doubled in size, about 2 hours and 30 minutes. During last 30 minutes of proofing, place a large Dutch oven in oven and preheat to 450°F.
3. Place dough on 2 stacked (16 x 12-inch) pieces of Reynolds Kitchens Unbleached Parchment Paper, and shape dough into a ball. Sprinkle top of dough lightly with more flour; gently rub to coat evenly. Using a bread lame or sharp knife, cut a shallow X in the top of the dough. Carefully lower dough into preheated Dutch oven, using edges of parchment as handles. Tuck ice cubes in between the layers of parchment paper. (This will create steam and give the bread a crispy crust.) Cover with lid.
4. Bake for 25 minutes. Remove lid; bake, uncovered, until dark golden brown and a thermometer inserted near center registers 190°F, 10 to 15 minutes more.
5. Remove bread from Dutch oven using parchment as handles. Let cool to room temperature on a wire rack, about 2 hours.

Bread-Baking Gear

Go pro with these tools

Lame
Pronounced "lahm," this sharp blade cuts cleanly through dough to create a neatly scored loaf.

Bench Scraper
A kitchen workhorse, this handy tool easily scoops up sticky doughs, sweeps flour off countertops, and helps precisely portion rolls and scones.

Proofing Basket
For a perfectly round loaf, turn to this coiled container to hold the dough as it rises.

COOKING SCHOOL

TIPS AND TRICKS FROM THE SOUTH'S MOST TRUSTED KITCHEN

Four Steps to a Beautiful Loaf

A Dutch oven is the key to our best-ever cinnamon-raisin bread (recipe, page 61).

1. SHAPE
Layer 2 pieces of parchment paper. Place dough on top; form into a ball, using both hands to tuck and drag dough until smooth and taut. Dust with flour, rubbing to coat.

2. SCORE
With a bread lame or sharp knife, cut a shallow X into the top of the ball of dough. You don't need to make it very deep.

3. TRANSFER
Using edges of parchment as handles, carefully lower dough into preheated Dutch oven. Tuck ice cubes in between parchment layers (do not let ice touch dough).

4. BAKE
Cover and bake 25 minutes. Remove lid, and continue baking until loaf is dark golden brown and a thermometer inserted into center registers 190°F, 10 to 15 minutes more.

April

BOUNTY

Pretty in Pink

Tart rhubarb adds a burst of brightness to these sweet recipes.

BROWN SUGAR SHORTCAKES WITH ROASTED RHUBARB

Brown Sugar Shortcakes with Roasted Rhubarb

ACTIVE 15 MIN. - TOTAL 35 MIN.

SERVES 4

Preheat oven to 450°F. Whisk together ¾ cup **heavy whipping cream**, 2 Tbsp. **light brown sugar**, 1 tsp. **vanilla paste or extract**, and 2 tsp. grated **lemon zest** in a medium bowl until smooth. Stir in 1¼ cups **self-rising flour** just until a shaggy dough forms. Use a ¼-cup measuring cup to scoop dough into 4 rounds; place on a parchment-lined baking sheet. Lightly brush tops with additional **heavy whipping cream.** Bake until lightly golden, 10 to 12 minutes; let cool 10 minutes. Whisk ¾ cup **heavy whipping cream,** 3 Tbsp. **light brown sugar,** and 2 tsp. **vanilla paste or extract** in a large bowl until soft peaks form. Slice shortcakes in half crosswise. Spoon 1 cup **Roasted Rhubarb** (recipe below) evenly on bottom halves of shortcakes; dollop with **whipped cream.** Drizzle with **rhubarb cooking juices,** and replace top halves of shortcakes.

YOGURT WITH ROASTED RHUBARB

Yogurt with Roasted Rhubarb

ACTIVE 5 MIN. - TOTAL 5 MIN.

SERVES 1

Spoon ¾ cup **plain whole-milk strained (Greek-style) yogurt** into a bowl. Top with ¼ cup **Roasted Rhubarb** (recipe below); drizzle with **rhubarb cooking juices.** Sprinkle with 1 Tbsp. chopped **raw pistachios** and torn **fresh mint leaves.**

Roasted Rhubarb

ACTIVE 10 MIN. - TOTAL 1 HOUR

SERVES 6

Preheat oven to 400°F. Cut peel from 1 **orange** into wide strips. Place ⅔ cup **granulated sugar** in a medium bowl. Using your fingers, rub orange peel strips, 3 **star anise,** and 1 **cinnamon stick** into sugar until sugar is fragrant. Cut 1 lb. **fresh rhubarb stalks** into 1½-inch pieces; arrange in a single snug layer in a 13 x 9-inch baking dish. Sprinkle with sugar mixture. Cover with foil, ensuring that foil does not touch rhubarb. Bake, covered, until sugar is partially dissolved, 12 to 15 minutes. Uncover, gently stir, and return baking dish to oven. Bake until rhubarb is tender but still holds its shape, about 5 minutes. Let cool 30 minutes in dish; remove orange peel strips, star anise, and cinnamon stick. Serve warm; or transfer rhubarb and cooking juices to an airtight container, and chill in refrigerator at least 2 hours or up to 3 days.

The Strange Delight of Pear Salad

It wouldn't be Easter without this old-school recipe.

IN THE SOUTH, we use the term "salad" quite liberally. If you've never attended a potluck with folding tables laden with cut-crystal platters bearing mysterious fruit-studded fluffs or shiny, gelatin-set "delights," I can see how these concoctions might cause you to raise an eyebrow. But as a Southerner, I know to expect far more than lettuce when salad is on the menu.

Of all the traditional dishes from the luncheons, get-togethers, and picnics of my childhood, there's one that reigns supreme: Open a can of pear halves (there's no place for fresh here), set them on your serving piece of choice (in my family, this means a deviled egg plate), dollop each with a hefty glob of mayonnaise (don't be shy!), and top with a generous sprinkle of shredded cheddar cheese. Et voilà! Pear Salad.

Some folks serve it on a bed of butter lettuce or with a maraschino cherry on top, but for my Nana, those frilly additions were unnecessary. I can't remember a meal at Nana's house when there wasn't Pear Salad on the table, and I know that if I were to go into my mama's pantry right now, I'd find a can or two of pears "just in case we need an extra side."

It's one of those dishes, like deviled eggs or a relish tray, that's always served at Easter, often shows up at weeknight suppers, or even suffices as a meal all on its own...if you're not too hungry. To some, the combination of pears, mayonnaise, and cheese might appear odd. But for me, this recipe tastes like home—and that's the cherry on top.

Pear Salad

ACTIVE 15 MIN. - TOTAL 15 MIN.

SERVES 12

Drain 3 (15-oz.) cans **pear halves.** (Note: some canned pears may be larger than others.) Pat pear halves dry with paper towels. Spoon at least 2 tsp. **mayonnaise** into each pear half (about ½ cup total). Top each half with shredded **sharp cheddar cheese** (about ½ cup total). Arrange pear halves over **butter lettuce** leaves, if desired, on a serving platter. Top pear halves with **whole maraschino cherries,** if desired.

Morning Glory

Mini croissants dress up this make-ahead casserole.

Blueberry-Croissant Breakfast Bake

ACTIVE 20 MIN. - TOTAL 1 HOUR, 30 MIN., PLUS 8 HOURS CHILLING

SERVES 12

- 1 cup powdered sugar, plus more for garnish
- 2 (8-oz.) pkg. softened cream cheese, divided
- 2 tsp. grated lemon zest plus 1½ Tbsp. fresh juice (from 1 lemon), divided
- 1 Tbsp. plus 1 tsp. vanilla extract, divided
- 2 cups fresh blueberries, divided
- ⅔ cup granulated sugar
- 2 cups half-and-half
- 4 large eggs, lightly beaten
- ½ tsp. kosher salt
- 14 mini croissants, divided
- Toasted sliced almonds

1. Whisk together powdered sugar, 1 package cream cheese, lemon zest, ½ tablespoon lemon juice, and 1 teaspoon vanilla in a large bowl until smooth. Stir in 1 cup blueberries, crushing slightly with a potato masher or fork, until well combined. Set aside.

2. In a separate large bowl, whisk together granulated sugar and remaining cream cheese until smooth. Gradually whisk in half-and-half, eggs, salt, and remaining 1 tablespoon lemon juice and vanilla extract until well combined. Set aside.

3. Cut 12 croissants in half crosswise. Place bottoms, cut sides up, in a 13 x 9-inch baking dish coated with cooking spray. Dollop with blueberry-cream cheese mixture; cover with croissant tops. Pour egg mixture over croissants.

4. Tear remaining 2 croissants into bite-size pieces; tuck in around sandwiches to fill any gaps. Sprinkle with remaining 1 cup blueberries. Cover and chill 8 to 12 hours.

5. Let stand at room temperature while oven preheats to 325°F. Bake, covered with foil, for 30 minutes. Remove foil; bake, uncovered, until golden brown and set, about 30 minutes more. Sprinkle with almonds; dust with powdered sugar.

SOUTHERN SHRIMP COCKTAIL

Staying Afloat

Louisiana shrimpers are fighting to preserve a historic Gulf industry amid tough economic times.

IT'S HARD TO nail down Dino Pertuit. I finally catch the Louisiana seafood legend early in the morning, and we chat while he drives back from a shrimping expedition, the phone call dropping at least three times along the way. His rich Cajun accent and the rumblings of his truck in the background make it hard for me to decipher everything he's saying. But one sentence stands out crystal clear: "I'm going to do it until I die," he says of shrimping. At 57, he's one of the younger ones who keep it going.

A third-generation shrimper, Pertuit has watched prices for his Gulf catch stagnate, but the hard work of harvesting has stayed the same. His shrimp commanded $3.50 a pound in the 1980s and today they still hover around that price—while the costs for everything else, like fuel and boat insurance, have gone up. His product remains highly coveted; he supplies to many of New Orleans' top restaurants, including Herbsaint and Cochon.

Louisiana native Lance Nacio has a slightly different approach to shrimping. He's been in the industry full-time for over 25 years and grew up in a trapping camp on Grand Bayou, an area that's accessible only by boat, where people spent winters capturing animals for fur and summers catching seafood. His great-grandfather immigrated to the United States from the Philippines and landed in Manila Village, a historic Filipino fishing community in Jefferson Parish. Nacio follows in his family's footsteps, alongside his son, David. "Shrimp is not just our industry—it's a way of life," reads his website.

Although he is passionate about continuing that legacy, I can hear in his voice that he is slightly exasperated as he prepares to travel to a multistate meeting with the Federal Trade Commission to discuss shrimp-labeling regulations. Nacio has been fighting for this industry almost as long as he's been in it. While he wades through the bureaucracy, he has wasted no time, turning to technology to overcome some of the challenges facing Gulf shrimpers. He's equipped his 55-foot boat with an onboard aluminum freezing plate that allows him to quickly preserve and package the thousands of shiny crustaceans his full nets dump on deck. He hand sorts the haul, picking out any finfish to be sold separately as well as the hidden soft-shell shrimp in the mix (that delicacy sells for $12 per pound).

The best way to lend shrimpers support is with your dollar, which is where trusted purveyors like Porgy's Seafood Market (in New Orleans' Mid-City) come in. Named after an oft-neglected bycatch, Porgy's offers lesser-known species of fish alongside shrimp, oysters, crabs, and seasonal delicacies like crawfish. The shop is run by restaurant veterans Caitlin Carney and Marcus Jacobs. Customers can buy seafood straight from the case or grab one of the mint green seats at the counter and enjoy it prepared by their kitchen. In the case of local shrimp, there's no hiding the flavor difference. "You can taste the salt of the marsh," says Jacobs. "There's something rugged, delicious, and very much of a place when you taste this shrimp." Nowhere is that clearer than in their shrimp rémoulade, served with humble saltines. And as if the flavor weren't a giveaway, you can watch as local shrimpers come in through the back and drop off their fresh catch in the kitchen while you dine. —Alana Al-Hatlani

Southern Shrimp Cocktail

ACTIVE 40 MIN. - TOTAL 40 MIN.
SERVES 6

SEASONED SHRIMP

- 2 cups dry white wine
- 1 garlic head, halved crosswise
- 1½ tsp. cayenne pepper
- 1 lemon, halved
- ¼ cup kosher salt
- 2 lb. jumbo peeled, deveined raw shrimp, tail-on

HORSERADISH RÉMOULADE

- ⅔ cup mayonnaise
- ¼ cup finely chopped mixed fresh tender herbs (such as chives, parsley, and tarragon), plus more for garnish
- ¼ cup prepared horseradish (from 1 [5.25-oz.] jar)
- 2 Tbsp. ketchup
- 1 Tbsp. hot sauce (such as Crystal)
- 1 Tbsp. whole-grain mustard

VIETNAMESE-STYLE COCKTAIL SAUCE

- ⅔ cup bottled chili sauce (such as Heinz)
- 1 Tbsp. fish sauce
- 1 Tbsp. fresh lime juice (from 1 lime)
- 1 Tbsp. sambal oelek (ground fresh chile paste)
- ¼ tsp. grated garlic (from 1 clove)
- Crispy fried shallots, for garnish
- Chopped fresh cilantro, for garnish

1. Prepare the Seasoned Shrimp: Stir together 3 quarts water, wine, garlic, and cayenne pepper in a medium pot. Squeeze lemon halves over mixture; add lemon halves to pot. Cover and bring to a boil over high. Uncover, stir in salt, and return to a boil. Reduce heat to medium-high, and gently simmer, undisturbed, until flavors meld, about 10 minutes.

2. Remove pot from heat, and add shrimp. Cook, stirring often, until shrimp are bright pink and just cooked through, 2 to 3 minutes. Drain in a colander, and rinse under cold running water to stop the cooking process. Pat shrimp dry. Cover and chill until ready to serve.

3. Prepare the Horseradish Rémoulade and Vietnamese-Style Cocktail Sauce: Stir together all ingredients for each sauce (except garnishes) in separate small bowls until combined. Garnish rémoulade with mixed fresh herbs, and garnish cocktail sauce with crispy fried shallots and fresh cilantro. Place Seasoned Shrimp over ice, and serve with sauces.

CAJUN SHRIMP SALAD

Pickled-Shrimp Toasts

ACTIVE 30 MIN. · TOTAL 30 MIN., PLUS 24 HOURS CHILLING

SERVES 4

- 1/3 cup white wine vinegar
- 1 Tbsp. pickling spice
- 1 1/2 tsp. kosher salt
- 6 (5-inch) tarragon sprigs, divided
- 1/4 cup plus 1 tsp. fresh lemon juice (from 2 lemons), divided
- 3/4 tsp. black pepper, divided
- 1/3 cup olive oil
- 1 Tbsp. Dijon mustard, divided
- 1 lb. large peeled, deveined cooked shrimp
- 1 cup thinly sliced crosswise, unpeeled mirliton (chayote squash)
- 1/2 cup thinly sliced red onion (from 1 small onion)
- 1/2 cup mayonnaise
- 1 Tbsp. brandy or cognac
- 4 (3/4-inch-thick) brioche bread slices (from 1 [15-oz.] loaf), toasted on both sides
- 2 Tbsp. thinly sliced and quartered watermelon radish rounds (from 1 small radish)

1. Add vinegar, pickling spice, salt, 4 tarragon sprigs, 1/4 cup lemon juice, and 1/2 teaspoon black pepper to a small saucepan. Cook over medium, stirring often, to dissolve salt. Remove from heat, and whisk in oil and 2 teaspoons Dijon mustard until combined.

2. Place shrimp, mirliton, and onion in a gallon-size ziplock plastic bag. Add vinegar mixture to the bag, shaking to coat. Press out as much air as you can; seal bag. Lay sealed bag flat on a plate in refrigerator, and chill at least 24 hours or up to 3 days, flipping bag occasionally.

3. Remove leaves from remaining 2 tarragon sprigs, and finely chop. Stir together mayonnaise, brandy, 1 tablespoon chopped tarragon leaves, and remaining 1 teaspoon each lemon juice, mustard, and 1/4 teaspoon black pepper in a small bowl until combined.

4. Remove 2 cups of the shrimp mixture from bag; drain and pat dry. Discard tarragon sprigs. Reserve remaining shrimp mixture for another use. Spread 2 heaping tablespoons mayonnaise mixture on 1 side of each bread slice. Arrange 1/2 cup shrimp mixture on each bread slice. Sprinkle with radish slices and remaining chopped tarragon. Serve immediately.

Cajun Shrimp Salad

ACTIVE 30 MIN. · TOTAL 30 MIN.

SERVES 4

- 1/4 cup olive oil, divided
- 1 lb. jumbo peeled, deveined raw shrimp, patted dry
- 2 3/4 tsp. Cajun seasoning (such as Emeril's), divided
- 1/2 tsp. kosher salt, divided
- 2 (3 oz. each) andouille sausages, chopped into 1/4-inch cubes (about 1 cup)
- 1 large shallot, thinly sliced (about 1/2 cup)
- 3 Tbsp. sherry vinegar
- 2 tsp. honey
- 1 tsp. whole-grain mustard
- 8 cups mixed salad greens
- 4 cocktail tomatoes (such as Campari), quartered
- 2 unpeeled Persian or mini cucumbers, sliced on an angle (about 1 cup)
- 1/4 cup chopped mixed fresh tender herbs (such as parsley, chives, and basil), plus more for garnish
- 2 Tbsp. fresh lemon juice (from 1 lemon)

1. Heat 2 tablespoons oil in a large skillet over medium-high until shimmering. While oil heats, toss shrimp with 2 1/2 teaspoons Cajun seasoning and 1/4 teaspoon salt until evenly coated. Add shrimp to hot oil in a single layer; cook, undisturbed, until bottom side is lightly golden brown, 2 to 3 minutes. Turn shrimp, and cook just until they are opaque throughout, about 1 minute. Transfer to a large plate, and wipe skillet clean.

2. Add andouille and 1 tablespoon oil to skillet, and cook over medium, stirring often, until browned and crisp in spots, about 7 minutes. Add shallot and remaining 1/4 teaspoon Cajun seasoning, and cook, stirring often, until shallot is just softened, about 2 minutes. Add vinegar, scraping bottom of skillet with a wooden spoon to release browned bits. Remove from heat; stir in 3 tablespoons water, followed by the honey and mustard. Set aside.

3. Toss together salad greens, tomatoes, cucumbers, fresh herbs, lemon juice, and remaining 1 tablespoon oil and 1/4 teaspoon salt in a large bowl until evenly coated. Arrange salad greens on a large platter, and top with cooked shrimp. Spoon andouille mixture over salad; garnish with additional chopped fresh herbs.

PICKLED-SHRIMP TOASTS

Easter Made Easy

Take menu planning off your plate with these impressive yet doable mains and sides.

Lamb Chops with Herby Pickle-Caper Relish

ACTIVE 20 MIN. - TOTAL 45 MIN.

SERVES 6

- 2 (1¼-lb.) racks of lamb (8 bones each)
- 2 tsp. kosher salt
- 2 tsp. black pepper
- 1 tsp. ground cumin
- 6 Tbsp. olive oil, divided
- ¾ cup finely chopped tender fresh herbs (such as parsley and cilantro)
- 3 Tbsp. nonpareil capers
- 3 Tbsp. finely chopped dill pickles plus ¼ cup pickle brine (from 1 [16-oz.] jar)
- 3 Tbsp. finely chopped scallions, white and light green parts only (from 4 scallions)
- 1 Tbsp. finely chopped red Fresno chile (from 1 small chile)
- 2 garlic cloves, grated (about 1 tsp.)

1. Preheat oven to 450°F. Use a knife to scrape the ends of the lamb-rack bones clean, if desired. Stir together salt, black pepper, cumin, and 1 tablespoon oil in a small bowl. Place lamb on a foil-lined baking sheet; rub spice mixture all over meat. Turn the lamb racks so bones are pointing down.

2. Roast in preheated oven until a meat thermometer registers 125°F (for medium-rare), 20 to 23 minutes. Transfer to a cutting board; let rest 10 minutes.

3. Stir together herbs, capers, pickles, pickle brine, scallions, chile, garlic, and remaining 5 tablespoons olive oil in a small bowl. Slice the lamb in between the bones. Arrange lamb chops on a serving platter; top with Herby Pickle-Caper Relish.

Whipped Potatoes with Brie

ACTIVE 20 MIN. - TOTAL 40 MIN.

SERVES 8

Cook 3 lb. peeled and chopped **gold potatoes** in a saucepan of boiling salted water until tender, 12 to 15 minutes. Drain; return to pan. Cook over medium-low until excess moisture has evaporated, 2 to 3 minutes. Add 1 cup **half-and-half**, 4 Tbsp. melted **unsalted butter**, 2 tsp. **kosher salt**, and ¼ tsp. each **ground nutmeg** and **dry mustard**; heat until steaming, about 4 minutes. Remove from heat; stir in 8 oz. cubed **Brie cheese** (rind trimmed and discarded). Beat with an electric hand mixer until creamy, about 1 minute. Spoon into a serving bowl; top with additional butter and **chopped chives.**

WHIPPED POTATOES WITH BRIE

LAMB CHOPS WITH HERBY PICKLE-CAPER RELISH

SALMON WITH CITRUS AND OLIVES

Salmon with Citrus and Olives

ACTIVE 20 MIN. - TOTAL 35 MIN.
SERVES 6

- 2½ tsp. paprika
- 1 tsp. ground coriander
- 6 Tbsp. olive oil, divided
- 2½ tsp. kosher salt, divided
- 1 tsp. black pepper, divided
- 2 tsp. grated lemon zest plus 2 Tbsp. fresh juice (from 1 lemon), divided
- 1 (2- to 2½-lb.) skinless salmon fillet (about 1½ inches thick)
- 4 small assorted oranges (such as navel, Cara Cara, or blood), divided
- 1 cup fresh flat-leaf parsley leaves
- 1 cup baby arugula
- 1 cup Castelvetrano olives, torn
- ½ cup thinly sliced shallot (from 1 large shallot)

1. Preheat oven to 300°F. Whisk together paprika, coriander, 3 tablespoons olive oil, 2 teaspoons salt, ¾ teaspoon pepper, and 1 teaspoon lemon zest in a bowl until smooth. Place salmon on a rimmed baking sheet lined with parchment paper. Rub spice mixture over fish. Drizzle with 2 tablespoons olive oil.
2. Bake in preheated oven until salmon flakes easily with a fork and registers 125°F in the thickest part (for medium), 20 to 25 minutes.
3. Grate zest from 1 of the oranges to yield ½ teaspoon. Use a knife to remove peel and pith of all 4 oranges; slice crosswise into rounds. Whisk together orange zest; remaining 1 teaspoon lemon zest; 2 tablespoons lemon juice; and remaining 1 tablespoon olive oil, ½ teaspoon salt, and ¼ teaspoon pepper in a large bowl. Add parsley, arugula, olives, shallot, and sliced oranges; toss to coat. Transfer salmon to a serving platter. Arrange citrus-and-olive mixture around salmon. Serve immediately.

Skillet-Roasted Radishes

ACTIVE 15 MIN. - TOTAL 30 MIN.
SERVES 4

Trim 2 (8-oz.) bunches **radishes with greens**; reserve greens. Halve radishes lengthwise; toss with 1 Tbsp. **olive oil**, ½ tsp. **kosher salt**, and ¼ tsp. **black pepper** in a 12-inch ovenproof skillet. Arrange radishes cut sides down; roast at 450°F until starting to soften, 10 minutes. Add 2 Tbsp. cubed **unsalted butter**, 3 sprigs **fresh thyme**, and 2 smashed **garlic** cloves to skillet. Continue roasting until radishes are tender, 10 to 12 minutes. Remove from oven; stir in 1½ tsp **apple cider vinegar**, ¼ tsp. **salt**, and reserved radish greens until wilted.

SKILLET-ROASTED RADISHES

Hot Honey Chicken Leg Quarters

ACTIVE 20 MIN. - TOTAL 55 MIN.

SERVES 6

- ½ cup honey
- 2 red Fresno chiles, stemmed and sliced
- 1 Tbsp. unsalted butter
- 2–3 tsp. hot sauce
- 2 tsp. Worcestershire sauce
- 6 chicken leg quarters (about 3¾ lb. total)
- 1 tsp. black pepper
- 1 tsp. onion powder
- 3 tsp. kosher salt, divided
- 2 Tbsp. canola oil, divided
- 1 red onion, peeled and cut into 6 wedges
- Thyme sprigs

1. Preheat oven to 425°F with rack in the upper third position. Bring honey, chiles, butter, hot sauce, and Worcestershire sauce to a simmer in a small saucepan over medium-low. Remove from heat. Cover and let stand 30 minutes.
2. Place chicken on a rimmed baking sheet; pat dry. Combine pepper, onion powder, and 2½ teaspoons salt in a bowl; sprinkle over chicken. Turn chicken skin side up; drizzle with 1½ tablespoons oil. Gently rub to coat. Roast in preheated oven 15 minutes.
3. Toss onion wedges with remaining ½ tablespoon oil and ½ teaspoon salt in a bowl. Tuck onion around chicken. Roast in preheated oven until thermometer inserted into thickest part of chicken registers 175°F, 20 to 25 minutes. Remove from oven; adjust oven to broil.
4. Brush some of the honey mixture over chicken and onion. Broil until browned, 2 to 3 minutes. Remove from oven; brush with honey mixture. Transfer chicken and onion to a serving platter; drizzle with remaining honey mixture. Garnish with thyme sprigs.

Crunchy Spring Salad

ACTIVE 20 MIN. - TOTAL 20 MIN.

SERVES 6

Whisk together ¼ cup **buttermilk,** 2 Tbsp. **mayonnaise,** 2 tsp. **Dijon mustard,** ½ tsp. **honey,** ½ tsp. **kosher salt,** and ¼ tsp. **black pepper** in a small bowl. Toss together 4 cups **baby gem** or chopped **romaine lettuce** leaves (from 2 heads), 3 cups halved **sugar snap peas,** 2 cups shredded **red cabbage,** 2 cups shaved **cucumber** ribbons (from 2 cucumbers), and ¼ cup **fresh mint** leaves in a large bowl. Drizzle with half of the dressing until coated. Transfer to a serving platter; sprinkle with 2 Tbsp. roasted salted **sunflower seeds.** Serve with remaining dressing.

CRUNCHY SPRING SALAD

HOT HONEY
CHICKEN
LEG QUARTERS

STUFFED PORK
LOIN WITH BACON
AND GREENS

Stuffed Pork Loin with Bacon and Greens

ACTIVE 35 MIN. - TOTAL 1 HOUR, 30 MIN.
SERVES 8

- **6 thick-cut bacon slices, finely chopped (about 1 cup packed)**
- **1 yellow onion, finely chopped (about 1½ cups)**
- **⅓ cup chopped marinated sun-dried tomatoes in oil (from 1 [8.5-oz.] jar)**
- **3 garlic cloves, finely chopped (about 1 Tbsp.)**
- **¾ tsp. plus 1 Tbsp. kosher salt, divided**
- **1¾ tsp. black pepper, divided**
- **2 bunches fresh mustard greens, stemmed and chopped (about 8 cups)**
- **¼ cup panko breadcrumbs**
- **1 (3-lb.) boneless pork loin roast**
- **2 Tbsp. stone-ground Dijon mustard**

1. Cook bacon in a large skillet over medium, stirring occasionally, until crisp, 10 to 12 minutes. Transfer bacon to a plate; reserve drippings in skillet. Add onion to skillet; cook over medium, stirring occasionally, until softened, 8 to 10 minutes. Add sun-dried tomatoes, garlic, and ¾ teaspoon each salt and pepper. Gradually add mustard greens, stirring until wilted, about 5 minutes. Remove from heat; stir in panko and cooked bacon. Let cool 10 minutes. Preheat oven to 350°F.

2. Place pork loin on a cutting board, fat side down. Slice lengthwise down center of loin, stopping about ¾ inch from bottom (do not cut all the way through). Open up loin like a book; repeat slicing process with each side. Cover loin with plastic wrap; pound to an even ¾-inch thickness.

3. Spread greens mixture over pork, leaving a 1-inch border. Starting at one long side, roll pork into a tight cylinder. Tie with kitchen twine at 1-inch intervals. Sprinkle with remaining 1 tablespoon salt and 1 teaspoon pepper.

4. Place loin seam side down on a rimmed baking sheet; brush evenly with mustard. Roast in preheated oven until a thermometer inserted into pork registers 145°F, 45 to 50 minutes. Transfer to a cutting board; let rest for 10 minutes before removing twine and slicing.

Lemon-Pepper Asparagus

ACTIVE 10 MIN. - TOTAL 10 MIN.
SERVES 4

Heat 1 Tbsp. **olive oil** and 1 Tbsp. **unsalted butter** in a large skillet over medium-high. Add 1 lb. trimmed **asparagus** and ½ tsp. each **kosher salt** and **black pepper.** Cook, tossing occasionally, until asparagus is tender-crisp, about 5 minutes. Remove from heat; add 1 Tbsp. each **fresh lemon juice** and **unsalted butter.** Toss until butter is melted and evenly coats asparagus. Garnish with grated **lemon zest.**

LEMON-PEPPER ASPARAGUS

Fried Chicken: A Love Story

No Southern dish feeds the soul like this one.

WHEN I WAS 6 YEARS OLD, I spent weekends with my grandma, Ava, so my mother could cook the Saturday shift at Red's Steakhouse and BBQ. Touches of mild dementia had already begun to show in Ava, but her daughters later referred to it, gently, as "that time, you know, when Mama was still all right."

Every Saturday morning, I'd sit at the kitchen table as she fried me the perfect chicken, because she loved me. She was nearsighted and a little bowlegged, so it was great entertainment to help her run one down in the yard. In her flower-print dress and heavy, sensible shoes, she'd cuss under her breath with every jerk and feint. She'd corner one, sooner or later; whack it on the head or neck with a broken broom handle; thank Jesus; and then scald, pluck, and clean it quickly, expertly. That is why you never ever name a chicken.

She would lightly dust the pieces with salt, flour, and a pinch of black pepper before frying them in lard in an ancient iron skillet. While cooking, she would talk nonstop to my grandpa Charlie Bundrum, who had been dead for seven years. Maybe she wasn't as all right as the grown-ups believed.

I thought she was perfect.

When it was done, she would fork the pieces out, set them on a chipped ceramic platter, and cover them with a clean white cloth, sewn out of flour sacks from the Great Depression. I waited in agony for it to cool and then sat on the vinyl rug in front of the black-and-white Philco television, watching cartoons and holding a chicken leg in one hand and a biscuit in the other.

Life has never been that good since. When I was done with a piece, I would take the bone, which was gnawed clean of everything, and—when my grandma was not looking—toss it behind the couch. I don't know why; I was 6. (Once a week, my mother would shove back the couch to pick up the bones and tell me never to do it again.) When Ava would see my empty hand, she'd drop another drumstick into it. "That boy sure likes his chicken," she would say to the open window, the willow trees, and the man I guess only she could see.

What made it so perfect, other than the love in it? In a word, restraint. My mother's recipe (below) is as close to Ava's as she can get these days. "Keep it simple," my mother says, though she does not claim that tarted-up chicken is all bad. "It's fine—for other people."
—Rick Bragg

Margaret Bragg's Fried Chicken

ACTIVE 35 MIN. - TOTAL 45 MIN.
SERVES 4

- **1 (4-lb.) whole frying chicken**
- **1 Tbsp. kosher salt**
- **1 tsp. black pepper**
- **2 cups all-purpose flour**
- **1–2 lb. lard, for frying (enough to form at least a 1-inch pool in the skillet)**

1. Cut the chicken into 8 pieces (2 each of breasts, thighs, wings, and drumsticks), being sure to save the liver, gizzards, back, neck, or anything else, even if you are not sure what it is. Salt and pepper all the pieces lightly. Using your hands, dust the damp pieces—top, bottom, and sides—as completely as you can with flour. Do not dredge in egg wash, etc. The point is to have a light, barely there crust. Cover and set aside.

2. In a large cast-iron skillet (or tall-sided cast-iron chicken fryer or Dutch oven), heat lard over medium-high until it liquefies, but do not turn the heat so high that it begins to smoke. Gently, carefully add the chicken pieces. Let them crisp for a moment, and then reduce the heat to medium. Do not worry about turning the chicken before you reduce the heat.

3. Over medium heat, cook the chicken between 20 and 25 minutes, turning it 4 times. (I am not sure what the science of this is; I guess it's just because my mother says so.) Add gizzards, liver, and other pieces about halfway through the process. Some people cook livers for only a few minutes, but my mother has such a fear of undercooked poultry—it's a cultural thing—that she crisps the organ meats a little more than necessary. In between gyrations, cover the skillet with a lid (again, being careful because steam can build up in just a few minutes). If you don't know whether your chicken is done, remove a thigh, cut into it, and look, being careful not to burn yourself or burn up the rest of the chicken. You can stick a meat thermometer into it if you have one and know how to use it, but in this you are on your own. We have never used one.

4. Let the chicken cool at least 10 minutes. The thighs retain heat, and I've seen them smoke when I've taken a bite, even after 10 minutes.

Fried and True

My mother's unconventional rules for perfect chicken

LEAN INTO LARD

You may be unable to bring yourself to fry your chicken in lard. It is not a sin to feel this way. My mother often fries hers using cooking oil. Some go with peanut oil. Others swear by Crisco. Very smart people will go on and on talking about burn ratios and such. I do not associate with them. Neither does my mother. She still uses lard a third of the time, for the sake of history.

CROWD THE SKILLET

Some cooks fry only a few pieces at a time to make sure the chicken crisps correctly, and they turn it only once. But my people do crowd the skillet. "I make sure there's just enough space," my mother explained. "It'll taste better, having it all cook together—white and dark meat, the liver, the bony pieces." She puts the bigger ones in the middle of the skillet and places the wings on the outside.

"Every Saturday morning, I'd sit at the kitchen table as [Ava] fried me the perfect chicken because she loved me." —Rick Bragg

A Slice of Sunshine

This easy-peasy lemon layer cake is baked in a single pan.

Lemon Buttermilk Cake

ACTIVE 45 MIN. - TOTAL 1 HOUR, 15 MIN., PLUS 2 HOURS, 35 MIN. COOLING AND CHILLING
SERVES 12

- 3 cups all-purpose flour
- 2 tsp. baking powder
- 1½ tsp. kosher salt, divided
- 1¼ cups whole buttermilk
- 2 tsp. vanilla extract
- 3 Tbsp. grated lemon zest plus 5 Tbsp. fresh lemon juice (from 6 lemons), divided
- 2 cups granulated sugar
- 1½ cups softened unsalted butter, divided
- 4 large eggs, at room temperature
- Lemon Cake Soak (recipe follows)
- 1 (8-oz.) pkg. cream cheese, softened
- 4½ cups powdered sugar
- 2–3 drops yellow liquid food coloring (optional)
- Lemon slices, for garnish (optional)

1. Preheat oven to 350°F. Coat a 13 x 9-inch baking pan with cooking spray. Line with parchment paper. Whisk together flour, baking powder, and 1 teaspoon salt in a medium bowl. Set aside. Stir together buttermilk, vanilla, and ¼ cup lemon juice in a large liquid measuring cup. Set aside.
2. Beat together granulated sugar and 2 tablespoons lemon zest in the bowl of a stand mixer fitted with a paddle attachment on low speed until fragrant, about 30 seconds. Add 1 cup butter; beat on medium speed until light and fluffy, about 2 minutes. Add eggs, 1 at a time, beating well after each addition and scraping down sides of bowl as needed.
3. With mixer on low speed, add flour mixture and buttermilk mixture alternately to butter mixture, beginning and ending with flour mixture, beating until just combined. Transfer batter to prepared pan; smooth into an even layer.
4. Bake in preheated oven until a wooden pick inserted in center comes out clean, 30 to 32 minutes. Let cool in pan on a wire rack for 15 minutes. Remove from pan onto rack, and discard parchment. Brush Lemon Cake Soak over warm cake. Let cool completely, about 90 minutes.
5. Beat together cream cheese and remaining ½ cup butter, 1 tablespoon each lemon zest and juice, and ½ teaspoon salt in the bowl of a stand mixer fitted with a paddle attachment on medium speed until smooth, about 1 minute. With mixer on low speed, gradually beat in powdered sugar until smooth and fluffy, about 3 minutes. Add food coloring, if desired; beat 30 seconds more.
6. Cut cake in half crosswise. Place 1 half on a serving plate; spread 1 cup frosting over top. Chill, uncovered, until frosting is firm, about 20 minutes. Place second cake half on top; spread remaining frosting over top and sides. Chill, uncovered, until frosting is firm, about 30 minutes; or refrigerate, covered, up to 3 days. Serve at room temperature. Garnish with lemon slices, if desired.

Lemon Cake Soak

ACTIVE 5 MIN. - TOTAL 5 MIN.
MAKES 6 TABLESPOONS

Stir together ¼ cup **fresh lemon juice** and ¼ cup **granulated sugar** in a small saucepan; cook over medium, stirring often, until sugar dissolves, about 2 minutes.

STACK IT UP
Turn the page for step-by-step tips for assembling the cake.

A lemon simple syrup brushed on the warm cake gives it a flavor boost and makes it extra moist, too.

COOKING SCHOOL

TIPS AND TRICKS FROM THE SOUTH'S MOST TRUSTED KITCHEN

One-Pan Wonder

Turn any sheet cake into a layered dessert in four simple steps.

1. SPLIT
Use a long, serrated knife to slice the cooled sheet cake in half crosswise to create 2 rectangles.

2. FROST
Place 1 half of the cake on a serving plate; spread 1 cup of the frosting evenly on top. Chill 20 minutes.

3. STACK
Carefully top with the remaining cake half. Line up the edges of the 2 halves so the sides are straight.

4. FINISH
Spread the remaining frosting over the top and sides of the cake. For neat slices, chill cake until the frosting is firm.

May

Gimme Chives!

More than a garnish, this member of the onion family adds fresh flavor to biscuits.

Chive Biscuits

ACTIVE 15 MIN. - TOTAL 45 MIN.
MAKES 12

Preheat oven to 425°F. Line a rimmed baking sheet with parchment. Stir together 3½ cups **soft wheat all-purpose flour,** 2 Tbsp. **granulated sugar,** 1 Tbsp. **baking powder,** 2 tsp. **kosher salt,** and ½ tsp. **baking soda** in a bowl. Using 2 forks, cut in 1¼ cups cold **butter** until crumbly. Stir in ½ cup each cold **buttermilk,** cold **sour cream,** and finely chopped **fresh chives** until a shaggy dough forms. Turn out dough onto a lightly floured surface; pat into a rectangle; cut into quarters. Stack quarters; pat down again into a rectangle. Repeat cutting and stacking once. Roll dough into a 9 x 7-inch rectangle; trim to create straight sides, if desired. Cut into 12 (2-inch) squares. Arrange squares ½ inch apart on prepared pan. Freeze until cold, about 10 minutes. Brush with 1 beaten **egg;** sprinkle with **flaky sea salt.** Bake until golden brown, about 15 minutes. Let cool 5 minutes; serve warm.

Chive Butter

ACTIVE 5 MIN. - TOTAL 5 MIN.
MAKES ABOUT 1 CUP

Stir together 1 cup softened **salted butter,** ½ cup finely chopped **fresh chives,** 1 tsp. grated **lemon zest,** and 1 tsp. **black pepper** in a small bowl until combined. Garnish with **flaky sea salt** and **fresh chive blossoms,** if desired.

LAY IT ON THICK
To make this spread extra delicious, use a European-style butter.

CHIVE BUTTER
CHIVE BISCUITS

Get the Ball Rolling

Turn a retro party staple into a festive Kentucky Derby appetizer.

SOME MIGHT call them old-fashioned, but I think that cheese balls deserve a comeback. At one time, you could find the herb- or pecan-covered mounds at every party you attended. Part of their allure is that until someone digs in, you never know what's inside—it could be spreadable cheese, deviled ham, or some secret concoction closely guarded by the cook.

Eventually, they fell out of fashion in favor of newfangled snacks, like whipped feta or baked brie. While I love these starters, too, there's something nostalgic and fun about the mysterious nature of a cheese ball. Regardless of the contents, each bite is flavorful, creamy, and crunchy. So to help bring this appetizer back in style, I gave it a modern makeover.

I often like to start by swapping out the traditional tray for a serving board, which is my go-to for grazing these days. This time, instead of using seasoned cream cheese or ham spread as the base, I chose pimiento cheese—the pâté of the South. I couldn't limit myself to just one coating, so I divided the mixture into five different balls. More choices are always better.

These Mini Pimiento Cheese Balls covered in chopped bacon, toasted pecans, fresh chives, fried onions, or everything bagel seasoning will make their debut at my Derby party this year, served with a few drizzles, including pepper jelly, cane syrup, and hot honey. I was lucky enough to attend the 148th running of the Kentucky Derby, when Rich Strike made the second-largest upset in the race's history. His win was completely unexpected, like this cheese ball revival that no one will see coming.

Mini Pimiento Cheese Balls

To make these easy appetizers ahead, wrap the uncoated balls in plastic or tuck them into a ziplock plastic bag. Refrigerate up to four days, and then just before serving, roll them in the coatings and accompany with sauces.

ACTIVE 15 MIN. - TOTAL 45 MIN.

SERVES 12

CHEESE BALLS

- 1 (8-oz.) pkg. cream cheese, softened
- 2 cups shredded extra-sharp cheddar cheese (about 8 oz.)
- 1 (4-oz.) jar diced pimientos, well drained
- 2 tsp. Worcestershire sauce
- 1/4 tsp. kosher salt
- 1/4 tsp. black pepper
- 1/4 tsp. smoked paprika
- 1/8 tsp. cayenne pepper

COATINGS

- 3/4 cup cooked and chopped bacon (from 10 slices)
- 3/4 cup chopped crispy fried onions (such as French's)
- 3/4 cup chopped toasted pecans
- 3/4 cup chopped fresh chives
- 1/2 cup everything bagel seasoning

EXTRAS

- Crackers, crudités, or toasted baguette slices, for serving
- 1/3 cup pepper jelly, heated in microwave to loosen
- 1/3 cup cane syrup
- 1/3 cup hot honey

1. Prepare the Cheese Balls: Using a rubber spatula, stir all ingredients until thoroughly combined. Using your hands, shape cheese mixture into 5 balls.

2. Spread your Coatings of choice on plates. Roll the Cheese Balls into the desired Coatings, pressing gently to cover completely. Refrigerate, uncovered, 30 minutes.

3. Place coated Cheese Balls in the center of a large tray or serving board, and surround them with crackers, crudités, or toasted baguette slices. Serve with small bowls of pepper jelly, cane syrup, and hot honey on the side.

Race-Day Refresher

No Derby party is complete without this classic cocktail.

Ivy's Mint Julep

ACTIVE 5 MIN. - TOTAL 20 MIN.

SERVES 1

Place a julep cup or freezer-safe glass in freezer; chill 15 minutes. Place 6 **fresh mint** leaves in serving cup; gently press leaves against cup with back of spoon to release flavors. Add 1 tsp. **powdered sugar** and 1 tsp. **water,** stirring gently until sugar is dissolved. Pack cup tightly with crushed **ice,** filling cup two-thirds full. Pour 2 oz. **bourbon** over ice; stir briskly. Add additional crushed **ice** to fill cup. Add 1 oz. **bourbon.** Garnish with **mint sprigs,** if desired.

MINI PIMIENTO
CHEESE BALLS

Cheers to Mom

Refreshing basil-infused limeade is a surprisingly sweet way to celebrate Mother's Day.

I AM BLESSED to live a short drive from my mother after more than a decade of being a plane trip away. Even though I see her more regularly now, it's not nearly as much as I'd like. With a busy fourth-grader in the house, my calendar is overpopulated with kids' birthday parties, music lessons, basketball practices, and my own commitments. And when my mom and I do spend time together, it's usually with our whole family.

Not long ago, I wanted some solo time with my mom, so I asked her out for lunch. And then I made a reservation at a nice restaurant about three hours away from where we live. I figured that six hours in the car would give us plenty of uninterrupted time to catch up. The meal was very good, but it was actually the drive that we enjoyed the most—we talked the whole way there and back.

It made me realize that time is the gift that every mother wants. But if you're lucky enough to have your mom close by, you don't have to go to such great lengths or spend way too much money on gas to be together.

This Mother's Day, make a pitcher of something refreshing over ice—like our Basil Limeade—grab some snacks, and set aside a few hours to visit with your mom without any distractions. (That means just you and her—and turn off your cell phone.) Of course, you can do this with an aunt, a grandmother, a sister, or any maternal figure in your life—or, if you are a mom, with your own children. Kids might not like to admit it, but they want quality time with you too.

Yes, cashmere socks and bouquets of tulips are nice (just in case my husband and child are reading this), but making memories with your mom is priceless.
—Lisa Cericola

Basil Limeade

ACTIVE 15 MIN. · TOTAL 35 MIN.
SERVES 4

- 2/3 cup granulated sugar
- 1 packed cup (1 oz.) basil sprigs, plus small sprigs for garnish
- 3/4 cup fresh lime juice (from 6 to 8 limes)
- Ice
- Lime wedges, for garnish

Bring sugar and ½ cup water to a simmer in a small saucepan over medium, stirring often to dissolve sugar. Remove from heat; add basil, and stir until submerged. Let basil syrup stand at room temperature until mixture is cool, about 20 minutes. Pour through a fine mesh strainer into a small pitcher; discard solids. Stir in lime juice and 3 cups water. Serve over ice, and garnish with small basil sprigs and lime wedges.

Frosty Basil Limeade

SERVES 4

Prepare basil syrup as directed in Basil Limeade recipe (left). Process syrup, 1 cup loosely packed fresh basil leaves, ¾ cup fresh lime juice, ½ cup water, and 6 cups ice cubes in a blender on low speed, gradually increasing speed, until thick and slushy, about 45 seconds. Garnish with a lime wheel and basil leaves.

Basil-Blueberry Limeade

SERVES 4

Prepare Basil Limeade (left) as directed, adding 1 cup fresh blueberries to sugar-water mixture. Bring to a simmer, remove from heat, and then smash berries with a fork before adding basil. Proceed with recipe. Serve over ice; garnish with basil sprigs and more blueberries.

Fruit Punch

Sweet-tart strawberry lemonade inspired these vibrant desserts.

NO-BAKE
BERRY-LEMON PIE
(PAGE 99)

STRAWBERRY-LEMONADE POPS (PAGE 100)

SWEET TIP
Resist the temptation to press the fresh berries into the batter; they will sink and settle as the cake bakes.

Sunken Strawberry-Lemon Cake

ACTIVE 30 MIN. - TOTAL 2 HOURS, 5 MIN.
SERVES 12

- Baking spray
- 1¼ cups granulated sugar
- ½ cup unsalted butter, softened
- 2 large eggs, at room temperature
- 2 tsp. vanilla extract
- 2½ cups all-purpose flour
- 1¾ tsp. baking powder
- ½ tsp. kosher salt
- ½ tsp. baking soda
- ⅔ cup sour cream, at room temperature
- ½ cup whole milk, at room temperature
- 2 Tbsp. grated lemon zest plus 2 tsp. fresh juice, plus lemon zest curls for garnish (from 3 lemons)
- 3½ cups hulled and quartered fresh ripe strawberries (from 2 [1-lb.] pkg.), divided
- 3 Tbsp. sparkling sugar
- Sweetened whipped cream

1. Preheat oven to 350°F. Coat a 13 x 9-inch baking pan with baking spray; set aside.

2. Beat granulated sugar and butter in a large bowl with an electric mixer on medium speed until fluffy, 3 to 4 minutes. With mixer on low speed, add eggs, 1 at a time, beating until combined after each addition. Beat in vanilla until combined.

3. Whisk together flour, baking powder, salt, and baking soda in a medium bowl until combined. Whisk together sour cream, milk, and lemon zest and juice in a separate medium bowl until combined. With mixer on low speed, add flour mixture to butter mixture alternately with sour cream mixture, beating until combined. Fold in 2 cups strawberries.

4. Spread batter evenly in prepared pan. Scatter remaining 1½ cups strawberries over top; do not press berries into batter. Sprinkle top with sparkling sugar.

5. Bake until a wooden pick inserted in center comes out clean about 35 minutes. Let cool in pan on a wire rack 1 hour. Slice and serve with whipped cream; garnish with lemon zest curls.

Strawberry-Lemon Pound Cake

Freeze-dried berries are best for this batter; they add flavor and color while keeping the cake tender.

ACTIVE 35 MIN. - TOTAL 3 HOURS, 50 MIN.

SERVES 8

CAKE

- Baking spray
- 1¼ cups granulated sugar
- ¾ cup unsalted butter, softened
- ⅓ cup packed light brown sugar
- 1½ Tbsp. grated lemon zest (from 3 lemons)
- 3 large eggs, at room temperature
- 2 cups all-purpose flour
- 1¼ tsp. ground cardamom
- ½ tsp. kosher salt
- ⅛ tsp. baking soda
- ½ cup sour cream, at room temperature
- 3 Tbsp. whole milk, at room temperature
- 2 tsp. vanilla extract
- ⅓ cup crushed freeze-dried strawberries (from 1 [1-oz.] pkg.)

GLAZE

- 1¼ cups powdered sugar
- ⅓ cup freeze-dried strawberries, plus more crushed freeze-dried strawberries for garnish (from 1 [1-oz.] pkg.)
- 2 Tbsp. unsalted butter, melted
- 2–3 Tbsp. whole milk, at room temperature

ADDITIONAL INGREDIENTS

- Sliced fresh strawberries
- Lemon slices

1. Prepare the Cake: Preheat oven to 325°F. Coat a 9 x 5-inch loaf pan with baking spray. Line bottom and sides of pan with parchment paper, leaving a 2-inch overhang on all sides; set aside.

2. Beat granulated sugar, butter, brown sugar, and lemon zest in a large bowl with an electric mixer on medium speed until fluffy, 3 to 4 minutes. With mixer on low speed, add eggs, 1 at a time, beating until combined after each addition.

3. Whisk together flour, cardamom, salt, and baking soda in a medium bowl. Whisk together sour cream, milk, and vanilla in a separate medium bowl. With mixer on low speed, gradually add the flour mixture to butter mixture alternately with sour cream mixture, beating until nearly combined. Fold in the freeze-dried strawberries until combined; spread batter into prepared pan, smoothing top with an offset spatula.

4. Bake until set and a wooden pick inserted in center comes out with a few moist crumbs, about 1 hour, 15 minutes, loosely covering with aluminum foil halfway through baking time, if needed. Using parchment as handles, immediately remove Cake from pan; let cool completely on a wire rack, about 2 hours.

5. Prepare the Glaze: Process powdered sugar and dried strawberries in a food processor until finely ground and well combined, about 30 seconds. Stir together powdered sugar mixture, butter, and 2 tablespoons milk in a medium bowl until combined. Gradually stir in remaining 1 tablespoon milk, ½ teaspoon at a time, until desired consistency.

6. Spoon Glaze over Cake; garnish with more crushed freeze-dried strawberries, sliced fresh strawberries, and lemon slices.

STRAWBERRY-
LEMONADE JELLY MOLD

SWEET TIP
For a smooth and shiny dessert, nudge the berries away from the edges of the pan before the gelatin sets.

Strawberry-Lemonade Jelly Mold

ACTIVE 25 MIN. - TOTAL 25 MIN., PLUS 8 HOURS CHILLING

SERVES 6

- 3 cups thinly sliced fresh ripe strawberries (from 1 [1-lb.] pkg.), plus fresh whole strawberries for garnish
- 1 (3-oz.) pkg. strawberry-flavor gelatin
- 1 (3-oz.) pkg. lemon-flavor gelatin
- 1¼ cups boiling water
- 1¼ cups cold lemon-lime soft drink (such as Sprite)
- Candied Lemon Slices (recipe, right)
- Fresh mint leaves

1. Coat a 5- to 6-cup Bundt pan with cooking spray. Add sliced strawberries to prepared pan in an even layer; set aside.
2. Whisk together strawberry and lemon gelatins in a large heatproof bowl. Gradually add boiling water to gelatin mixture, gently whisking until dissolved, about 2 minutes. Stir in soft drink; let stand until foam on top dissipates, about 10 minutes.
3. Gradually pour gelatin mixture over strawberries in prepared pan. Chill, uncovered, until beginning to set, about 20 minutes. For a smoother exterior, gently move strawberries away from pan edges, allowing area to refill with gelatin. Chill until set, at least 8 hours.
4. To unmold, fill a large bowl with hot water; carefully dip bottom of pan in water for 10 seconds. Place a serving plate upside down over pan. Holding plate and pan together firmly, carefully invert. Slowly remove pan. Garnish with Candied Lemon Slices, whole strawberries, and mint leaves.

Candied Lemon Slices

ACTIVE 30 MIN. - TOTAL 1 HOUR, 10 MIN., PLUS 8 HOURS DRYING

SERVES 6

- 14 (¼-inch-thick) seeded lemon slices (from 2 lemons)
- 2½ cups granulated sugar

1. Add water to a medium skillet to a depth of 1 inch. Add lemon slices, and bring to a boil over medium-high; do not stir. Drain through a fine mesh strainer, and discard cooking liquid; set lemon slices aside. (Do not wipe skillet clean.)
2. Bring granulated sugar and 2¼ cups water to a boil in same skillet over medium-high, stirring often. Add drained lemon slices; reduce heat to a simmer over medium-low. Cook, turning occasionally, until pulp is glassy, 45 to 50 minutes.
3. Remove lemon slices using tongs, and place in an even layer on a wire rack set over a large baking sheet. (Reserve lemon syrup for another use.) Let lemons stand, uncovered, until slightly dry but still sticky, at least 8 hours or up to 24 hours. Use immediately, or store in an airtight container in refrigerator up to 1 week.

No-Bake Berry-Lemon Pie

(Photo, page 92)

ACTIVE 50 MIN. - TOTAL 1 HOUR, 10 MIN., PLUS 4 HOURS CHILLING

SERVES 8

- 1½ cups loosely packed, finely ground crumbs of shortbread cookies (such as Lorna Doone; from 1 [10-oz.] pkg.)
- ¼ cup packed light brown sugar
- 2 tsp. grated lemon zest (from 1 lemon), divided, plus lemon zest curls for garnish
- 6 Tbsp. salted butter, melted
- 1 (3.4-oz.) pkg. lemon-flavor instant pudding and pie filling (such as Jell-O)
- 1 cup cold whole milk
- 1 (8-oz.) pkg. cream cheese, softened
- 1½ cups heavy whipping cream
- ½ cup unsifted powdered sugar
- ¼ cup strawberry-flavor gelatin (from 1 [3-oz.] pkg.)
- ½ cup boiling water
- Halved fresh strawberries

1. Generously coat a 9-inch pie plate with cooking spray. Stir together cookie crumbs, brown sugar, and 1 teaspoon zest in a medium bowl until well combined; add butter, stirring until combined. Press into bottom and up sides of prepared pie plate. Freeze while preparing filling.
2. Whisk together pudding mix, whole milk, and remaining 1 teaspoon zest in a medium bowl until well combined, about 2 minutes. Beat cream cheese in a large bowl with an electric mixer on medium speed until smooth, about 1 minute. Add pudding mixture, and beat on medium-low speed until well combined, about 30 seconds. Spread pudding mixture into prepared crust. Chill until slightly firm, about 30 minutes.
3. During last 15 minutes of chilling, beat cream and powdered sugar in a large bowl with an electric mixer on medium speed until stiff peaks form, 3 to 4 minutes. Place gelatin in a small heatproof bowl; add boiling water, and whisk until dissolved, about 2 minutes. Whisk 2 tablespoons whipped cream into gelatin mixture until combined. With mixer on medium speed, gradually add gelatin mixture to whipped cream in a steady stream, beating until combined.
4. Spread 2 cups cream mixture over pudding mixture. Chill, uncovered, until set, at least 4 hours or up to 18 hours. Refrigerate remaining cream mixture in an airtight container until ready to serve.
5. Stir reserved cream mixture until smooth. Pipe or spread over pie as desired. Garnish with strawberries and lemon zest curls. Cover and refrigerate up to 3 days, if desired.

Best-Ever Strawberry Lemonade

ACTIVE 15 MIN. - TOTAL 15 MIN.
SERVES 8

- 6 large lemons
- 1 lb. fresh strawberries (4 cups), plus more for garnish
- 1¼ cups granulated sugar
- Ice
- Fresh mint leaves

1. Cut the ends from 5 lemons. Stand each cut lemon on a cut side. Cut peel and pith from lemons; discard peel and pith. Quarter each peeled lemon, and place in a blender. Slice remaining 1 lemon, and reserve for garnish.
2. Hull fresh strawberries. Place strawberries, sugar, and 2 cups water in blender with lemon quarters; blend on HIGH until almost fully pureed, 30 seconds to 1 minute. Pour through a fine mesh strainer into a pitcher, and discard solids. Stir in 2½ cups more water.
3. Serve over ice, and garnish with reserved lemon slices, fresh mint leaves, and more fresh strawberries.

BEST-EVER STRAWBERRY LEMONADE

Strawberry-Lemonade Pops

(Photo, page 93)

Don't have ice-pop molds? Use 3-ounce paper cups, and secure each stick in the center with masking tape.

ACTIVE 15 MIN. - TOTAL 15 MIN., PLUS 8 HOURS FREEZING
MAKES 8 TO 10

- 1 lb. fresh strawberries, hulled and halved (about 4 cups)
- ⅓ cup granulated sugar
- 2 tsp. grated lemon zest plus ¼ cup fresh juice (from 1 lemon)
- ⅓ cup strawberry jam
- Ice-pop sticks

1. Place strawberries, sugar, and lemon zest and juice in a blender. Blend until smooth, about 1 minute. Add jam; blend until just combined, about 10 seconds.
2. Pour into 8 to 10 (3-ounce) ice-pop molds; cover with mold lids, and insert ice-pop sticks. Freeze until solid, at least 8 hours or up to 2 weeks. To serve, run the molds under warm water for a few seconds and gently pull pops from molds.

Strawberry-Lemonade Sorbet

ACTIVE 10 MIN. - TOTAL 20 MIN., PLUS 8 HOURS FREEZING
SERVES 8

- 4 cups frozen whole strawberries (from 1 [32-oz.] pkg.)
- ½ cup honey
- 2 tsp. grated lemon zest plus ¼ cup fresh juice (from 1 lemon)

Place strawberries in a food processor; let berries sit at room temperature 10 minutes. Pulse until coarsely chopped, about 10 pulses. Scrape down sides of bowl, and add honey and lemon zest and juice. Process until smooth and creamy, about 2 minutes. Transfer to a resealable freezer-safe (1-quart) container. Cover and freeze until firm, about 8 hours.

Strawberry-Lemonade Sorbet Float

Place a 3- to 4-Tbsp. scoop **Strawberry-Lemonade Sorbet** in a coupe glass. Top with chilled **Prosecco**, **lemon slices**, and halved **fresh strawberries**.

STRAWBERRY-LEMONADE SORBET FLOATS

SWEET TIP
Swap out the Prosecco for a non-boozy bubbly, such as lemon-lime or orange soda, for a kid-friendly treat.

The Great Southern Slaw Trail

In small towns across the Tennessee River Valley, this everyday side is a source of local pride.

SEVERAL YEARS AGO, a friend called me and said, "I'd give anything to have some of your Papaw's red slaw right now. I'd even trade you some of my pool-hall slaw." That stopped me in my tracks. I said, "Pool-hall slaw? Tell me more."

If the idea of a lengthy conversation about coleslaw seems strange, I get it. This dish is often the lone bowl of cabbage on the potluck table someone feels obligated to bring but few people actually eat. But if you're from certain corners of the South, it's so much more than a boring side. It says something about the place you call home.

From my (apparently limited) understanding, all the coleslaw variations could be counted on one hand: mayonnaise, mustard, vinegar, buttermilk, and my treasured red. In my hometown of Scottsboro, Alabama, the last kind is served atop hot dogs, not as a side. Its origins are murky. Some say it was first made at a five-and-dime shop on the city's downtown square in the 1950s. Not so, according to my grandfather, who managed the store around that time. And the family behind Payne's Sandwich Shop & Soda Fountain says they've been slinging this slaw since the 1940s. Whatever its story may be, this oddball, ketchup-laden condiment is a point of pride for our small town. People journey there from other states, other countries even, seeking a bite of it.

POOL-HALL SLAW

My friend's pool-hall slaw has an equally ambiguous pedigree. It was created and popularized in Fayetteville, Tennessee. While that's only a little over 60 miles from Scottsboro, the recipe couldn't be more different from the one I grew up eating. Local lore points to Honey's Restaurant, a downtown billiard hall turned full-time diner. With a sunny hue from yellow mustard, it has a unique balance of sweet and sour flavors that work well on a hamburger, which is how you'll typically find it served.

I realized I'd only scratched the surface of these community-famous variations. In February 2024, Tennessee named hot slaw its first official state food and declared the city of Cleveland the dish's capital. Located east of Chattanooga, Cleveland is less than 100 miles away from Scottsboro, yet this slaw was also a total mystery to me. Credited as being introduced at the Star Vue Theatre, it's traditionally made with raw onion and jalapeños (pickled or fresh) and falls into the condiment category as well. After that, I came across yet another one—red, in fact—that was born in Lexington, North Carolina, and meant to be eaten with barbecue.

After visiting these towns, walking their squares, and tasting more than my fair share of slaw-topped burgers and hot dogs, it all started to come together. These recipes and their stories were never intended to be claims to fame; they cropped up at a drive-in theater in Cleveland and at a soda fountain in Scottsboro as small but significant bids for local identity. Through the decades, folks have held them close for what they've meant to the community, to their families, and to their sense of place—something a little different and a lot special. —Kimberly Holland

Pool-Hall Slaw

ACTIVE 30 MIN. - TOTAL 30 MIN.

MAKES ABOUT 10 CUPS

Whisk together 1 cup **distilled white vinegar,** ⅓ cup **apple cider vinegar,** ⅓ cup **granulated sugar,** ⅓ cup **yellow mustard,** 2 tsp. **mustard seed,** 2 tsp. **crushed red pepper,** 2 tsp. **kosher or seasoned salt,** 1 tsp. **ground turmeric,** and 1 tsp. **black pepper** in a large bowl until combined. Stir in 8 cups grated **green cabbage,** 2 cups finely chopped **red bell pepper,** 2½ cups grated **carrot,** 2 cups grated **yellow onion,** and ¼ cup finely chopped **fresh jalapeño** until evenly coated. Serve immediately, or cover and refrigerate up to 3 days.

Hot Slaw

ACTIVE 20 MIN. - TOTAL 20 MIN.

MAKES ABOUT 6 CUPS

Whisk together ½ cup **mayonnaise,** 3 Tbsp. **yellow mustard,** and ¼ cup **pickled jalapeño liquid** (from 1 [12-oz.] jar pickled jalapeño slices) in a large bowl. Stir in 8 cups grated **green cabbage,** ½ cup grated **yellow onion,** and ⅔ cup **pickled jalapeño slices.** Season with 1 tsp. **kosher salt,** plus more to taste. Serve immediately, or cover and refrigerate up to 3 days.

Red Slaw

ACTIVE 15 MIN. - TOTAL 15 MIN.

MAKES ABOUT 6 CUPS

Whisk together 1½ cups **ketchup,** 2 Tbsp. **yellow mustard,** and 1½ tsp. **hot sauce** in a large bowl until combined. Stir in 8 cups grated **green cabbage** until evenly coated. Add more **hot sauce,** if desired. Serve immediately, or cover and refrigerate up to 3 days.

HOT SLAW

RED SLAW

Simply Delicious

These four low-effort dinners practically cook themselves.

Mississippi Chicken Kebabs

Inspired by our reader-favorite Mississippi Pot Roast, these six-ingredient skewers are great for cookouts or weeknight dinners.

ACTIVE 30 MIN. - TOTAL 1 HOUR

SERVES 6

- 2 (1-oz.) envelopes ranch dressing mix
- 2 (1-oz.) envelopes au jus gravy mix (such as Knorr)
- 1 (16-oz.) jar whole pepperoncini peppers, divided
- ½ cup canola oil, divided, plus more for grill grates
- 3¾ lb. boneless, skinless chicken breasts, cut into 1½-inch cubes
- 2 red onions, cut into 1½-inch pieces
- 12 (10-inch) skewers
- Chopped fresh parsley, for garnish

1. Stir together ranch dressing mix, gravy mix, ¼ cup pepperoncini brine, and ¼ cup oil in a large bowl. Add chicken pieces, and toss to coat; cover and let stand at room temperature for 30 minutes.
2. Meanwhile, preheat grill to medium-high (400°F to 450°F). Thread chicken, pepperoncini peppers, and onion pieces onto skewers. Drizzle with remaining ¼ cup oil.
3. Place kebabs on oiled grates; grill, covered, turning every 2 minutes, until a thermometer inserted into chicken registers 165°F, about 10 minutes total. Garnish with chopped parsley.

Blackened-Shrimp Tacos with Shortcut Slaw

(Photo, page 106)

Already prepped shrimp and bagged coleslaw mix help this supper come together in under half an hour.

ACTIVE 25 MIN. - TOTAL 25 MIN.

SERVES 8

- ½ cup mayonnaise
- ¼ cup rice vinegar
- 2 Tbsp. granulated sugar
- ¾ tsp. kosher salt
- 1 tsp. black pepper, divided
- 1 (16-oz.) pkg. coleslaw mix (about 6 cups)
- 3 Tbsp. Cajun seasoning (such as Emeril's)
- 2½ lb. large peeled and deveined raw shrimp, patted dry (tails removed)
- 3 Tbsp. canola oil, divided
- 16 (6-inch) corn tortillas, warmed
- 2 avocados, peeled and sliced
- Lemon wedges and hot sauce, for serving

1. Whisk together mayonnaise, vinegar, sugar, salt, and ½ teaspoon pepper in a medium bowl. Add slaw mix, and toss to coat. Set aside. Stir together Cajun seasoning and remaining ½ teaspoon pepper in another medium bowl. Add shrimp; toss to coat.
2. Heat a large cast-iron skillet over high until starting to smoke, 3 to 5 minutes. Add 1 tablespoon oil and about one-third of the shrimp; cook, undisturbed, until shrimp have developed a dark brown crust, about 2 minutes. Cook, stirring occasionally, until shrimp are opaque and crust darkens, 1 to 2 more minutes. Transfer to a plate; repeat process with remaining oil and shrimp.
3. Divide slaw evenly among tortillas; top with shrimp and avocado slices. Serve with lemon wedges and hot sauce.

Farm Stand Pasta Salad

(Photo, page 107)

Fresh herbs and warm-weather vegetables shine in this adaptable recipe.

ACTIVE 30 MIN. - TOTAL 40 MIN.

SERVES 8

- 12 oz. uncooked rotini or fusilli pasta
- ⅓ cup fresh lemon juice (from 2 lemons)
- ⅓ cup extra-virgin olive oil
- 2 tsp. honey
- 2 tsp. kosher salt, plus more for pasta water
- 1 tsp. Dijon mustard
- ½ tsp. black pepper
- 2 zucchini or yellow squash, sliced into ¼-inch-thick half-moons (about 4 cups)
- 2¼ cups fresh corn kernels (from 3 ears)
- 1 pt. cherry tomatoes, halved
- ½ cup thinly sliced red onion (from 1 onion)
- 1 (8-oz.) block feta cheese, cut into ½-inch cubes (about 2 cups)
- ½ cup chopped fresh mixed herbs (such as chives, tarragon, and dill), plus more for garnish

1. Cook pasta in a large pot of boiling salted water according to package directions for al dente. Drain; rinse pasta under cold water until no longer hot, about 2 minutes. Let cool to room temperature, about 10 minutes.
2. Meanwhile, whisk together lemon juice, oil, honey, salt, mustard, and pepper in a large bowl. Add zucchini, corn, tomatoes, and onion; toss to coat. Let stand 10 minutes, tossing occasionally.
3. Add cooled pasta, feta, and herbs to vegetable mixture; gently toss to combine. Garnish with additional herbs.

MISSISSIPPI CHICKEN KEBABS

BLACKENED-SHRIMP TACOS
WITH SHORTCUT SLAW
(PAGE 104)

FARM STAND
PASTA SALAD
(PAGE 104)

Our Easiest Slow-Cooker Barbecue Sandwiches

Country-style pork ribs get fall-apart tender in less time than a large roast.

ACTIVE 15 MIN. - TOTAL 6 HOURS, 15 MIN.

SERVES 8

- 3 Tbsp. light brown sugar
- 1 Tbsp. garlic powder
- 1 Tbsp. onion powder
- 2½ tsp. kosher salt
- 1½ tsp. black pepper
- 1 tsp. smoked paprika
- 5 lb. bone-in (or 3 to 4 lb. boneless) country-style pork ribs, patted dry
- 1 sweet onion, thinly sliced lengthwise (about 2½ cups)
- 1 (16-oz.) bottle barbecue sauce, divided
- 8 hamburger buns
- Coleslaw
- Dill pickle chips

1. Stir together light brown sugar, garlic powder, onion powder, kosher salt, black pepper, and smoked paprika in a small bowl; rub all over ribs.

2. Preheat grill to medium-high (400°F to 450°F). Place ribs on oiled grates; grill, uncovered, until lightly charred on all sides, about 2 minutes per side. (Alternatively, preheat a cast-iron skillet or grill pan over high; cook ribs in batches until browned, 2 to 3 minutes per side.)

3. Place onion in bottom of a 6-quart slow cooker; top with ribs. Drizzle with ½ cup barbecue sauce. Cover and cook on LOW for 6 hours or HIGH for about 3½ hours until meat shreds easily.

4. Use 2 forks to shred ribs in slow cooker, discarding any bones. Stir pork together with onion and any residual juices in slow cooker. Drain and discard all but ½ cup of the juices. Stir in 1 cup of the barbecue sauce.

5. Serve pulled pork on buns with coleslaw, dill pickle chips, and remaining barbecue sauce.

OUR EASIEST SLOW-COOKER BARBECUE SANDWICHES

Oldie but Goodie

There's a reason olive oil cake has been around for centuries.

Lemon Olive Oil Cake

ACTIVE 15 MIN. - TOTAL 1 HOUR, PLUS 1 HOUR, 45 MIN. COOLING
SERVES 10

- 2 cups all-purpose flour
- 2 tsp. baking powder
- 1 tsp. kosher salt
- 1¼ cups granulated sugar
- 2 tsp. grated lemon zest plus 2 Tbsp. fresh juice (from 1 lemon), divided
- 1 cup extra-virgin olive oil
- ¾ cup whole buttermilk, at room temperature
- 3 large eggs, at room temperature
- 1 tsp. vanilla extract
- Powdered sugar, for topping

1. Preheat oven to 325°F. Grease a 9-inch round cake pan (with 2-inch-tall sides) with cooking spray; line bottom with parchment. Whisk together flour, baking powder, and salt in a medium bowl. Set aside.

2. Place granulated sugar and lemon zest in a large bowl, and rub zest and sugar between your fingers to release oils from zest. Whisk in olive oil, buttermilk, eggs, vanilla, and lemon juice until smooth.

3. Whisk in flour mixture until combined. Transfer batter to prepared pan. Bake until a wooden pick inserted in center comes out clean, 45 to 50 minutes.

4. Let cool in pan for 15 minutes; remove from pan, and transfer to a wire rack to cool completely, about 1 hour, 30 minutes. Dust with powdered sugar, as desired, just before serving.

FANCY IT UP
Use a stencil from a crafts store to create a pretty design with the powdered sugar.

LEMON OLIVE OIL CAKE

Two Tasty Variations

Blueberry-Ginger Olive Oil Cake

(Photo, page 2)

Follow recipe as directed through Step 1. In Step 2, add 1 Tbsp. grated fresh ginger to the granulated sugar and zest. Proceed with the remainder of Step 2 as directed. In Step 3, after transferring batter to pan, top with 1 cup fresh blueberries. Continue with recipe as directed.

Cherry-Pistachio Olive Oil Cake

(Photo, page 2)

Follow recipe as directed through Step 2. In Step 3, after transferring batter to pan, top with 1 cup fresh (or thawed frozen) pitted cherries (patted dry) and ¼ cup chopped unsalted dry-roasted pistachios. Continue with recipe as directed.

Dipping into Summer

Whether you're heading to the beach or a cookout, this 10-minute appetizer will be a crowd-pleaser.

Picnic Dip

ACTIVE 10 MIN. - TOTAL 10 MIN.
SERVES 12

- 1/2 cup (4 oz.) cream cheese, at room temperature
- 1 (16-oz.) container sour cream, at room temperature
- 1 1/2 cups shredded sharp cheddar cheese (about 6 oz.)
- 3/4 cup pickled diced jalapeños, drained (from 1 [12-oz.] jar), plus more for garnish
- 1 1/2 tsp. garlic powder
- 1/4 tsp. cayenne pepper
- 1 cup chopped cooked bacon, divided
- Crudités or potato chips, for serving

1. Whisk cream cheese until smooth. Add sour cream; whisk until combined. Fold in cheddar, pickled jalapeños, garlic powder, cayenne, and 3/4 cup of the bacon.

2. Transfer to a serving bowl, and garnish evenly with additional jalapeños and remaining 1/4 cup bacon. Serve cold or at room temperature with crudités or potato chips.

Skinny Dip

If you're watching calories or just want to lighten things up, try this slimmed-down version of our Picnic Dip recipe.

ACTIVE 10 MIN. - TOTAL 10 MIN.
SERVES 12

Prepare the recipe as directed, substituting 1/2 cup **reduced-fat cream cheese** and 1 (16-oz.) container **reduced-fat sour cream** for the full-fat cream cheese and sour cream. Serve with **crudités** for dipping instead of chips.

Omelets to Order

Light, fluffy, and prepared in a flash, here's how to make this morning standby.

Folded Omelet

ACTIVE 15 MIN. - TOTAL 15 MIN.
SERVES 1

- 4 large eggs
- ½ tsp. kosher salt
- ¼ tsp. black pepper, plus more for garnish
- 1 Tbsp. unsalted butter
- ½ oz. crumbled goat cheese (about 2 Tbsp.), plus more for garnish
- 1 Tbsp. chopped fresh tender herbs (such as chives, tarragon, and dill), plus more for garnish

1. Whisk together eggs, salt, and pepper in a medium bowl; set aside.
2. Melt butter in a 10-inch nonstick skillet over medium-high until foamy. Reduce heat to medium-low. Add egg mixture, and cook, stirring gently and scraping bottom of skillet in a circular motion using a rubber spatula, until large curds begin to form and bare spots appear on bottom of skillet, about 45 seconds. Tilt skillet so eggs fill bare spots; scrape cooked eggs down from sides of skillet, and cook until just set, about 30 seconds. Remove from heat.
3. Sprinkle goat cheese and herbs over half of the cooked egg mixture; cover and let stand until fully set, about 1 minute. Fold omelet in half over cheese and herbs. Gently transfer to a plate, and garnish with more black pepper, goat cheese, and herbs.

A FRENCH TWIST

Unlike our Folded Omelet, the French version is rolled into a cylinder. It has a tender, soft center and no browning on the outside. Traditionally, it's finished with finely chopped chives and sometimes a flourish of flaky salt. Although seemingly simple on the surface, the rolled technique can be tricky to master, while the American method is easy to pull off with a well-greased pan. See Cooking School (page 112) for a step-by-step omelet lesson.

Egg White Omelet

In Step 1, separate egg yolks from egg whites (reserve yolks for another use); whisk whites until frothy, about 30 seconds. Whisk in ¼ cup shredded **sharp cheddar cheese** with salt and pepper. Proceed with recipe as directed. In Step 3, omit goat cheese; replace with ¼ cup shredded **sharp cheddar cheese**. Proceed with remainder of Step 3, garnishing with more shredded **sharp cheddar cheese**, pepper, and herbs.

Denver Omelet

Cook ⅓ cup each diced **sweet onion**, **bell pepper**, and **smoked ham** in 1 Tbsp. **unsalted butter** in a 10-inch nonstick skillet over medium, stirring often, until vegetables are tender, about 5 minutes. Transfer to a bowl; set aside. Wipe skillet clean. Proceed with recipe as directed through Step 2. In Step 3, omit goat cheese and herbs; replace with ½ cup shredded **Monterey Jack cheese** and ½ cup reserved onion mixture. Proceed with remainder of Step 3, garnishing with black pepper and remaining onion mixture.

COOKING SCHOOL

TIPS AND TRICKS FROM THE SOUTH'S MOST TRUSTED KITCHEN

An Eggcellent Omelet

We've cracked the code on this breakfast staple.

1. BEAT
Whisk together the eggs, kosher salt, and black pepper in a bowl until smooth, about 30 seconds. There shouldn't be any streaks of egg white.

2. STIR
Melt butter in a nonstick skillet over medium-high (swirl to evenly distribute). Reduce heat; add egg mixture. Cook, gently stirring using a rubber spatula, until some ribbons form.

3. TILT
Swirl the skillet so that uncooked eggs fill in the bare spots. Scrape cooked eggs down from the sides of the pan, and cook until just set, about 30 seconds. Remove from heat.

4. FOLD
Sprinkle desired fillings evenly over half of the cooked eggs; cover and let stand until fully set, about 1 minute. Fold the omelet in half, and gently slide it onto a plate. Serve immediately.

June–July

Naturally Sweet

The smooth-skinned cousins to peaches, juicy nectarines require no peeling at all.

Mixed Green Salad with Pickled Nectarines

ACTIVE 15 MIN. - TOTAL 45 MIN.
SERVES 6

Cook 1 cup **apple cider vinegar,** 1 cup **water,** ½ cup **granulated sugar,** and ¾ tsp. **kosher salt** in a saucepan over medium-high, stirring occasionally, until sugar dissolves and mixture comes to a boil. Remove from heat. Add 3 cups thinly sliced **firm-ripe nectarines.** Let stand at least 30 minutes or up to 1 hour. Reserve ¼ cup pickling liquid in a small bowl, and then drain nectarines. Whisk together reserved pickling liquid, ¼ cup **extra-virgin olive oil,** 1 Tbsp. **Dijon mustard,** 1 Tbsp. **apple cider vinegar,** ¼ tsp. **kosher salt,** and ⅛ tsp. **black pepper** in small bowl to make dressing. Gently toss together 6 oz. **spring mix salad greens,** ¼ cup crumbled **goat cheese,** drained nectarines, and dressing in a large bowl. Sprinkle with ⅓ cup plain **granola.**

MIXED GREEN SALAD WITH PICKLED NECTARINES

Nectarine Smoothies

ACTIVE 5 MIN. - TOTAL 5 MIN.
SERVES 2

Process 2 cups **ice,** 1½ cups chopped **very ripe nectarines,** ¼ cup **coconut water,** ¼ cup **fresh orange juice,** and 1½ Tbsp. **honey** in a blender until smooth, about 1 minute. Pour evenly into 2 glasses; garnish with **fresh nectarine slices,** if desired.

Honey-Glazed Grilled Nectarines

ACTIVE 15 MIN. - TOTAL 30 MIN.
SERVES 6

Cut 6 **firm-ripe nectarines** in half lengthwise; remove pits. Stir together ½ cup **honey,** 2 Tbsp. **fresh orange juice,** and ½ tsp. **orange zest** in a small bowl; reserve 3 Tbsp. mixture for grilling. Brush nectarines all over with remaining honey mixture. Grill on oiled grates over medium-high (400°F to 450°F), covered, until softened, about 10 minutes, flipping halfway through and brushing with reserved honey mixture. Let cool slightly, about 5 minutes. Serve with **vanilla ice cream,** and garnish with **fresh mint leaves.**

HONEY-GLAZED GRILLED NECTARINES

FAMILY TREE
One gene sets nectarines apart from peaches, and it's the reason they don't have fuzzy skin.

A Festive Gathering

On Juneteenth, North Carolina chef Ricky Moore brings the community together with a picnic.

RICKY MOORE still calls himself a cook, despite being a James Beard Award–winning chef. It's a small detail that says a lot about his humble spirit. As the owner of Saltbox Seafood Joint in Durham, North Carolina, he's become an evangelist for local seafood and the power of collaboration in the kitchen. It's the latter that inspired his annual Juneteenth celebration, called the Durmnik (Durham picnic) because, as he says, "The idea of Juneteenth is community."

This holiday commemorates the reading of General Order No. 3 on June 19, 1865. Even though the Emancipation Proclamation had been issued about two and half years prior, this was when the news of freedom first made it to an estimated 250,000 enslaved people in Texas. From then on, the day became one for celebration, although it wasn't established as an official holiday across the United States until 2021.

Moore's Durmnik gathering highlights several North Carolina chefs, and each prepares a dish to contribute to the event's to-go lunch boxes. Offerings include flavors from around the world, which is by design. "When you have a picnic, get-together, or party, you've got a bunch of [different] people bringing something to the table," he says.

Last year, Moore made his Trini-Style "Soused" North Carolina Shrimp, Cucumber, Corn, and Peppers (recipe, page 119), which he describes as the "great-grandmama of pickled shrimp." Served ice-cold, it's ideal on a hot, humid summer day. The term "soused" refers to marinating an ingredient in a pickling liquid, like these shrimp dressed in a seasoned lime juice brine. It's also a nod to Caribbean souse, a cold dish made with pigs' feet. Moore says you either love souse or you don't, but he adds that it shouldn't rattle Southerners. "How many times do you go into a corner store [in the South] and see pickled pigs' feet?" he asks, drawing on the connection between the African diaspora and Southern foodways.

Take the green seasoning in the recipe: Moore likens it to the "holy trinity" of Cajun cooking–onion, celery, and bell pepper. Although its formula varies across the Caribbean, green seasoning is generally composed of onion, peppers, scallions, garlic, and chadon beni–an herb related to cilantro that is often sold as culantro and has a bold citrus flavor. If you're not up for all that chopping, he says Walkerswood (a Jamaican food brand) makes a good store-bought alternative.

Alongside his own cooking, the roster of talented chefs bring their own tastes to the picnic. Moore considers it one way to pay his success forward. "There's enough room for everyone to be recognized," he says, calling himself a cheerleader for the local culinary up-and-comers.

The 2024 Durmnik lineup also featured Sweet-and-Sour Watermelon Salad (recipe, page 119) from Sera Cuni of The Root Cellar Cafe & Catering in Chapel Hill and Cafe Root Cellar in Pittsboro. This refreshing combo calls for cubes of melon and the pickled rind. To wash it all down, Adrian Lindsay of Missy Lane's Assembly Room in Durham mixed up the spirit-free cocktail A Mockery (recipe, page 119), which is infused with hibiscus tea, cherry juice, and sage. The hibiscus lends it a holiday hue, as red drinks are an important symbol of Juneteenth, tied to West African beverages made from this flower or kola nuts.

Moore hopes to continue to grow the event each year and include more people. But at the end of the day, he says, "If I'm able to have a platform to showcase folks and everybody gets a win, that's super fulfilling for me."

TRINI-STYLE "SOUSED" NORTH CAROLINA SHRIMP, CUCUMBER, CORN, AND PEPPERS (PAGE 119)

A MOCKERY

SWEET-AND-SOUR
WATERMELON SALAD

A Mockery

Recipe by Adrian Lindsay of Missy Lane's Assembly Room in Durham

ACTIVE 5 MIN. - TOTAL 5 MIN.

SERVES 1

- 1 cup cold hibiscus tea, brewed according to package directions (such as Traditional Medicinals)
- ½ cup tart cherry juice
- 1½ Tbsp. (¾ oz.) fresh lemon juice (from 1 lemon)
- 1 Tbsp. (½ oz.) orgeat or almond syrup (such as Monin)
- 1 Tbsp. (½ oz.) Sage Simple Syrup (recipe follows)
- Ice
- Lemon slices
- Fresh sage leaves

Stir first 5 ingredients in a 16-ounce glass filled with ice until chilled and combined, about 15 seconds. Garnish with lemon slices and sage leaves.

Sage Simple Syrup

ACTIVE 10 MIN. - TOTAL 1 HOUR, 10 MIN.

MAKES ABOUT ¾ CUP

Bring ½ cup water to a boil in a saucepan over high. Remove from heat. Add ½ cup granulated sugar; stir until dissolved, about 30 seconds. Add 5 fresh sage leaves; cover and let steep at room temperature about 1 hour. Discard sage. Refrigerate in an airtight container up to 1 week.

Alongside his own cooking, the roster of talented chefs bring their own tastes to the picnic. Moore considers it one way to pay his success forward. "There's enough room for everyone to be recognized," he says.

Sweet-and-Sour Watermelon Salad

Recipe by Sera Cuni, chef and owner of The Root Cellar Cafe & Catering in Chapel Hill and its sister restaurant in Pittsboro

ACTIVE 30 MIN. - TOTAL 1 HOUR

SERVES 6

DRESSING

- ½ cup fresh lime juice (from 4 limes)
- 3 Tbsp. light brown sugar
- 2 Tbsp. finely chopped garlic
- 1 Tbsp. finely chopped fresh ginger (from 1 [2-inch] piece)
- ½ cup olive oil
- 1 tsp. kosher salt
- ½ tsp. black pepper

SALAD

- 1 (5-lb.) seedless watermelon, peeled and cut into ½-inch cubes (about 10 cups)
- 4 shallots, thinly sliced (about ¾ cup)
- 2 red jalapeño or serrano chiles, thinly sliced (seeded if less heat is desired, about ½ cup)
- 1 cup chopped fresh cilantro leaves and tender stems (from 1 bunch)
- ½ cup drained watermelon-rind pickles (homemade or store-bought)
- ¼ cup chopped fresh mint, plus more for garnish
- 3 Tbsp. chopped Thai basil

1. Prepare the Dressing: Whisk together lime juice, brown sugar, garlic, and ginger in a medium bowl until combined. Whisking constantly, gradually add oil until combined. Whisk in salt and pepper. Set Dressing aside, or cover and refrigerate up to a week.
2. Prepare the Salad: Toss together watermelon, shallots, red jalapeños or serranos, cilantro, watermelon-rind pickles, mint, basil, and Dressing in a large bowl until combined. Cover and refrigerate 30 minutes or up to 12 hours. Garnish with mint just before serving.

Trini-Style "Soused" North Carolina Shrimp, Cucumber, Corn, and Peppers

(Photo, page 117)

Recipe by Ricky Moore, chef and owner of Saltbox Seafood Joint in Durham

ACTIVE 40 MIN. - TOTAL 2 HOURS, 45 MIN.

SERVES 6

- 1 lb. large, peeled and deveined, fresh raw shrimp, tails removed
- 1 cup fresh corn kernels (from 1 ear)
- 2 cucumbers, thinly sliced (about 5 cups)
- 1 white onion, thinly sliced (about 2¼ cups)
- 1½ cups thinly sliced roasted red peppers (from 1 [16-oz.] jar)
- 5 Tbsp. fresh lime juice (from 3 limes)
- 3 Tbsp. thinly sliced fresh chadon beni or cilantro, plus more for garnish
- 2 Tbsp. chicken bouillon granules
- 1 Tbsp. kosher salt
- 1 Tbsp. Caribbean green seasoning (such as Walkerswood)
- 2 tsp. finely chopped garlic (from 2 garlic cloves)
- 1 tsp. Jamaican hot pepper sauce (such as Grace), plus more to taste

1. Place a steamer basket inside a medium pot. Fill pot with about ½ inch of water, ensuring there is at least 1 inch between basket bottom and waterline. Cover and bring to a boil over high. Reduce heat to medium; add shrimp and corn to steamer basket. Cover and cook, undisturbed, until shrimp are cooked and corn is tender, 5 to 7 minutes. Remove steamer basket from pot. Let cool 5 minutes.
2. Stir together cucumbers, onion, roasted red peppers, 1½ cups water, lime juice, chadon beni or cilantro, bouillon, salt green seasoning, garlic, and hot pepper sauce in a large bowl. Add cooked shrimp and corn; cover and refrigerate for 2 hours or up to 24 hours.
3. Taste and add more Jamaican hot pepper sauce, if desired. Garnish with fresh chadon beni or cilantro. Serve at room temperature or chilled.

Gone Fishin'

Reel in family and friends with this classic Southern feast.

EVERY SUMMER for the better part of 60 years, my extended family gathered for a week at a state park near Sardis, Mississippi. Matriarchs and patriarchs, aunts, uncles, and cousins would come from all around the South—Jackson, Memphis, and even Virginia—to tighten the weave that the long year had loosened.

Early in the morning, before my grandmother started frying bacon, the baritone sputter of an outboard motor would fracture the only stillness Sardis Lake would see that day. Moments later, a metal jon boat would glide by with my grandfather on the back bench seat with one hand on the tiller handle, the cresting V of the boat's wake rippling the serene water behind him. I was never much of a fisherman, but every so often, I would tag along to check the trotline. Sometimes the haul was a generous bounty; other times it was slim pickings.

Each family was responsible for one supper during the time together. But our final feast was always a fish fry, and the men were in charge. They would fish all week long, at dawn and dusk and anytime in between, hoarding their catch for the big night. The guys cleaned their spoils while everyone else bustled about, fixing the sides, making iced tea, and lighting citronella candles.

When the frying was done and all of the kids had been called up, we'd gather on the hillside and tuck into our supper. Perched in folding chairs and balancing paper plates in our laps, we'd visit in between bites of cornmeal-crusted catfish, bass, and bream. As the sun melted into the lake and lightning bugs began blinking in the giant oaks overhead, I understood why summer is better in the South.

You can't turn back the clock, but you can revisit the past. Whether you go with fresh or saltwater fish, whether you choose to doctor up your hush puppies and okra or keep them classic, these recipes can help you relive your best summer memories—or make new ones you'll come to cherish just as much.
—Josh Miller

What's the Catch?

Our flexible recipe works with different varieties of fish. Here are six rules to fry by.

1. Not all white-fleshed fish are the same. The ideal type is firm and has a mild flavor. Our top picks are redfish, catfish, and snapper, but other tasty options include cod, flounder, and perch.

2. Look for fillets that are ½ to ¾ inch thick so they will cook evenly and won't fall apart when frying. If the piece tapers at one end, just trim the thin portion to even it out.

3. Run your finger along each fillet to check for bones, and remove any that you notice.

4. Steer away from using fish that are strongly flavored (salmon) or dense (tuna or swordfish), because they're more difficult to fry.

5. If you don't live near the coast, frozen seafood is fine. Thaw it thoroughly in the refrigerator, and pat it dry before cooking. For the best texture, avoid using fish that's been frozen for more than three months.

6. Buy fresh fish right before you plan to cook it. Try not to store it in the fridge for more than two days.

HOT TIP
First time frying fish? Our step-by-step tutorial on page 144 breaks down the process for the best results.

CRACKER-CRUSTED FRIED FISH (PAGE 123)

FRIED PICKLED OKRA (PAGE 123)

TEXAS CAVIAR

CREAMED-CORN HUSH PUPPIES

Texas Caviar

Coleslaw may be the classic side for a fish fry, but give this super easy dip a try. The combination of crunchy fresh veggies with convenient canned goods will make it your new favorite for potlucks, picnics, and cookouts.

ACTIVE 15 MIN. - TOTAL 15 MIN.
SERVES 8

Dice 2 **red tomatoes**, 2 **green tomatoes**, 1 **green bell pepper**, 2 seeded **jalapeños**, half of a **yellow onion**, and ½ cup **fresh cilantro** leaves; add to a large bowl. Stir in 2 (14-oz.) cans drained **black-eyed peas**, 1 (15.5-oz.) can drained **white hominy**, 1 (8-oz.) bottle **Italian salad dressing**, and 2 minced **garlic** cloves; stir to combine. Serve with **tortilla chips**.

Creamed-Corn Hush Puppies

Adding sweet summer corn to this batter transforms the usual hush puppies, giving them a light and tender texture.

ACTIVE 30 MIN. - TOTAL 30 MIN.
SERVES 6 TO 8

- Vegetable or peanut oil
- 2 Tbsp. unsalted butter
- ½ cup finely chopped yellow onion (from 1 onion)
- 1¼ cups corn kernels (from 2 ears), chopped
- 2 tsp. kosher salt, divided, plus more to taste
- ½ cup plus 1½ tsp. all-purpose flour, divided
- ⅔ cup heavy whipping cream
- 1 Tbsp. granulated sugar
- ¾ cup plain yellow cornmeal
- 1½ tsp. baking powder
- ¼ tsp. garlic powder
- 2 Tbsp. whole buttermilk
- 2 large eggs, lightly beaten
- Lemon wedges, for serving

1. Heat 2 inches of oil in a large Dutch oven over medium to 350°F.
2. Melt butter in a large skillet over medium. Add onion; cook, stirring often, until translucent, about 3 minutes. Add corn and 1 teaspoon salt; cook, stirring occasionally, until corn is tender, about 5 minutes. Sprinkle 1½ teaspoons flour over mixture; cook, stirring constantly, until combined, about 30 seconds. Gradually add cream and sugar; cook, stirring constantly, until sauce thickens and coats corn, 1 to 2 minutes. Remove from heat; set aside to cool slightly, about 5 minutes.
3. Stir together cornmeal, baking powder, garlic powder, and remaining ½ cup flour and 1 teaspoon salt in a large bowl until well combined. Add buttermilk, eggs, and cooled corn mixture; stir until just combined. (Mixture will resemble a thick pancake batter.)
4. Working in several batches, carefully add heaping tablespoons of batter to hot oil. Cook, turning occasionally, until golden brown on all sides, about 3 minutes. Transfer hush puppies to a wire rack set over a rimmed baking sheet; season with salt to taste. Serve with lemon wedges.

Fried Pickled Okra

(Photo, page 121)

Because of its dense interior, okra is a tricky vegetable to season evenly—the crispy coating is often the star. By starting with the pickled kind instead of fresh, this recipe builds flavor from the inside out.

ACTIVE 30 MIN. - TOTAL 30 MIN.
SERVES 8

- Vegetable or peanut oil
- 1 (16-oz.) jar pickled okra, drained
- 1¼ cups all-purpose flour, divided
- 1 Tbsp. whole buttermilk
- 1 large egg, lightly beaten
- ½ cup plain yellow cornmeal
- 1½ tsp. kosher salt, plus more to taste
- ¾ tsp. baking powder
- ¾ tsp. garlic powder

1. Heat 2 inches of oil in a large Dutch oven over medium to 350°F. Slice pickled okra in half lengthwise. Pat dry with paper towels; set aside.
2. Place ½ cup flour in a shallow bowl. Whisk together buttermilk and egg in another shallow bowl. Stir together cornmeal, salt, baking powder, garlic powder, and remaining ¾ cup flour in a third shallow bowl.
3. Dredge 1 piece of okra in flour, shaking off excess. Dip in egg mixture, allowing excess to drip off. Dredge okra in cornmeal mixture, pressing to coat all sides. Place breaded okra on a plate or baking sheet; repeat with remaining okra.
4. Working in several batches, fry okra, turning occasionally, until golden brown, 2 to 3 minutes. Repeat with remaining okra, allowing oil to return to temperature between batches. Transfer fried okra to a paper towel-lined plate to drain; sprinkle with salt to taste. Serve warm.

Cracker-Crusted Fried Fish

(Photo, page 121)

Fans of cornmeal-coated fish will enjoy this version that's even crispier. Also sold as cracker meal, the simple breading of crushed saltines and seasonings gives the fillets an extra-savory crunch.

ACTIVE 20 MIN. - TOTAL 30 MIN.
SERVES 6

- Vegetable or peanut oil
- 1 cup whole buttermilk
- 2 large eggs, lightly beaten
- 1 tsp. hot sauce
- 6 (4-oz.) skinless fish fillets, such as red snapper or catfish
- 1 cup finely crushed saltine crackers (about 25 crackers)
- 1¼ tsp. kosher salt, plus more to taste
- 1 tsp. garlic powder
- 1 tsp. paprika
- 1 tsp. black pepper
- ½ tsp. cayenne pepper
- Coleslaw and lemon wedges, for serving

1. Heat 2 inches of oil in a large Dutch oven over medium to 350°F. Whisk together buttermilk, eggs, and hot sauce in a large bowl. Add fish; let marinate 10 minutes.
2. Stir together crushed crackers, kosher salt, garlic powder, paprika, black pepper, and cayenne pepper in a shallow bowl. Remove 1 fillet from buttermilk mixture, allowing excess to drip off. Transfer fillet to cracker mixture, pressing to coat. Gently shake off excess; place breaded fillet on a plate. Repeat with remaining fish.
3. Working in several batches, carefully add fish to hot oil. Fry, turning occasionally, until golden brown and cooked through, 3 to 4 minutes, allowing oil to return to temperature between batches. Transfer fried fish to a wire rack set over a rimmed baking sheet lined with paper towels; season with salt to taste. Serve warm with coleslaw and lemon wedges.

Peach Perfect

These simple desserts celebrate the South's favorite stone fruit.

IN EARLY AUGUST 1992, I was dashing out the door to fly to Boston to meet Julia Child. Yes, that Julia Child. She was about to celebrate her 80th birthday, and I had secured an interview at her Cambridge, Massachusetts, home. Before I left my Atlanta house and locked the front door, I panicked because this interview had come together so fast that I hadn't thought of bringing her a hospitality gift.

I glanced at the fruit bowl on the kitchen counter and quickly grabbed the largest, most fragrant Georgia peach, blushing deep coral red like those late-summer varieties do. Then I swaddled it in paper towels and placed it gently in my purse.

In Julia's kitchen, we roasted chicken and tossed a green salad for lunch and sipped a chilled Sauvignon Blanc as we cooked. After the meal, I sheepishly pulled out the peach and said something like, "from my Georgia kitchen to yours." Julia held my gift carefully like it was a newborn. She cooed about peaches in her warbling voice, how she loved the white varieties of France, and then she sliced it onto a plate for us to share.

That peach thrilled her—and saved me. Peaches do that. On their own, they can transform the simplest meals into memories. They leave their flavor behind in recipes for warm-weather preserves, boldly imprint their fragrance into homemade ice cream or pound cake, and fill cobblers and sonkers to the top of the pan effortlessly with all their wonderful juices. I just can't imagine a summer without Southern peaches, whether cooking with them or devouring one as I lean over the kitchen sink so the sweet, tart juices are free to run down my arm to my elbow.

Although California is the largest U.S. producer of peaches, the best flavor can be found in Southern varieties. The earliest ones will likely be clingstone types (the pit hangs onto the fruit's flesh), making them a little fussy to slice. They don't have the deep flavor that late-season freestone ones do, but both kinds work in these recipes.

Whether they're a variety from Upcountry South Carolina; reliable Georgia Elbertas; bright Redhavens from Chilton County, Alabama; or even the kind grown around Cleveland, Tennessee, peaches are the greatest gifts of a Southern summer. Here are my favorite ways to enjoy them.
—Anne Byrn

Julia held my gift carefully like it was a newborn. She cooed about peaches in her warbling voice, how she loved the white varieties of France, and then she sliced it onto a plate for us to share.

PEACH SONKER
(PAGE 130)

BUTTERMILK PANNA COTTA WITH CARAMEL PEACHES (PAGE 130)

THE ULTIMATE PEACH SUNDAES (PAGE 131)

PEACH POUND CAKE
(PAGE 131)

Peach Sonker

(Photo, page 126)

ACTIVE 1 HOUR · TOTAL 1 HOUR, 45 MIN., PLUS 1 HOUR COOLING

SERVES 12

CRUST

- **2½ cups unbleached all-purpose flour, plus more for work surface**
- **1 Tbsp. baking powder**
- **½ tsp. kosher salt**
- **14 Tbsp. cold unsalted butter, cubed**
- **⅔ cup whole milk**

FILLING

- **2½ Tbsp. unbleached all-purpose flour**
- **1¼ cups plus 2 Tbsp. granulated sugar, divided**
- **7½ cups peeled and sliced peaches (from 12 to 15 medium peaches)**
- **2 Tbsp. unsalted butter, cut into small pieces**
- **1 large egg**

MILK DIP

- **6 Tbsp. granulated sugar**
- **2½ tsp. cornstarch**
- **1 pinch kosher salt**
- **1½ cups whole milk**
- **1 tsp. vanilla extract**

1. Prepare the Crust: Place flour, baking powder, and salt in a food processor; pulse to combine, about 4 pulses. Scatter butter on top of flour mixture, and pulse 8 or 9 times until crumbly and butter is the size of small peas. Add milk, and pulse until dough comes together into a mass, 8 to 10 pulses. Turn dough out onto a lightly floured work surface, and cut in half. Cover 1 dough half; set aside for the top.

2. Roll out remaining dough half into a 22 x 4-inch rectangle. Cut rectangle in half lengthwise to create 2 strips. Press 1 of the dough strips halfway around the interior sides of a 13 x 9-inch baking dish. Repeat with remaining dough strip, pressing ends together to form a dough border inside the perimeter of the baking dish (there is no bottom crust). Set aside. Preheat oven to 375°F with rack in middle position.

3. Prepare the Filling: Stir together flour and 1¼ cups sugar in a large bowl. Add peaches; toss to combine. Spoon peaches and any juices in bowl into baking dish, spreading into an even layer, and dot with butter.

4. Roll out remaining dough half into a 12½ x 8½-inch rectangle. Cut about 20 random holes in the pastry using a 1- to 1½-inch round cutter; remove and discard dough rounds. To transfer dough to baking dish, carefully fold sheet of dough in half and then in half again. Gently unfold dough over the peach mixture, covering the filling completely. Whisk egg and 2 teaspoons water in a small bowl until combined; brush top of pastry with egg mixture. Sprinkle remaining 2 tablespoons sugar evenly over top.

5. Bake until bubbly and golden, 55 to 60 minutes, loosely covering with aluminum foil to prevent overbrowning, if needed.

6. Prepare the Milk Dip: Whisk together sugar, cornstarch, and salt in a large saucepan. Whisk in milk. Bring to a boil over medium, whisking often. Cook, whisking constantly, until thickened, about 2 minutes. Remove from heat; whisk in vanilla. Transfer to a bowl; set aside. Let sonker cool on a wire rack 1 hour. (Filling will remain fairly loose.) Serve warm with Milk Dip on the side.

Buttermilk Panna Cotta with Caramel Peaches

(Photo, page 127)

ACTIVE 50 MIN. · TOTAL 1 HOUR, 25 MIN., PLUS 8 HOURS CHILLING

SERVES 8

PANNA COTTA

- **1½ tsp. unflavored gelatin (from 1 [¼-oz.] envelope)**
- **1 cup heavy whipping cream**
- **½ cup granulated sugar**
- **1 tsp. grated lemon zest (from 1 lemon)**
- **1 pinch kosher salt**
- **2 cups whole buttermilk**
- **1 tsp. vanilla extract**

CARAMEL PEACHES

- **1 cup granulated sugar**
- **1 lb. firm-ripe peaches (about 4 peaches), peeled and sliced**
- **½ cup warm water**

1. Prepare the Panna Cotta: Place 2 tablespoons water in a bowl, and sprinkle gelatin on top. Stir; let stand 10 minutes.

2. Meanwhile, place cream, sugar, lemon zest, and salt in a saucepan over medium; bring just to a simmer, stirring constantly to dissolve sugar, 3 to 4 minutes. Remove from heat. Whisk in gelatin mixture until dissolved. Whisk in buttermilk and vanilla.

3. Divide buttermilk mixture evenly among 8 (5- to 6-ounce) heatproof custard cups. Place on a tray. Chill, uncovered, until firm, 8 hours or up to 3 days.

4. Prepare the Caramel Peaches: Fill a large heatproof bowl about halfway with ice and cold water; set aside. Place sugar in a heavy saucepan or medium stainless-steel skillet. Heat over medium, stirring around edges and swirling pan to mix melted sugar with unmelted sugar, until amber in color but not smoking, 4 to 6 minutes. Remove from heat; place saucepan in bowl with ice water until caramel cools and thickens slightly, 3 to 4 minutes. (Sugar mixture may solidify.)

5. Place peaches in a medium bowl. Heat pan of caramel over low; carefully pour warm water into pan. Cook over low, stirring often, slowly, and patiently, until caramel dissolves into water and creates a sauce, 10 to 15 minutes. Remove from heat, and let cool slightly, 5 to 10 minutes.

6. Pour caramel sauce over sliced peaches, stirring until combined; let stand at room temperature 30 minutes or up to 4 hours.

7. Spoon some of the Caramel Peaches over Panna Cotta; serve immediately with any extra Caramel Peaches on the side.

Peach Pound Cake

(Photo, page 129)

ACTIVE 25 MIN. · TOTAL 1 HOUR, 55 MIN., PLUS 1 HOUR COOLING

SERVES 12

- **1 cup unsalted butter, at room temperature, plus more for pan**
- **3 cups all-purpose flour, plus more for pan**
- **2½ cups granulated sugar**
- **5 large eggs, at room temperature**
- **2 tsp. vanilla extract**
- **½ tsp. almond extract (optional)**
- **¾ tsp. kosher salt**
- **¼ tsp. baking powder**
- **½ cup sour cream, at room temperature**
- **1¼ cups finely chopped, unpeeled peaches, drained and patted dry (from 3 to 4 peaches)**

1. Preheat oven to 325°F with rack in middle position. Butter and flour a 10-inch tube pan, and set aside.
2. Place sugar and butter in a large bowl; beat with an electric mixer on medium speed until light in color and fluffy, 4 to 5 minutes. Add eggs, 1 at a time, beating until incorporated. Beat in vanilla and almond extracts, if desired.
3. Whisk together flour, salt, and baking powder in a medium bowl. Add a third of the flour mixture to butter mixture; beat on low speed until just incorporated. Add half of the sour cream, mixing until just incorporated. With mixer running, alternate adding flour mixture and sour cream, beginning and ending with flour mixture. Fold in peaches.
4. Spoon and spread batter evenly in prepared pan. Bake until top is golden brown and springs back when lightly pressed in the center, 1 hour, 15 minutes to 1 hour, 20 minutes. Let cool in pan on a wire rack 15 to 20 minutes. Run a knife around edges of cake to loosen; remove from pan, and let cool right side up on wire rack for 1 hour.

Iron-Skillet Peach Ice Cream

(Photo, page 128)

ACTIVE 40 MIN. · TOTAL 2 HOURS, 5 MIN., PLUS 16 HOURS, 30 MIN. COOLING, CHILLING, AND FREEZING

SERVES 8

- **2¼ to 2½ lb. peaches (6 to 8 peaches)**
- **1 pinch kosher salt**
- **1¼ cups granulated sugar, divided**
- **1½ cups whole milk**
- **4 large egg yolks**
- **1½ cups heavy whipping cream**

1. Preheat oven to 350°F. Peel and slice peaches; place in a medium bowl along with any juices to yield about 3 cups. Stir in salt and ½ cup sugar. Transfer peach mixture to a 10- or 12-inch cast-iron skillet; cook over medium, stirring constantly, until sugar dissolves, 2 to 3 minutes. Remove from heat; transfer skillet to oven. Bake until juices are lightly syrupy, 25 to 35 minutes, stirring once halfway through cook time. Remove skillet from oven, and use a potato masher to crush peaches until nearly smooth. Transfer to a medium heatproof bowl, and cool to room temperature, 1½ to 2 hours.
2. While peach mixture cools, heat milk in a medium saucepan over low, stirring often, until steam rises and small bubbles begin to form around edges of pan (but do not boil), about 8 minutes. Meanwhile, whisk together egg yolks and remaining ¾ cup sugar in a large bowl. Gradually pour half of the hot milk mixture into yolk mixture, whisking rapidly to combine. Whisk in remaining milk, and return mixture to saucepan. Cook over medium-low, stirring constantly, until mixture slightly thickens and lightly coats the back of a spoon, about 5 minutes. Remove from heat, and transfer custard to a large heatproof bowl. Loosely cover with plastic wrap, and chill, stirring occasionally, until cold, about 1 hour.
3. Once peaches and custard have cooled, whisk peaches and heavy cream into custard mixture. Cover with plastic wrap, and chill overnight (at least 12 hours) or up to 20 hours.
4. When ready to make the ice cream, pour the cold custard mixture into a 2-quart or larger ice-cream machine canister; churn mixture according to the manufacturer's instructions until it reaches a soft-serve ice-cream consistency, about 1 hour. Transfer to a freezer-safe container, and freeze until firm and scoopable, 3 to 4 hours.

The Ultimate Peach Sundaes

(Photo, page 128)

ACTIVE 25 MIN. · TOTAL 25 MIN.

SERVES 4

- **4 (½-inch-thick) slices Peach Pound Cake (recipe left)**
- **2 cups peeled and sliced peaches (from 2 to 3 large peaches)**
- **2 Tbsp. granulated sugar, plus more to taste**
- **8 scoops Iron-Skillet Peach Ice Cream (recipe left), divided**
- **Sweetened whipped cream**

1. Cut the Peach Pound Cake slices into ½-inch cubes; set aside.
2. Toss the sliced peaches with sugar in a medium bowl until well combined. Taste the mixture, add more sugar, if desired. Set peach mixture aside.
3. Divide half of the cake cubes among 4 goblets, large wineglasses, or small bowls. Top each serving with 1 scoop of the Iron-Skillet Peach Ice Cream. Spoon half of the peaches and their juices over the ice cream in the goblets. Repeat the sundae layers once with the remaining cake cubes, ice cream, and peach mixture. Top sundaes with sweetened whipped cream, and drizzle with any leftover peach juices, if desired. Serve immediately.

Mary Jo's Sun-Cooked Peach Preserves

My aunt Mary Jo Ellis had an unconventional way of preserving peaches—she let the sun do most of the work. The juices evaporate, leaving soft slices of glistening fruit behind to spread onto warm biscuits or toast.

ACTIVE 55 MIN. · TOTAL 1 HOUR, 25 MIN., PLUS AT LEAST 12 HOURS SUN-COOKING AND OVERNIGHT CHILLING

MAKES 4 TO 6 HALF-PINT JARS

- 6 cups peeled and sliced peaches (from 10 to 12 peaches)
- 4 cups granulated sugar
- 3 Tbsp. fresh lemon juice (from 2 lemons)

1. Place peach slices, sugar, and lemon juice in a large (5-quart) stainless-steel or enameled saucepan; stir to combine. Let stand until sugar is dissolved, about 30 minutes.

2. Bring peach mixture to a boil over medium-high, stirring occasionally. Reduce heat to medium-low, and simmer, stirring occasionally, 8 minutes. Remove from heat.

3. Transfer peaches and their juices to a clean 2-quart glass dish or bowl with a transparent lid (to allow the sunlight in). Place on a table outdoors for at least 6 hours of full sun, stirring once or twice.

4. At the end of the day, bring peaches inside; cover and refrigerate. Depending on the amount of liquid in the peaches and the intensity of the sun, the preserves should come together in 2 to 3 days (with 6 hours of full sunlight each day). The peach slices will look translucent, and the juices should thicken, though they will not thicken as much as store-bought peach preserves. (For thicker results, simmer preserves in a saucepan on the stove until desired consistency is reached.)

5. Pack preserves into 4 to 6 sterilized half-pint jars, leaving ¼-inch headspace at the top. Secure with sterilized lids and jar rims; store in the refrigerator. Preserves will keep in the fridge for 2 to 3 weeks.

STOVETOP-ONLY VARIATION: Make preserves through Step 1. In Step 2, heat saucepan over medium-high; bring mixture to a boil, stirring occasionally. Reduce heat to medium-low, and cook, stirring occasionally and skimming foam off top, until peaches are translucent and a candy thermometer registers 220°F, 20 to 30 minutes. (To check consistency, place some of the peach mixture on a heatproof plate; freeze 10 minutes. Remove plate; run a spoon through mixture. It should be thick enough to hold a trail that flows back together very slowly.) Remove from heat. Omit Steps 3 and 4. Proceed with Step 5 as directed.

Chill Out

Keep the oven off, and whip up this five-ingredient icebox dessert.

No-Bake Chocolate Pie

ACTIVE 20 MIN. - TOTAL 25 MIN., PLUS 2 HOURS CHILLING

SERVES 10

- 20 cream-filled chocolate sandwich cookies (such as Oreo, from 1 [13.29-oz.] pkg.), plus more crushed cookies for garnish
- ½ cup butter, divided
- 1¼ cups heavy whipping cream
- 1 (12-oz.) pkg. semisweet chocolate chips (such as Ghirardelli)
- Sweetened whipped cream, for serving

1. Grease a 9-inch pie plate with cooking spray, and set aside. Process chocolate sandwich cookies into fine crumbs in a food processor, about 45 seconds. Microwave ¼ cup butter in a small bowl on HIGH until melted, about 30 seconds. With food processor running, add melted butter; pulse until well combined, about 15 seconds more.

2. Transfer crumb mixture to prepared pie plate. Firmly press crumbs into bottom and up sides of pie plate in an even layer. Freeze 15 minutes.

3. Meanwhile, heat cream in a saucepan over medium until steaming; do not boil. Pour hot cream over chocolate chips in a large heatproof mixing bowl; let stand 3 minutes. Gently whisk chocolate mixture until smooth. Cut remaining ¼ cup butter into small pieces, and add to chocolate mixture. Stir until butter is completely melted and incorporated.

4. Pour chocolate mixture into chilled crust, spreading in an even layer (it will come right up to the top). Chill pie, uncovered, until set, about 2 hours. Top with whipped cream just before serving. Sprinkle with additional crushed cookies.

The Thrill of Grilling

These smokin' hot recipes will make you want to cook everything outdoors.

BLESS MY GRILL'S HEART. When the summer heat reaches its peak, there's nothing I won't put it through. Those hardworking burners have baked pies and cheese straws, boiled pasta and potatoes, and even fried chicken and okra. Trust me—when you live in a 100-year-old house with an ancient air conditioner, you'll do just about anything to avoid turning your oven on until October.

Truthfully, I'm grateful for this "hardship." In addition to opening my eyes to my grill's versatility, it has taught me how joyful it can be to cook outdoors. I'm free from the worry of spatters, spills, and boilovers—I've even been known to fling spent lemon rinds into the bushes, which I recommend if you haven't tried.

These recipes show you all the cool things that your grill can do, from adding a smoky char to deviled eggs, slaw, and potato salad to baking the best peach cobbler you've ever tasted. It's time to fire things up and enjoy grilling again. —Josh Miller

TENNESSEE ONION BURGERS (PAGE 139)

GRILLED DEVILED EGGS
SMOKY POTATO SALAD
CHARRED CABBAGE-AND-CARROT SLAW

Grilled Deviled Eggs

These aren't your grandma's deviled eggs. Be sure to brush the whites generously with oil to help them release from the grill grates with ease.

ACTIVE 35 MIN. - TOTAL 35 MIN.

SERVES 12

- **12 hard-cooked eggs, peeled and cut in half lengthwise**
- **6 Tbsp. mayonnaise**
- **2 tsp. Dijon mustard**
- **1½ tsp. hot sauce**
- **¾ tsp. kosher salt**
- **¼ tsp. black pepper, plus more for garnish**
- **2 tsp. vegetable oil**
- **Pickled red onions**
- **Chopped fresh chives**

1. Preheat a gas grill to medium-high (400°F to 450°F). While grill preheats, separate egg yolks from egg whites. Place egg yolks in a bowl; mash with a fork until crumbly. Add mayonnaise, mustard, hot sauce, salt, and black pepper; stir until smooth. Place in a piping bag or a ziplock plastic bag; refrigerate until ready to use.

2. Brush cut sides of egg whites with oil. Working in batches of 4 to 6 egg whites at a time, place egg whites, cut sides down, on oiled grates; grill, uncovered, until grill marks form, about 1 minute. Carefully remove from grill, and place on a platter. Repeat process with remaining egg whites.

3. Pipe egg yolk mixture into grilled egg whites; top with pickled red onions, chives, and additional black pepper. Serve immediately.

Smoky Potato Salad

Boiling the potatoes first guarantees that they'll come off the grill fork-tender with a crispy exterior.

ACTIVE 40 MIN. - TOTAL 1 HOUR, 15 MIN.

SERVES 12

- **3 lb. red baby new potatoes, scrubbed and halved lengthwise (about 8 cups)**
- **¾ cup apple cider vinegar, divided**
- **5 tsp. kosher salt, divided**
- **8 thick-cut bacon slices, cut into 1-inch pieces (about 2 cups)**
- **¼ cup packed light brown sugar**
- **3 Tbsp. whole-grain mustard**
- **½ tsp. black pepper, plus more for garnish**
- **1 Tbsp. finely chopped garlic (from about 3 garlic cloves)**
- **¼ cup chopped mixed tender herbs (such as parsley, basil, chives, and dill), plus more for garnish**

1. Bring potatoes, ¼ cup apple cider vinegar, 4 teaspoons salt, and enough tap water to cover the potatoes by 1 inch to a boil in a large Dutch oven over medium-high. Boil over medium-high, undisturbed, until tender-crisp, about 12 minutes. Drain well.

2. Preheat a gas grill to medium-high (400°F to 450°F). Place parcooked potatoes, cut sides down, on oiled grates; grill, uncovered and undisturbed, until tender and charred, about 5 minutes. Remove from grill, and place on a baking sheet; set aside.

3. Place bacon in a large skillet, and heat over medium. Cook, stirring occasionally, until crispy, 12 to 15 minutes. Using a slotted spoon, transfer bacon to a paper towel-lined plate, and set aside. Reserve 2 tablespoons drippings in the skillet, and save remaining drippings for another use. Add brown sugar, mustard, black pepper, remaining ½ cup vinegar, and remaining 1 teaspoon salt to reserved drippings in skillet; cook over medium, stirring often and scraping up any browned bits, until mixture is slightly thickened, about 2 minutes. Add garlic; cook, stirring constantly, until fragrant, about 1 minute. Stir in herbs and reserved potatoes and bacon until well coated. Remove skillet from heat, and garnish with additional herbs and black pepper; serve warm or at room temperature.

Charred Cabbage-and-Carrot Slaw

Slaw is often an afterthought at cookouts, but this one steals the show with its tangy dressing and smoky crunch.

ACTIVE 40 MIN. - TOTAL 45 MIN.

SERVES 12

- **¼ cup mayonnaise**
- **2 Tbsp. granulated sugar**
- **2 Tbsp. fresh orange juice (from 1 orange)**
- **1 Tbsp. apple cider vinegar**
- **1 Tbsp. kosher salt**
- **1 tsp. onion powder**
- **1 tsp. black pepper**
- **2 Tbsp. vegetable oil**
- **1 tsp. smoked paprika**
- **1 small head red cabbage, quartered with core intact**
- **2 cups matchstick carrots (from 1 [10-oz.] bag)**
- **1 cup golden raisins**
- **½ cup chopped smoked almonds, plus more for garnish**
- **Chopped fresh flat-leaf parsley**

1. Preheat a gas grill to medium (350°F to 400°F). While grill is preheating, whisk together mayonnaise, sugar, orange juice, vinegar, salt, onion powder, and black pepper in a large bowl.

2. Whisk together oil and smoked paprika in a small bowl; brush over cabbage. Place cabbage on oiled grates; grill, covered, turning occasionally, until charred and softened, 15 to 20 minutes. Remove from grill; let stand until cool enough to handle, about 5 minutes. Remove and discard cores; thinly slice cabbage. Add cabbage, carrots, raisins, and almonds to mayonnaise mixture in large bowl; toss until coated. Garnish with parsley and additional almonds; serve warm or at room temperature.

GRILLED PEACH COBBLER

Grilled Peach Cobbler

This versatile dessert can be made with fresh plums, nectarines, or even pineapple. For extra summer flavor, fold in a cup of blackberries with the peaches at the end of Step 2.

ACTIVE 45 MIN. - TOTAL 1 HOUR, 35 MIN.

SERVES 8

- **4 lb. fresh unpeeled peaches, halved and pitted (about 8 large)**
- **2 Tbsp. cornstarch**
- **2 Tbsp. bourbon**
- **1 Tbsp. fresh lemon juice (from 1 lemon)**
- **1 tsp. ground cinnamon**
- **1 cup plus 6 Tbsp. packed light brown sugar, divided**
- **3/4 tsp. kosher salt, divided**
- **1 cup all-purpose flour**
- **3/4 tsp. baking powder**
- **1/4 tsp. baking soda**
- **1/4 cup cold unsalted butter, cubed**
- **6 Tbsp. whole buttermilk**
- **Vanilla ice cream, for serving**

1. Preheat a gas grill to medium-high (400°F to 450°F) on 1 side; keep other side unlit. Place peaches, cut sides down, on oiled grates over lit side of grill. Grill, uncovered and undisturbed, until charred, about 4 minutes. Remove from grill, and place on a cutting board; let stand until cool enough to handle, about 5 minutes. Slice into 1-inch-thick wedges.

2. Stir together cornstarch, bourbon, lemon juice, cinnamon, 1 cup brown sugar, and ½ teaspoon salt in a 12-inch cast-iron or enamel-coated skillet until evenly combined. Gently fold in peaches until coated; set aside.

3. Whisk together flour, baking powder, baking soda, 4 tablespoons brown sugar, and remaining ¼ teaspoon salt in a medium bowl. Using a pastry blender or 2 forks, cut in butter until mixture is crumbly. Stir in buttermilk until just combined. Crumble flour mixture over peach mixture in skillet; sprinkle with remaining 2 tablespoons brown sugar. Place skillet on unlit side of grill. Close the grill lid; bake, rotating skillet a quarter turn every 10 minutes, until the filling is bubbly and the topping is golden brown, about 45 minutes. Let cool 10 minutes. Serve warm with vanilla ice cream.

Tennessee Onion Burgers

(Photo, page 135)

Inspired by one of our favorite side dishes, these cheesy, buttery onions are a tasty way to raise your burger game.

ACTIVE 45 MIN. - TOTAL 1 HOUR, 25 MIN.

SERVES 8

- **2½ lb. sweet onions (about 3 large onions), cut crosswise into ¼-inch-thick slices and separated into rings (about 11 cups)**
- **2 tsp. dried Italian seasoning**
- **½ tsp. dry mustard**
- **2½ tsp. seasoned salt, divided**
- **¼ cup unsalted butter, cubed**
- **2 cups shredded sharp cheddar cheese (from 1 [8-oz.] pkg.)**
- **2 lb. 80/20 ground beef**
- **½ tsp. black pepper**
- **8 sesame seed hamburger buns**
- **Toppings: green leaf lettuce, tomato slices, cooked bacon slices, pickle chips**

1. Preheat oven to 350°F. Coat a 13 x 9-inch baking dish with cooking spray; set aside.

2. Place the onions in a large bowl. Sprinkle with Italian seasoning, dry mustard, and 1 teaspoon seasoned salt; toss gently to coat. Arrange onions in an even layer in prepared baking dish. Scatter butter over onions; sprinkle with shredded cheddar. Cover with aluminum foil; bake until onions are soft, about 40 minutes. Remove and discard foil. Bake until top is golden, about 30 minutes.

3. Meanwhile, preheat a gas grill to medium-high (400°F to 450°F). While grill preheats, mix together ground beef, black pepper, and remaining 1½ teaspoons seasoned salt in a large bowl until just combined, being careful not to overwork. Divide beef mixture into 8 equal portions (about 4 ounces each). Form each into a ½-inch-thick patty (about 3½ inches in diameter). Place patties on oiled grates. Grill, uncovered, flipping once halfway through cook time, until desired degree of doneness is reached, 2 minutes per side for medium-rare to 4 minutes per side for medium-well. Remove burgers from grill. Place on a platter, and cover loosely with foil. Set aside.

4. Place buns, cut sides down, on oiled grates; grill, uncovered, until toasted, about 1 minute. Place 1 burger on each toasted bottom bun; add cooked onions, desired toppings, and top buns.

OVER EASY

Better Than the Bakery

Buttermilk makes these berry muffins extra tender and fluffy.

Blackberry Muffins with Lemon-Buttermilk Glaze

ACTIVE 20 MIN. - TOTAL 1 HOUR, 20 MIN.

MAKES 1 DOZEN

- 3/4 cup granulated sugar
- 1/2 cup unsalted butter, melted
- 2 large eggs, at room temperature
- 3 tsp. grated lemon zest (from 1 large lemon), divided, plus more for garnish
- 1 tsp. baking powder
- 1/2 tsp. baking soda
- 2/3 cup plus 1 Tbsp. whole buttermilk, divided
- 2 1/2 tsp. vanilla extract, divided
- 1/2 tsp. kosher salt, plus a pinch, divided
- 2 1/2 cups all-purpose flour
- 2 cups fresh blackberries, halved (from 1 [10-oz.] pkg.)
- 2 Tbsp. turbinado sugar (optional)
- 3/4 cup powdered sugar

1. Preheat oven to 400°F. Line a 12-cup muffin tray with paper liners; set aside.
2. Whisk together granulated sugar, melted butter, eggs, 2 teaspoons lemon zest, baking powder, baking soda, 2/3 cup buttermilk, 2 teaspoons vanilla, and 1/2 teaspoon salt in a large bowl until smooth. Gently fold flour and blackberries into granulated sugar mixture until no streaks of flour remain (batter will be thick).
3. Spoon batter into prepared muffin wells, about 1/3 cup per well. Sprinkle tops with turbinado sugar, if using.
4. Bake until tops are golden and a wooden pick inserted in center comes out clean, about 18 minutes. Let cool in pan 5 minutes; transfer to a wire rack, and let cool 30 minutes.
5. Stir together powdered sugar and remaining 1 tablespoon buttermilk, 1 teaspoon lemon zest, 1/2 teaspoon vanilla, and pinch of salt in a small bowl until smooth. Drizzle over cooled muffins; sprinkle with more lemon zest, if desired.

SNACK TIME

Good Catch

Upgrade happy hour with this stir-together appetizer inspired by the Gulf Coast.

TEST KITCHEN TIP
Can't find the right tuna? In a pinch, add a dash of liquid smoke.

Smoked-Tuna Dip

ACTIVE 10 MIN. - TOTAL 10 MIN.
SERVES 8

- 4 oz. cream cheese, softened
- 2 tsp. grated lemon zest plus 2 tsp. fresh juice (from 1 lemon), divided, plus lemon wedges for serving
- 2 Tbsp. minced shallot (from 1 shallot)
- 2 Tbsp. chopped fresh chives, plus more for garnish
- 2 Tbsp. drained nonpareil capers, coarsely chopped
- 1/4 tsp. kosher salt
- 1/4 tsp. freshly ground black pepper
- 4 (2.5-oz.) pouches smoked tuna (such as Bumble Bee), drained
- Fresh flat-leaf parsley leaves
- Assorted crackers
- Hot sauce

1. Whisk together cream cheese and lemon juice in a bowl until smooth. Stir in zest, shallot, chives, capers, salt, and pepper. Stir in half of tuna until well combined. Fold in remaining tuna until just combined.

2. Transfer to a small serving bowl; garnish with chives and parsley. Serve dip with crackers, hot sauce, and lemon wedges.

Dog Days

Three spins on a summertime favorite burst with flavor.

Viet-Cajun Style Hot Dogs

ACTIVE 30 MIN. - TOTAL 1 HOUR

SERVES 8

- ½ cup matchstick carrots
- 3 radishes, cut into matchsticks (about ½ cup)
- ½ cup seasoned rice vinegar
- 1 jalapeño, halved, seeded, and thinly sliced
- ½ tsp. grated lime zest plus 1 Tbsp. fresh juice, divided (from 1 lime)
- 2 Tbsp. chopped fresh cilantro, plus more for garnish
- 1 Tbsp. chopped fresh mint, plus more for garnish
- ⅔ cup mayonnaise
- 2 Tbsp. Sriracha sauce
- 2 (12-oz.) pkg. andouille sausage links
- 8 brioche hot dog buns, toasted

1. Stir together carrots, radishes, vinegar, jalapeño, and lime zest in a bowl. Cover and chill 30 minutes. Drain carrot mixture; stir in cilantro and mint. Set aside. Stir together mayonnaise, Sriracha, and lime juice in a separate bowl; set aside.

2. Place andouille in a large cast-iron skillet over medium; cook, turning occasionally, until lightly charred and heated through, 10 to 15 minutes. Place 1 sausage link in each bun. Top with carrot slaw, drizzle with mayonnaise mixture, and garnish with herbs.

ALABAMA HOT DOGS

Alabama Hot Dogs

ACTIVE 15 MIN. - TOTAL 25 MIN.

SERVES 8

Preheat grill to medium-high (400°F to 450°F). Stir together 1 cup **mayonnaise**; 2 Tbsp. **apple cider vinegar**; 1 tsp. each **horseradish**, **black pepper**, and **Worcestershire sauce**; ¾ tsp. **garlic powder**; and ½ tsp. each **salt** and **hot sauce** in a bowl. Grill 8 (7-inch-long) **hickory-smoked sausages**, uncovered, turning often, until lightly charred, about 6 minutes. Divide among 8 **buns**; top with mayonnaise mixture and **pickle relish**.

BACON-WRAPPED HOT DOGS

Bacon-Wrapped Hot Dogs

ACTIVE 30 MIN. - TOTAL 30 MIN.

SERVES 8

Tightly wrap 8 **beef hot dogs** with 8 slices **center-cut bacon** (1 each). Cook in a large cast-iron skillet over medium, turning occasionally, until bacon is crispy, about 18 minutes. Meanwhile, stir together 1 cup **pico de gallo** and ¼ cup chopped **cilantro** in a bowl; set aside. Divide bacon-wrapped hot dogs among 8 **buns**; drizzle with **yellow mustard**. Top with pico de gallo mixture and **pickled jalapeño** slices, if desired.

VIET-CAJUN STYLE HOT DOGS

Strawberry Frosé

Cool off with this frosty cocktail.

ACTIVE 5 MIN. - TOTAL 4 HOURS, 5 MIN.
SERVES 4

Combine 1 (750-milliliter) bottle **dry rosé wine**, 1 cup thawed **strawberries in syrup**, and 2 Tbsp. **vodka** in a 1-gallon ziplock plastic freezer bag. Seal bag; freeze until almost solid, 4 to 6 hours. If desired, spoon mixture into a blender; blend until smooth. Pour into 4 glasses, and garnish with **fresh strawberries**.

Crispy Fried Fish in a Flash

Fry like a pro with our foolproof technique (recipe, page 123).

1. SOAK THE FISH
Whisk together buttermilk, eggs, and hot sauce in a large bowl. Add the fillets, and submerge completely. Marinate at room temperature for 10 minutes.

2. MAKE A SEASONED DREDGE
Stir crushed saltine crackers, salt, garlic powder, paprika, black pepper, and cayenne pepper in a wide, shallow bowl or pie plate until well combined.

3. COAT IT EVENLY
Remove fish from buttermilk mixture, allowing excess to drip off. Transfer to cracker mixture, pressing to coat both sides. Gently shake off excess.

4. DON'T CROWD THE POT
Add a few fillets at a time to the hot oil. Fry, turning occasionally, until golden brown and cooked through, 3 to 4 minutes. Let oil return to temperature after each batch.

August

BOUNTY

Aw, Shucks

During peak season, corn shines in both sweet and savory recipes.

Mexican Street Corn Pasta Salad

ACTIVE 25 MIN. - TOTAL 35 MIN.
SERVES 6

Preheat a gas grill to medium-high (400°F to 450°F). Brush 4 **medium ears fresh corn** with 1 Tbsp. **canola oil;** sprinkle evenly with 1 tsp. **kosher salt.** Place corn on oiled grates; grill, uncovered and turning often, until charred in spots and tender, 8 to 10 minutes. Let corn stand until cool enough to handle, about 15 minutes. Cut off kernels, and discard cobs. Whisk together ⅔ cup **mayonnaise,** ¼ cup **crema Mexicana,** 2 tsp. minced **garlic,** 1½ tsp. **ancho chile powder,** ½ tsp. **ground cumin,** and ½ tsp. **kosher salt** in a large bowl. Stir in 1 (1-lb.) pkg. cooked **orecchiette pasta,** corn kernels, ½ cup crumbled **Cotija cheese,** ½ cup finely chopped **onion,** ⅓ cup chopped **mild pickled jalapeño chiles** plus 2 Tbsp. **liquid from jar,** and ¼ cup chopped **fresh cilantro** until evenly combined. Garnish with more **ancho chile powder, Cotija cheese,** and **fresh cilantro.**

NO-CHURN CORN ICE CREAM

No-Churn Corn Ice Cream

ACTIVE 30 MIN. - TOTAL 30 MIN., PLUS 3 HOURS CHILLING AND 6 HOURS FREEZING
SERVES 6

Cut kernels from 3 **large ears fresh yellow corn** to yield 2¼ cups, reserving cobs. Place corn kernels and cobs, 2 cups **heavy whipping cream,** 1 (14-oz.) can **sweetened condensed milk,** and ⅛ tsp. **kosher salt** in a large Dutch oven. Bring to a simmer over medium; reduce heat to medium-low, and simmer, stirring constantly, until kernels are just tender, about 6 minutes. Transfer mixture to a large heatproof bowl. Chill in refrigerator, uncovered and stirring occasionally, until cold, about 3 hours. Remove corn cobs, scraping any liquid back into bowl before discarding. Strain corn mixture using a fine mesh strainer into a large bowl, pressing to release as much liquid as possible. Whisk in 2 Tbsp. **light corn syrup** and ¼ tsp. **vanilla extract.** Reserve kernels in an airtight container in refrigerator for garnish, if desired. Beat cream mixture with an electric mixer on medium speed until aerated and fluffy, about 6 minutes. Spread mixture in a freezer-safe 9- x 5-inch loaf pan. Place plastic wrap directly on surface. Freeze until firm, at least 6 hours or up to 1 week. Garnish scoops with reserved kernels and **fresh basil,** if desired.

Lost Treasure in Old Cookbooks

Regional recipe collections are filled with hidden gems.

WITH THEIR distinctive spiral bindings and often torn and food-spattered paper covers, my beloved community cookbooks quietly distinguish themselves from the surrounding tomes on my shelves. Bearing names like *The Black Family Reunion Cookbook* (from the National Council of Negro Women) and *Cane River Cuisine: Louisiana's Finest Recipes* (from the Service League of Natchitoches), they are snapshots of a time and place.

Titles created in the mid-20th century feature dishes like glistening, jiggly aspics and cheese balls enrobed in crushed pecans. Thumbing through them is a delight—a trip down cooking's memory lane. Today's offerings often tout the virtues of various superfoods or devices like Instant Pots and air fryers. But no matter the era, a lot of the dishes have been passed down for generations within families. Publishing them is a way to honor the cooks and ensure the recipes aren't lost to time.

Many of these books, like *Charleston Receipts* and *River Road Recipes*, were produced by local Junior League chapters (some even have multiple editions) and have become culinary classics. However, I prefer the quirky ones that began life as fundraisers for small churches, fraternal organizations, school alumni associations, and other groups. They, as much as the annual outpouring of cookbooks from more familiar and larger publishing houses, give a sense of the scope of the country's changing culinary landscape. In them, I have found some real gems, like the coconut crisps from *Culinary Masterpieces from the Wolmer's Kitchens*, a 2010 compilation of Jamaican and international recipes from an American alumni association of a legendary Jamaican school.

As a founding member of the Southern Foodways Alliance, I'd definitely be remiss if I didn't mention the organization's 2015 contribution to the genre, *The Southern Foodways Alliance Community Cookbook*. I am always tickled when folks say that they've made and enjoyed my super simple instructions for spiced pecans, which are included in the book. But my favorite in the collection is the fried chicken from chef Austin Leslie of New Orleans' Chez Hélène. Topped with a "confetti" of garlic and parsley and served with dill pickle slices, the chicken was called an homage "to heart and home and skillet" by the book's editors, Sara Roahen and John T. Edge. It is certainly that and (dare I say it?) almost as good as my mother's.
—Jessica B. Harris

Austin Leslie's Confetti Chicken

ACTIVE 45 MIN. - TOTAL 1 HOUR, 55 MIN.
SERVES 6 TO 8

- 2 Tbsp. black pepper
- 2 Tbsp. Cajun seasoning
- 4 tsp. kosher salt
- 1 (3- to 4-lb.) whole chicken, cut into 8 to 10 pieces
- Peanut oil
- 1 large egg, beaten
- 1 (12-oz.) can evaporated milk
- 1 cup all-purpose flour
- 1 garlic clove, minced (1 tsp.)
- 1 small bunch flat-leaf parsley, finely chopped (1/4 cup)
- 8-10 dill pickle chips

1. Combine pepper, Cajun seasoning, and salt in a large bowl. Place chicken in bowl; turn to coat. Place seasoned chicken in a single layer on a baking sheet; chill, uncovered, at least 1 hour or up to 24 hours.
2. Pour oil into a deep skillet or large Dutch oven to a depth of at least 3 inches; heat oil to 350°F. Meanwhile, remove chicken from refrigerator; let stand while oil preheats. Line a baking sheet with a wire rack, and set aside.
3. Whisk together egg, evaporated milk, and 1 cup water in a large bowl. Place flour in a shallow bowl. Working in batches, dip chicken in egg mixture, letting excess drip off; place in flour, turning to coat completely.
4. Place 3 or 4 pieces in skillet at a time, adjusting heat as needed to maintain oil temperature at 335°F. Cook, turning twice, until deep golden brown and a thermometer inserted into thickest portion registers 165°F, 12 to 15 minutes for thighs, and 15 to 18 minutes for breasts. Transfer to prepared baking sheet; tent loosely with foil while cooking remaining chicken.
5. Let fried chicken rest on wire rack 10 minutes. Stir together garlic and parsley in a small bowl. Top chicken with pickles; sprinkle with parsley mixture.

AUSTIN LESLIE: A LOUISIANA LEGEND

A fixture on the New Orleans food scene for almost half a century, chef Austin Leslie was instantly recognizable thanks to his signature muttonchop whiskers and always-present captain's hat. In his later years, he cooked in celebrated eateries such as Jacques-Imo's and Pampy's Creole Kitchen. But he was probably best known as the chef at Chez Hélène, the Creole restaurant started by his aunt, who sold it to him in 1975. This spot was even the inspiration for a 1980s TV show called *Frank's Place*. Twenty years ago, Leslie passed away in Atlanta after being rescued from Hurricane Katrina. His book *Austin Leslie's Creole-Soul* is out of print, but it's worth a spot on your shelf if you can find it.

IVY ODOM AND HER
GRANDMOTHER JUDY
FAISON MAKE TEA CAKES
IN IVY'S KITCHEN.

Baking with Nana

My sweetest memories were made in my grandma's Georgia kitchen.

THEY CAME TO EVERY piano recital, choir performance, award ceremony, and even the few sporting events I reluctantly tried as a child. (I quickly learned sports were not my strong suit and I should stick to more artsy endeavors.) I went out to eat with Papa on Tuesday nights and played bingo with Nana at the country club on Thursdays.

So many of my happiest moments involved the two of them, but my most cherished memories are the ones from their house. I spent many Friday nights over at Nana and Papa's. I can remember waking up to the smell of bacon frying and grits bubbling on the stove. Every time I make bacon in my own house now, which has original heart pine flooring like Nana and Papa's house did, there is something about the smell that takes me back to Saturday mornings on Faison Road. The Golf Channel would always be playing in the background; the soft claps were the soundtrack to our slow Saturdays. We'd play out in the yard or in the playhouse Papa had built just for his three grandchildren, while Nana made a lunch of pimiento cheese, salad, fried chicken, and sliced tomatoes. In the afternoons, we crowded around the breakfast table to make tea cakes or make pot holders on antique red metal looms. Nana taught me to cross-stitch and tat; Papa taught me how to hit a golf ball and drive a lawn mower. So much of who I am today is because of afternoons with them.

Papa passed away a few years ago, and there isn't a day that goes by that I don't miss him. I'm lucky enough to get to see Nana every time I go back home to Moultrie, and I'm even luckier that she (reluctantly) agreed to come to Birmingham to cook with me in my own kitchen for a photo shoot.

We made tea cakes (which you can find below), still one of my favorites from her recipe collection. While she loves to cook, it took a few glass bottle Coca-Colas to convince her to smile for the camera. I'll forever be thankful for the chance to capture that afternoon forever in my new cookbook, *My Southern Kitchen*. She might not admit it, but she had (almost) as much fun as we used to on our treasured Saturdays together. —Ivy Odom

Nana's Tea Cakes

ACTIVE 20 MIN. - TOTAL 50 MIN.
MAKES ABOUT 4 DOZEN COOKIES

- 3½ cups all-purpose flour
- 2 cups granulated sugar
- 2 tsp. baking powder
- 1 tsp. kosher salt
- 1 cup butter, cut into ½-inch pieces, at room temperature
- 2 large eggs, lightly beaten
- 1 Tbsp. vanilla extract

1. Preheat oven to 400°F. Line 2 baking sheets with parchment paper. Whisk together flour, sugar, baking powder, and salt in a large bowl. Add butter pieces to bowl; mix with hands, pinching butter into flour mixture with your fingers until it resembles chunky wet sand. Add eggs and vanilla into flour mixture, and mix well with hands until dough comes together into a smooth ball.
2. Roll dough, about 1 tablespoon at a time, into gumball-size balls, and place on prepared baking sheets about 1 inch apart. Bake 7 to 9 minutes or until lightly golden brown and set, rotating baking sheets halfway through. Let cool completely on wire racks, about 20 minutes.

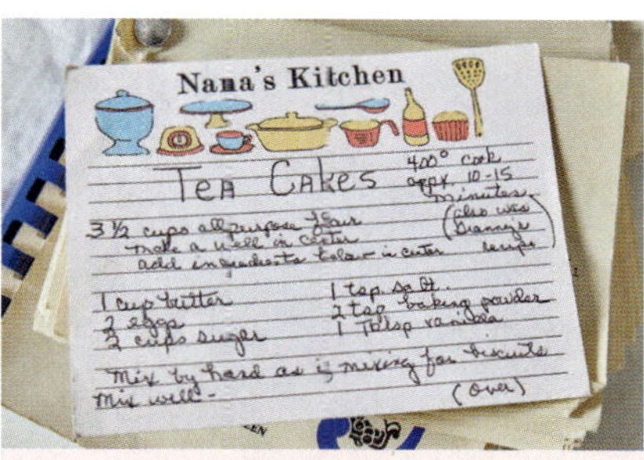

Two Takes on Tea Cakes

Although I followed her handwritten recipe card exactly during the photo shoot, Nana couldn't stop herself from telling me I was doing it all wrong. The recipe card gives two different instructions. Option one: "Roll the dough into balls about the size of a gumball, and place on a baking sheet." Or option two: "Roll the dough, and use a small round cutter (or shot glass) to cut the cookies." The problem is that these two methods give very different results. One is thinner and more wafer-like; the other is thicker and chewier. Growing up, we always rolled and cut our tea cakes, but the thinner ones got a little too crisp for my liking. When I tried the gumball method, I much preferred the chewier cookie. So that's what I call for in this recipe.

However, when I started forming the gumballs during the photo shoot, Nana immediately took over and said the thinner, rolling-pin method was better. If you look at the photos, you can see us each doing them our own way. We had everyone on set try them, and it was split on which style of cookie people favored. According to her, my version isn't a true tea cake, but it does taste good. Since we couldn't agree, I'll let y'all decide which you like best.

NANA'S TEA CAKES (PAGE 151)

One of the things I'm most thankful for about my childhood is that we lived in the same town as my mama's parents.

SUPPERTIME

Garden Party

Tomatoes and basil team up for dinner in a flash.

PEPPERONI PIZZA WITH BASIL OIL

FLAVOR UP
Use leftover Basil Oil on grilled vegetables, or toss with pasta—hot or cold.

Pepperoni Pizza with Basil Oil

ACTIVE 20 MIN. - TOTAL 40 MIN.
SERVES 4

- 1 tomato, sliced ¼ inch thick (about 1 cup)
- ¼ tsp. kosher salt
- ¼ cup Basil Oil (recipe follows), divided, plus more for serving (optional)
- 1 lb. fresh pizza dough, at room temperature
- ¼ cup tomato sauce (from 1 [8-oz.] can) or pizza sauce
- 1 garlic clove, grated (about ½ tsp.)
- 1 (8-oz.) ball fresh mozzarella cheese, sliced or torn (about 1½ cups)
- 6 slices pepperoni or soppressata
- Fresh basil leaves, for garnish

1. Preheat oven to 450°F. Place tomato slices on a paper towel–lined plate, and sprinkle evenly with salt. Set aside.
2. Brush a 12-inch cast-iron skillet with 2 tablespoons Basil Oil. Stretch or roll dough into a 13-inch circle; place it in the bottom and about 1 inch up sides of the skillet. Brush dough with 1 tablespoon Basil Oil. Pat tomato slices dry with paper towels.
3. Stir together tomato sauce, garlic, and remaining 1 tablespoon Basil Oil. Spoon sauce mixture over crust in skillet, leaving a ½-inch border around edge. Top with mozzarella, tomato slices, and pepperoni.
4. Place skillet over medium-high; cook until bottom just begins to set and edges begin to puff, 3 to 4 minutes. Transfer to oven; bake until golden brown and cooked through, 16 to 18 minutes. Garnish with basil leaves. Drizzle with additional Basil Oil before serving, if desired.

Basil Oil

ACTIVE 5 MIN. - TOTAL 5 MIN.
MAKES ABOUT ½ CUP

Process 1 cup firmly packed **fresh basil** leaves, ½ cup **olive oil,** and 1 **garlic clove** in a blender until smooth, about 2 minutes. Season with ½ tsp. **kosher salt** and ¼ tsp. **black pepper.** Store in an airtight container in refrigerator up to 24 hours.

Pasta with Fresh Tomato-Basil Sauce

(Photo, page 156)
ACTIVE 20 MIN. - TOTAL 20 MIN.
SERVES 4

- 3 Tbsp. extra-virgin olive oil
- 2 lb. multicolored cherry tomatoes (about 3 pints)
- 6 garlic cloves, thinly sliced (about 2 Tbsp.)
- ½ cup sun-dried tomatoes in oil (from 1 [10-oz.] jar), chopped
- Pinch of crushed red pepper (optional)
- 1 Tbsp. kosher salt
- 1 lb. uncooked bucatini or vermicelli pasta
- ½ cup grated Parmesan cheese (about 2 oz.), plus more for garnish
- 2 Tbsp. unsalted butter
- ½ cup chopped fresh basil, plus more basil leaves for garnish

1. Heat oil in a large skillet over medium-high. Add cherry tomatoes, garlic, sun-dried tomatoes, and crushed red pepper (if desired). Cover and cook, stirring occasionally, until tomatoes release their juices, about 12 minutes. Use the back of a spoon to crush tomatoes.
2. While tomatoes cook, bring a large pot of water to a boil over high; add salt. Cook pasta according to package directions for al dente, about 10 minutes. Reserve 1½ cups cooking water; drain pasta.
3. Add cooked pasta, Parmesan, butter, and ½ cup reserved cooking water to skillet with tomatoes; toss to combine. Add more cooking water, if needed, to reach a saucy consistency. Cook over medium, stirring constantly, until sauce clings to pasta, about 3 minutes. Remove from heat. Stir in chopped basil. Garnish with additional Parmesan and basil leaves, if desired.

Tomato-Basil Chicken

(Photo, page 157)
ACTIVE 20 MIN. - TOTAL 35 MIN.
SERVES 4 TO 6

- 2 cups multicolored cherry or grape tomatoes, halved
- 1 lb. heirloom tomatoes, sliced (about 3 cups)
- 1 red onion, thinly sliced (about 1½ cups)
- ⅓ cup packed chopped fresh basil, plus more for garnish
- 1 serrano chile, thinly sliced
- ½ cup red wine vinegar
- ¾ cup plus 1 Tbsp. extra-virgin olive oil, divided
- 3½ tsp. kosher salt, divided
- 1 tsp. black pepper, divided
- 6 (5-oz.) boneless, skinless chicken breast cutlets
- 1 tsp. garlic powder
- 1 tsp. Italian seasoning
- Crusty bread, for serving

1. Preheat a grill to high (450°F to 500°F). Combine tomatoes, red onion, basil, serrano chile, vinegar, ¾ cup olive oil, 2 teaspoons salt, and ½ teaspoon black pepper in a glass or ceramic 13- x 9-inch baking dish. Let stand at room temperature while preparing chicken.
2. Brush chicken with remaining 1 tablespoon oil; season with garlic powder, Italian seasoning, and remaining 1½ teaspoons salt and ½ teaspoon black pepper. Place chicken on oiled grates; grill, uncovered, until an instant-read thermometer inserted into thickest portion of chicken registers 160°F, 3 to 4 minutes per side.
3. Nestle cooked chicken into dish with tomato mixture; spoon juices over chicken. Let stand at room temperature 15 to 30 minutes. Garnish with more fresh basil; serve with crusty bread.

PASTA WITH FRESH TOMATO-BASIL SAUCE (PAGE 155)

TOMATO-BASIL CHICKEN
(PAGE 155)

Heirloom Tomato-and-Mozzarella Salad

ACTIVE 10 MIN. - TOTAL 10 MIN.

SERVES 4

- **2 lb. ripe heirloom tomatoes, sliced 1/4 inch thick (if large) or halved (if small)**
- **8 oz. fresh mozzarella cheese, sliced 1/4 inch thick (about 1 1/2 cups)**
- **1/2 cup packed fresh basil leaves**
- **1 tsp. flaky sea salt**
- **1/2 tsp. black pepper**
- **1 Tbsp. rice vinegar**
- **2 Tbsp. Basil Oil (recipe, page 155)**

Place tomato slices or halves on a large platter. Tuck in mozzarella slices around tomatoes. Sprinkle with basil, and season with salt and pepper. Drizzle with vinegar and Basil Oil just before serving.

The New Fried Green Tomato

Crunchy, golden slices of squash make the perfect starter.

DRY BEFORE YOU FRY
Salt the squash slices prior to dredging to draw out extra moisture and concentrate the vegetable's flavor.

Fried Squash with Creamy Herb Dipping Sauce

ACTIVE 30 MIN. - TOTAL 45 MIN.

SERVES 6

- 3 yellow crookneck squash or zucchini, sliced into ⅓-inch-thick rounds (about 5 cups)
- 2½ tsp. kosher salt, divided, plus more to taste
- ⅓ cup mayonnaise
- ⅓ cup sour cream
- 3 Tbsp. chopped fresh tender herbs (such as dill, chives, and parsley), plus more for garnish
- 1 tsp. white wine vinegar
- ⅔ cup whole buttermilk, divided
- 1 tsp. garlic powder, divided
- ½ tsp. black pepper, divided
- 3 large eggs
- 1½ cups self-rising cornmeal
- 1 cup dry breadcrumbs
- Peanut oil, for frying

1. Sprinkle squash slices with 1 teaspoon salt, and let stand for 15 minutes. Meanwhile, stir together mayonnaise, sour cream, herbs, vinegar, ⅓ cup buttermilk, ½ teaspoon salt, ½ teaspoon garlic powder, and ¼ teaspoon pepper. Refrigerate sauce until ready to serve.
2. Whisk together eggs and remaining ⅓ cup buttermilk in a wide shallow bowl. Place cornmeal, breadcrumbs, and remaining 1 teaspoon salt, ½ teaspoon garlic powder, and ¼ teaspoon pepper in a separate shallow bowl.
3. Pour oil to a depth of ½ inch in a large cast-iron skillet; heat over medium-high to 375°F. Thoroughly pat squash slices dry. Working in batches, dredge squash in cornmeal mixture, shaking off excess. Dip in egg mixture, allowing excess to drip off. Dredge in cornmeal mixture again, pressing to coat. Place in a single layer on a plate or a baking sheet.
4. Working in 3 batches, place squash in hot oil. Cook, turning occasionally, until crisp and golden brown, 2 to 3 minutes. Transfer to a paper towel–lined plate. Sprinkle with more salt to taste. Transfer squash to a platter, and serve with dipping sauce garnished with more chopped fresh herbs.

CHOCOLATE CHIP
ICE-CREAM SANDWICHES

Summer in a Sandwich

Skip the ice-cream parlor and whip up these nostalgic desserts.

Chocolate Chip Ice-Cream Sandwiches

ACTIVE 30 MIN. - TOTAL 1 HOUR, 10 MIN., PLUS 3 HOURS FREEZING

MAKES 18

- 2¾ cups all-purpose flour
- 1 Tbsp. cornstarch
- 1 tsp. kosher salt
- 1 tsp. baking soda
- ½ tsp. baking powder
- 1 cup unsalted butter, softened
- 1 cup packed light brown sugar
- ½ cup granulated sugar
- 2 large eggs, at room temperature
- 2 tsp. vanilla extract
- 1 (10-oz.) pkg. miniature semisweet chocolate chips (about 1⅔ cups), plus more for rolling
- 4½ cups vanilla ice cream (from 1 [1½-qt.] container)

1. Preheat oven to 375°F. Line 2 rimmed baking sheets with parchment paper. Whisk together flour, cornstarch, salt, baking soda, and baking powder in a large bowl; set aside.

2. Place butter and both sugars in another large bowl; beat with an electric mixer on medium speed until light and fluffy, about 3 minutes, scraping down sides of bowl as needed. Add eggs, 1 at a time, beating until combined; add vanilla. Reduce speed to medium-low; gradually beat in flour mixture until just combined, about 1 minute. Fold in chocolate chips.

3. Scoop dough into 1½-tablespoon portions; roll into 36 balls. Place 1 inch apart on prepared pans. Bake in batches until cookies are light golden brown, 10 to 12 minutes. Remove from oven. Let rest on pans 5 minutes; transfer cookies to wire racks, and let cool 15 minutes. Repeat baking process with remaining dough balls.

4. To assemble, let ice cream stand at room temperature until slightly softened, about 5 minutes. Using a ¼-cup scoop or measuring cup, scoop ice cream onto bottom sides of 18 cookies. Cover with remaining cookies, top sides up; gently press to flatten ice cream. Place ice-cream sandwiches on a baking sheet. Cover with plastic wrap, and freeze until ice cream is solid, at least 3 hours or up to 24 hours (the longer, the better). Roll sides of each sandwich in more chocolate chips. Transfer to an airtight container, and freeze up to 3 months.

BIRTHDAY CAKE ICE-CREAM SANDWICHES

BUTTER-PECAN ICE-CREAM SANDWICHES

Pick Your Flavor

Add color and crunch with two fun twists on the classic.

Birthday Cake Ice-Cream Sandwiches

In Step 2, substitute ¾ cup **rainbow sprinkles** for chocolate chips. In Step 4, substitute **birthday cake ice cream** for vanilla ice cream. Roll sandwiches in more **rainbow sprinkles**, if desired.

Butter-Pecan Ice-Cream Sandwiches

In Step 2, substitute 1⅔ cups finely chopped **pecans** for chocolate chips. In Step 4, substitute **butter-pecan ice cream** for vanilla ice cream. Roll sandwiches in more finely chopped **pecans**, if desired.

These big-batch sandwiches are perfect for a crowd, but also make a grab-and-go breakfast for any day of the week when you make a batch and freeze them.

Good to Go

Ta-da! Serve up these special egg sandwiches to company.

Big-Batch English Muffin Breakfast Sandwiches

ACTIVE 15 MIN. - TOTAL 1 HOUR, 15 MIN.
MAKES 12

- 18 large eggs
- 1 cup whole milk
- 2 tsp. kosher salt
- 1 tsp. black pepper
- 2 cups hot water
- 12 English muffins, split
- 24 sharp Cheddar cheese slices
- 12 thick-cut bacon slices, cooked and cut in half

1. Preheat oven to 325°F with racks in upper third and lower third positions. Generously coat a 13- x 9-inch baking dish with cooking spray; place dish on a large rimmed baking sheet.

2. Whisk eggs in a large bowl until smooth. Whisk in milk, salt, and pepper. Pour mixture into prepared baking dish. Place in oven on lower rack; carefully pour hot water around dish on baking sheet (to create a water bath). Bake until eggs are just set, 30 to 35 minutes. Carefully remove baking dish from baking sheet, and let cool 5 minutes. Run a knife around edges of baking dish to loosen the egg mixture; cut into 12 even portions (about 2½ x 3 inches each).

3. Preheat oven to broil. Place muffin halves on a baking sheet, cut sides up. Top each of 12 muffin halves with 1 slice of cheese; broil until cheese is melted, about 1 minute. Transfer untopped muffin halves to a plate; set aside.

4. Using a spatula, place an egg portion on each cheese-topped muffin half; cover with another slice of cheese. Broil until cheese is melted, about 1 minute. Remove from oven; top with bacon and reserved muffin halves. See step-by-step tips on page 164.

FREEZING POINTERS
Prepare recipe through Step 3, omitting cheese. Omit Step 4. To assemble, top each of 12 muffin halves with 1 cheese slice, 1 egg portion, another cheese slice, and 2 bacon pieces. Cover with remaining muffin halves. Wrap each sandwich in foil. Transfer to a ziplock freezer bag; freeze up to 2 months. To reheat, remove foil. Wrap sandwich in a paper towel. Microwave on HIGH until hot, about 1 minute and 30 seconds.

A Few Tasty Toppings

The options are endless—here are three ways to mix it up.

Spicy Tex-Mex

Replace the Cheddar with slices of **pepper Jack cheese.** Omit the bacon, and top each sandwich with **salsa** and sliced **avocado.**

Ultimate Veggie

Omit the Cheddar; spread **goat cheese** on the bottom muffin half and on top of the egg. Replace the bacon with **sautéed mushrooms** and **spinach.**

Deli Style

Omit the Cheddar and bacon; spread **cream cheese** on the bottom muffin half. Top with egg, thinly sliced **red onion, smoked salmon,** and **arugula.**

COOKING SCHOOL

TIPS AND TRICKS FROM THE SOUTH'S MOST TRUSTED KITCHEN

Big-Batch Breakfast

How to make egg sandwiches for a crowd—or the freezer (recipe, page 163).

1. BEAT
Whisk eggs, milk, salt, and black pepper in a large bowl until smooth. Pour mixture into a greased baking dish, and place on a large rimmed baking sheet.

2. BAKE
To help the eggs cook gently, carefully pour hot water into the baking sheet to create a water bath. Bake until just set, about 30 minutes. Let cool slightly, about 5 minutes.

3. ASSEMBLE
Run a knife around baked egg mixture to loosen; slice into 12 portions. Top toasted muffin halves in this order: cheese, egg, cheese, bacon, and remaining muffin half.

4. FREEZE
Wrap each sandwich tightly ir foil; freeze in a ziplock plastic bag up to 2 months. To reheat, remove foil, wrap sandwich in a paper towel, and microwave on HIGH until hot, about 1 minute and 30 seconds.

September

BOUNTY

Branch Out

Make tart crabapples into sweet preserves you can enjoy year-round.

EXTRA KICK
Harvested from July to November, this fruit is also used to make cider and flavor bourbon.

PEANUT BUTTER BREAKFAST COOKIES (PAGE 169)

What a Treat

Greet the day with a cookie for breakfast.

IN OUR HOUSE, like many others, there are weekday breakfasts and weekend breakfasts. The latter is all about indulgence and slowing down. I look forward to an unhurried Saturday morning when I can flip pancakes in my pajamas or have people over for a big spread with a pile of bacon, a fruit salad, and a beautiful casserole at the center of the table.

Weekday mornings, on the other hand, are about speed and sustenance. Everyone needs to eat something to fuel their brains and bodies before they race off to work or school. Some days there's oatmeal or cereal with berries, and other days a toaster waffle is eaten in the car. Every so often, someone goes to the Dunkin' drive-through and lets their kid eat a bag of Munchkins doughnut holes. (Okay, fine...it's me.)

Could the two breakfast worlds ever combine? My vision was to create a grab-and-go option that's a little bit decadent without being a total sugar bomb. And I didn't want it to come from a box or a package. Enter the breakfast cookie. More wholesome than a muffin or a bowl of cornflakes, it's packed with enough whole grains, pecans, and fruit to keep you going throughout the morning—but it still tastes like a treat. And if you have someone with a food allergy or an aversion to nuts in the family, you can tweak this recipe to suit your needs, like in the two variations shown at right.

Bake a batch on Sunday, and you'll be set for a whole week of easy breakfasts—just add a cup of coffee or a glass of milk. If a delicious cookie can't get you out of bed in the morning, I don't know what will. —Lisa Cericola

Coconut-Pecan Breakfast Cookies

ACTIVE 35 MIN. - TOTAL 1 HOUR, 50 MIN.
MAKES 1½ DOZEN

- 1 cup granulated sugar
- ½ cup unsalted butter, softened
- 1 large egg, at room temperature
- ½ cup mashed very ripe banana (from 1 banana)
- ¼ cup pure maple syrup
- 1 cup all-purpose flour
- ⅔ cup whole wheat flour
- 1½ tsp. ground cinnamon
- 1 tsp. baking soda
- ¾ tsp. kosher salt
- 2 cups uncooked old-fashioned regular rolled oats
- 1¼ cups chopped toasted pecans, divided
- ¾ cup sweetened flaked coconut, divided
- ¾ cup semisweet chocolate chips, divided

1. Preheat oven to 350°F. Line 3 rimmed baking sheets with parchment paper.
2. Beat sugar and butter in a large bowl with an electric mixer on medium speed until fluffy, 2 to 3 minutes, stopping to scrape down sides as needed. Add egg, banana, and maple syrup; beat on medium speed until combined, about 1 minute.
3. Whisk together all-purpose flour, whole wheat flour, cinnamon, baking soda, and salt in a medium bowl. With mixer on low speed, gradually add flour mixture to sugar mixture, beating until nearly combined, about 45 seconds. Stir in oats, 1 cup pecans, ½ cup coconut, and ½ cup chocolate chips.
4. Divide dough into 18 mounds (about ¼ cup each) on prepared baking sheets, spacing 2½ inches apart. Press mounds to a ¾-inch thickness using damp hands. Sprinkle tops evenly with remaining ¼ cup each pecans, coconut, and chocolate chips; lightly press into dough.
5. Bake until edges are just set and centers are still slightly soft, 12 to 14 minutes. Let cool on baking sheets 5 minutes. Transfer to wire racks; let cool completely, about 30 minutes.

Peanut Butter Breakfast Cookies

(Photo, page 170)
ACTIVE 35 MIN. - TOTAL 1 HOUR, 50 MIN.
MAKES 1½ DOZEN

Prepare recipe as directed, substituting ½ cup **creamy peanut butter** for butter in Step 2. In Step 3, substitute 1 cup chopped **peanuts** for pecans. In Step 4, press dough to a ½-inch thickness, and substitute ¼ cup **peanuts** for pecans. Proceed as directed.

Apple-Spice Breakfast Cookies

(Photo, page 171)
ACTIVE 35 MIN. - TOTAL 1 HOUR, 50 MIN.
MAKES 1½ DOZEN

Prepare recipe as directed, substituting ½ cup **applesauce** for banana in Step 2. In Step 3, stir ½ tsp. **allspice** into flour mixture; substitute ½ cup chopped **apple chips** for chocolate chips. In Step 4, substitute ¼ cup **apple chips** for chocolate chips; proceed as directed.

APPLE-SPICE BREAKFAST COOKIES (PAGE 169)

TRADITIONS

It All Started with Catfish Stew

Literary luminary John T. Edge's mother's family recipe finds new life.

I GREW UP IN GEORGIA in the late 1960s and early 1970s on barbecue pork that was doused in a ketchup-blushed vinegar sauce and hot dogs that were smothered with cinnamon-spiked chili and crowned with sweet slaw. By my thirties, I had learned to enjoy scooping up Ethiopian okra stew with injera and mopping up Indian collards with corn roti.

For much of my life, whenever I talked about my favorite foods, I mentioned restaurant dishes like those. That changed in the late 2010s, as my wife, Blair Hobbs, and I got our son, Jess, ready for college. We realized that he didn't know enough about my mother, Mary Beverly Evans Edge, whose life, cut short by alcoholism, ended 11 days before Jess was born.

My memoir, *House of Smoke*, begins when I was a boy, with my mother running out the back door of our home, bound for the dark woods, and me frantically giving chase. The story I tell spans the Deep South, from that Clinton, Georgia, house where a Confederate general once lived to Columbia, South Carolina, where my parents met, and resolves in Oxford, Mississippi, where Blair and I choose to live and work. Across time and place, *House of Smoke* moves toward a reckoning with the troubled South that shaped my worldview and an appreciation for the many gifts my beautiful and tragic mother bestowed. And it all started with a recipe for catfish stew.

When Blair began to cook this dish in Oxford, she made a path to welcome my mother back into our lives. She based it on the recipe my mom wrote in cursive on three-hole-punch paper. Framed and mounted to the left of our stove above three bottles of Tabasco sauce and a couple of jars of chili crisp, that recipe was inspired by the one my mother's father, Jesse Clifton Evans, cooked at his fish camp on the Edisto River near Orangeburg, South Carolina.

To make her stew, Blair substituted bacon, cured by our friend Allan Benton, for the streak o' lean my mother favored. And she borrowed techniques from Edna Lewis and Scott Peacock, who included a version in their book, *The Gift of Southern Cooking*. With every adaptation, Blair's stew has become a truer reflection of the people who came before me, the stories I've inherited and worked to rewrite, and the rich life we now live in Oxford.

Each time I look at the cover of *House of Smoke*, painted by my friend Noah Saterstrom, I think about our family recipe. Noah based the artwork on a picture of my mother, standing at the stove in the kitchen of our house back in Clinton, stirring a pot of what I would like to believe was catfish stew. To make the image work for the cover, he had to paint her out of the scene. But each time Blair cooks her version in Oxford, my mother steps back into the frame—and isn't that what we all want out of an heirloom recipe? —John T. Edge

Blair's Catfish Stew

ACTIVE 30 MIN. · TOTAL 1 HOUR
SERVES 10

- **2 Tbsp. unsalted butter**
- **2 thick-cut bacon slices, chopped (for a heaping ½ cup)**
- **1 yellow onion, chopped (about 2 cups)**
- **3 celery stalks, sliced (about 1 cup)**
- **4 garlic cloves, minced (about 1½ Tbsp.)**
- **2 tsp. dried thyme**
- **1 tsp. dried basil**
- **7 red new potatoes, cut into ½-inch pieces (about 2½ cups)**
- **3 carrots, peeled and thinly sliced crosswise (about 2 cups)**
- **1 (14-oz.) can diced tomatoes**
- **2 tsp. kosher salt, divided, plus more to taste**
- **1 tsp. black pepper, divided, plus more to taste**
- **6 cups water**
- **1 cup dry white wine**
- **4 scallions, green parts only, chopped (about ½ cup)**
- **3 chicken bouillon cubes (such as Wyler's)**
- **2 lb. catfish fillets (we love Simmons)**
- **1–2 Tbsp. honey (optional)**
- **½ cup chopped fresh flat-leaf parsley**
- **Hot sauce (such as Tabasco)**

1. Heat butter and bacon in a large Dutch oven over medium-high; cook, stirring often, until bacon begins to brown, about 7 minutes. Add onion, celery, garlic, thyme, and basil. Cook, picking up any browned bits from bottom of Dutch oven using a wooden spoon, until mixture sputters, releases its water, and then cooks off and sizzles and onion is translucent, about 10 minutes.
2. Add new potatoes, carrots, tomatoes, 1½ teaspoons of the kosher salt, and ½ teaspoon of the pepper to Dutch oven. Stir and bring to a boil over medium-high. Add water, white wine, scallions, and bouillon cubes.
3. Turn down heat in Dutch oven to medium-low to maintain a simmer; cover with a lid (leaving a crack for steam), and cook until potatoes are tender, 15 to 20 minutes.
4. Lightly sprinkle catfish fillets with remaining ½ teaspoon each of salt and pepper. Cut fillets in half, if needed, to help them fit in Dutch oven without crowding. Gently lay fillets in Dutch oven, and cook until you can cut fillets into chunks with the side of a spoon, 6 to 10 minutes, depending on thickness of fillets. (Do not overcook, or the chunks of catfish will turn to feathers.) Season one final time, as needed, with additional salt and pepper to taste; gently stir in honey (if using).
5. Serve stew in bowls; garnish with parsley, and splash with hot sauce, as needed.

In Praise of Pole Beans

Beloved throughout Appalachia, these hearty legumes are always worth the fuss.

BEFORE I WAS OLD ENOUGH TO RIDE A BIKE, my grandparents taught me how to string and break bushels of beans from their garden. We ate what we could each summer and then canned or dried all that our basement shelves could hold—enough to carry us through the long and snowy winters of the Blue Ridge Mountains.

It's hard to overstate the elemental importance of beans in Appalachian cuisine. My family, like many others, tended to rows of those that flourished in our climate, with colorful names like Rattlesnake, Pink Tip, Fat Man, cornfield, half-runner, cutshort, and greasy beans (which have naturally shiny green hulls and look as though they've been burnished with oil). I think of these heirloom legumes collectively as pole beans (or runner beans), though I understand that some actually grow on bushes that rarely get more than a couple feet high. They send out vines that can reach 12 feet in length and must be tied to trellises or trained to climb poles to keep them from overtaking the rest of the crops. Native Americans—the land's original master gardeners—grew them near cornstalks to support the vines as part of a companion-planting technique known as the Three Sisters, which also included using squash as a ground cover.

Whether pole or bush, these beans stand apart from the ordinary green kind. More than a vegetable side dish, they are a satisfying, nutritious source of protein destined for the center of our plates. They aren't picked until the hulls are bumpy and nearly bursting with meaty beans, with tough, ropy strings running down each side. Then they must be strung and snapped into bite-size lengths or shelled out individually—all by hand. This labor is a price gladly paid for their incomparable flavor.

I learned to fix beans by watching family members. My childhood apprenticeship took place under the carport after supper every night during the peak season. Seated in a semicircle of aluminum-framed lawn chairs, we'd stay at it until moths started batting at the porch lights. It's a scene that many Southern families know well and still hold dear. To this day, working up a mess of beans soothes and centers me. It requires mindfulness but not rapt attention, so I can multitask and watch TV or carry on a conversation—plus I can literally see what I've accomplished at the end of the session, an industrious pastime.

People who've never tasted pole beans left on the vine until plump might wonder if they're worth the effort. Yes, they are. Run-of-the-mill green beans don't have the same special taste and texture. Farmers' markets are often the best sources for them, as are home gardeners and seed savers who value superior flavor and biodiversity. Those who can't get their hands on Appalachian heirloom varieties might find a similar local specialty. If we continue to buy and eat these beans, people will have reason to keep growing them. I'm doing my part by pulling as many strings as I can. —Sheri Castle

Old-Fashioned Pole Beans and New Potatoes

ACTIVE 30 MIN. - TOTAL 1 HOUR, 30 MIN.

SERVES 4 TO 6

- **4 oz. thick-cut bacon slices (about 3 slices), cut crosswise into ½-inch strips**
- **1 yellow onion, chopped (about 1½ cups)**
- **2 tsp. kosher salt**
- **2 cups chicken broth**
- **1 lb. fresh pole beans, strings removed, broken into bite-size lengths (about 4 cups)**
- **12 oz. very small new potatoes (such as red bliss or Baby Dutch Yellow), scrubbed and halved**
- **2 Tbsp. apple cider vinegar**
- **2 tsp. granulated sugar**
- **½ tsp. black pepper**
- **2 Tbsp. finely chopped fresh parsley**
- **1 Tbsp. fresh thyme leaves**

1. Cook bacon in a large high-sided skillet over medium-high, stirring often, until it begins to render or fat begins to look translucent, about 3 minutes. Reduce heat to medium-low, and cook until bacon is fully rendered, browned, and crisp, 10 to 15 minutes. With a slotted spoon, transfer bacon to a paper towel–lined plate, reserving drippings in skillet. Set bacon aside.

2. Stir onion and salt into reserved drippings, and increase heat to medium-high; cook, stirring often, until onion is softened, about 5 minutes. Stir in broth and beans. Bring to a boil over medium-high; reduce heat to medium-low, and simmer until beans are nearly tender, about 20 minutes.

3. Scatter potatoes over top of beans, and push them down with a spoon to submerge in liquid. Cover and simmer over medium-low until potatoes and beans are tender, 20 to 25 minutes. Remove from heat.

4. Stir in vinegar, sugar, and pepper; let stand, uncovered, 5 minutes. Sprinkle with parsley, thyme, and reserved bacon.

OLD-FASHIONED POLE BEANS AND NEW POTATOES

BRAISED POLE BEANS IN SMOKY TOMATO SAUCE (PAGE 177)

HERBED SHELL BEANS AND GARLICKY GREENS ON GRILLED BREAD

Herbed Shell Beans and Garlicky Greens on Grilled Bread

ACTIVE 25 MIN. - TOTAL 1 HOUR, 45 MIN.
SERVES 6

HERBED SHELL BEANS

- 3½ cups shelled fresh beans (such as lady peas; about 1 lb. shelled beans from 3 lb. unshelled beans)
- 2½ tsp. kosher salt, divided
- 4 (6-inch) thyme sprigs
- 2 (6-inch) sage sprigs
- 1 (6-inch) rosemary sprig
- 1 fresh bay leaf
- 2 garlic cloves, crushed
- 3 Tbsp. extra-virgin olive oil
- 2 Tbsp. double-concentrated tomato paste (such as Cento)
- 1 Tbsp. finely chopped fresh sage
- ½ tsp. black pepper

GARLICKY GREENS

- 3 Tbsp. extra-virgin olive oil
- 1 yellow onion, thinly sliced (about 1½ cups)
- 1 tsp. dark brown sugar
- ¾ tsp. kosher salt, divided
- 3 garlic cloves, thinly sliced (about 3 Tbsp.)
- Pinch of crushed red pepper, plus more for sprinkling
- 12 loosely packed cups stemmed and shredded kale or other hardy greens (from 2 bunches)
- 3-4 Tbsp. sherry vinegar
- Black pepper to taste

GRILLED BREAD

- 6 (¾-inch-thick) large, sturdy bread slices (such as sourdough)
- Extra-virgin olive oil, for brushing and drizzling
- ¼ tsp. kosher salt
- ¼ tsp. black pepper

1. Prepare the Herbed Shell Beans: Rinse beans to remove any bits of hull and stickiness; pour them into a medium saucepan. Cover to a depth of 1 inch with cool water. Add 2 teaspoons salt. Drop in thyme, sage, and rosemary sprigs; bay leaf; and garlic.
2. Bring just to a boil over medium-high, reduce heat to medium-low, and simmer until al dente, about 40 minutes. (The beans must stay submerged, so add a splash of water as they cook, if needed.)
3. Whisk in oil and tomato paste. Cook at a bare simmer over medium-low until beans are soft and creamy and liquid reduces and thickens a bit, about 25 minutes.
4. Remove from heat, stir in remaining ½ teaspoon salt, and let stand at least 10 minutes to give beans time to absorb it.
5. Discard herb sprigs and bay leaf. Stir in finely chopped sage and black pepper. (The beans can be made up to 3 days ahead. Cool, cover, and store in refrigerator; reheat before serving.)
6. While beans cook, prepare the Garlicky Greens: Heat oil in a large skillet over medium-high. Stir in onion, brown sugar, and ½ teaspoon salt. Cook, stirring often, until softened and golden, 5 to 8 minutes. Stir in garlic and crushed red pepper, and cook, stirring constantly, until fragrant, about 1 minute.
7. Add kale, 1 large handful at a time, and cook, tossing constantly with tongs, until slightly wilted before adding more. Cook, tossing often, until greens are tender, about 5 minutes. Remove from heat.
8. Stir in 3 Tbsp. vinegar and remaining ¼ teaspoon salt. Add more vinegar and black pepper to taste. Keep warm.
9. When ready to serve, prepare the Grilled Bread: Preheat a grill pan over medium-high until very hot. Brush or drizzle both sides of bread generously with oil. Cook until bread turns crisp and toasty and grill marks form, about 1 minute per side. Sprinkle bread slices evenly with salt and pepper.
10. To serve: Divide Grilled Bread among plates. Top with Herbed Shell Beans and Garlicky Greens; garnish with additional drizzled olive oil and crushed red pepper. Serve immediately so bread remains crisp.

KITCHEN TIP
Pole beans must be cooked until fully tender, far longer than ordinary stringless green beans. It's like the difference between braising short ribs and searing a rare steak.

Braised Pole Beans in Smoky Tomato Sauce

(Photo, page 175)
ACTIVE 30 MIN. - TOTAL 1 HOUR, 30 MIN.
SERVES 4 TO 6

- ¼ cup unsalted butter
- 1 large yellow onion, very finely chopped (about 2 cups)
- 1½ tsp. kosher salt, divided
- 2 garlic cloves, finely chopped (about 2 tsp.)
- ¾ tsp. smoked paprika
- ½ tsp. black pepper
- ¼ tsp. ground cardamom
- ¼ tsp. ground ginger
- 1 (14.5-oz.) can fire-roasted crushed tomatoes (about 2 cups)
- 1½ lb. fresh pole beans, strings removed, broken in half (about 8 cups)
- 2 Tbsp. fresh lemon juice (from 1 lemon)

1. Melt butter in a large saucepan over medium. Stir in onion and 1 teaspoon kosher salt; cook, stirring often, until onion is softened, about 5 minutes. Stir in garlic, smoked paprika, black pepper, cardamom, and ginger; cook, stirring constantly, until fragrant, about 1 minute.
2. Stir in tomatoes and ½ cup water; bring to a simmer over medium-high. Stir in fresh pole beans, and return to a simmer. Reduce heat to medium-low, cover, and cook at a low simmer, stirring occasionally, until beans are tender, about 1 hour. (The beans must stay very moist in a gently bubbling sauce, so add another ¼ cup water, if needed.)
3. Stir in lemon juice and the remaining ½ teaspoon salt. Serve warm.
Make-ahead note: The flavor of these beans deepens over time. Let cool, uncovered, to room temperature, about 30 minutes. Transfer to a covered container, and store in the refrigerator up to 3 days.

Late-Summer Minestrone with Pesto-Parmesan Croutons

ACTIVE 1 HOUR - TOTAL 1 HOUR, 40 MIN.

SERVES 6 TO 8

- 1/4 cup extra-virgin olive oil
- 1 yellow onion, chopped (about 1 1/2 cups)
- 1 carrot, chopped (about 1/2 cup)
- 1 Tbsp. kosher salt, divided
- 4 garlic cloves, thinly sliced (about 1/4 cup)
- 1 Tbsp. dried Italian seasoning
- 6 cups chicken broth (preferably bone broth) or vegetable stock
- 3 (2-oz.) Parmesan cheese rinds
- 1 large fresh bay leaf
- 2 cups pole beans, strings removed, broken into bite-size lengths (about 8 oz.)
- 1 cup shelled fresh beans (such as lady peas)
- 2 cups diced yellow squash and/or zucchini (from 1 squash)
- 2 cups diced tomatoes or halved cherry tomatoes (from 1 large beefsteak tomato or 1 pt. cherry tomatoes)
- 1 1/2 cups fresh corn kernels (from 2 ears)
- 1 cup chopped green cabbage (preferably savoy; from 1 small cabbage)
- 1 cup loosely packed fresh basil leaves
- 1 Tbsp. hot sauce
- Black pepper to taste
- Pesto-Parmesan Croutons (recipe follows)

1. Heat oil in a large saucepan over medium until shimmering. Stir in onion, carrot, and 2 teaspoons salt. Cook, stirring occasionally, until beginning to soften, about 5 minutes. Stir in garlic and Italian seasoning, and cook, stirring constantly, until fragrant, about 1 minute.

2. Stir in broth, Parmesan rinds, bay leaf, pole beans, and shell beans; bring to a simmer over medium-low. Cook, stirring occasionally, until shell beans are almost tender, about 30 minutes.

3. Stir in squash, tomatoes, corn, and cabbage. Simmer, stirring occasionally, until all vegetables are just tender, about 10 minutes.

4. Remove from heat. Discard Parmesan rinds and bay leaf. Stir in basil, hot sauce, black pepper to taste, and remaining 1 teaspoon salt.

5. Top with Pesto-Parmesan Croutons before serving.

Pesto-Parmesan Croutons

ACTIVE 10 MIN. - TOTAL 20 MIN.

SERVES 8

- 1/4 cup extra-virgin olive oil
- 1/4 cup basil pesto
- 4 cups bite-size ciabatta pieces (from 1 [1-lb.] ciabatta loaf)
- 1/4 cup Parmesan cheese, shredded (about 1 oz.)

1. Preheat oven to 400°F. Line a rimmed baking sheet with parchment paper.

2. Stir together oil and pesto in a large bowl. Add ciabatta pieces, and toss well to coat. Spread in a single layer on prepared baking sheet.

3. Bake until crisp and browned on edges, about 8 minutes, stirring halfway through bake time.

4. Sprinkle with Parmesan, and bake until cheese melts and turns golden, 2 to 3 minutes. Serve warm or at room temperature. Store in an airtight container at room temperature up to 1 day.

LATE-SUMMER MINESTRONE WITH PESTO-PARMESAN CROUTONS

The Icing on the Cake

We celebrate—and simplify—the South's most finicky frosting.

ULTIMATE CARAMEL FROSTING (PAGE 182)

If you've ever made a caramel cake from scratch, you have a war story. Whether it's your first attempt or your 50th, the fickle icing tries the patience of even the most experienced cooks.

From grandmothers who've made it for countless birthdays and potlucks to professional pastry chefs and celebrated cookbook authors, most Southerners approach this beloved yet confidence-shaking dessert with a sense of trepidation. "It's a heck of a lot of trouble," says Anne Byrn, best-selling author of *Baking in the American South*. "But if you make a good caramel cake, you get to whine about how much trouble it was."

If you get it right–or even close–one bite of that sweet icing with a little balancing bitterness of almost-burnt sugar outshines any and all curveballs and cussing that happen along the way. The rich flavor and texture make it better than any buttercream.

"When the icing is smooth and the sugar is the perfect level of caramelized, it makes your taste buds respond, 'Ah, this is special,' " says Judy Miller, an everyday Southern baker who happens to be my mom. Her mother taught her how to make this treasured dessert–one that challenges her to this day. "Caramel icing is my nemesis," she says. "It knows when you need it to work the most, and it'll turn on you just out of spite."

Although there are countless recipes for caramel, they all depend on the same thing: caramelized sugar. Whether you're relying on an experienced eye or a candy thermometer, this process demands certain things from the cook–namely time and careful attention. The sugar's shift in color from golden to amber is subtle, fast, and crucial. "You almost need to know what you're looking for before you ever begin," Byrn says.

But sometimes–even when you do everything correctly–the frosting has other plans. "It's not going to work out the same every time because of the temperature of the kitchen or of the ingredients," Byrn notes. "Sugar and flour are very porous, and we live in a humid environment."

Cheryl Day, who owned Savannah's now-closed Back in the Day Bakery and is the award-winning author of *Cheryl Day's Treasury of Southern Baking*, agrees with Byrn. Like so many of us, she has endured her fair share of failures in pursuit of the ideal caramel. Describing the icing, Day says, "She's got a personality. She's sassy, finicky, and demands respect–and she'll humble you as well."

Day spent long afternoons with her mother learning the secrets of her family's Southern kitchen. "Cooking is an art; baking is a science," she says. "My ancestors were intuitive and knew how to fix a problem if something went wrong." But Day says that a lack of wisdom and experience shouldn't discourage you from making caramel icing. "It's something that takes practice and a lot of patience," she explains. "You'll get better at it the more you do it."

That brings us to the recipe that unfolds on the following pages. We've published plenty of caramel cakes over the years, from classic ones to quick and easy options and every variation in between. For this version, we set out to create an icing that hearkens back to traditional flavor while avoiding the inherent pitfalls of this notoriously nuanced confection.

After several weeks of experimentation, 16 meticulous tests, and lots of deliberation among the best bakers in the *Southern Living* Test Kitchen, we're proud to share this frosting recipe that–believe it or not–can be made a day or two ahead and spread on cake layers (or cupcakes) with ease. While it may not be the exact version that you grew up with, we've worked hard to make it more foolproof than most. In the words of my mama, who had the tough job of trying three iterations of this cake, "It's tasty–and pretty darn close." –Josh Miller

Ultimate Caramel Frosting

(Photo, page 181)

In Mississippi and other places in the South, caramel cake is often topped with a looser icing that's spooned over the layers while it's still warm, but it can harden quickly. We created this recipe to be more forgiving and easier to spread—even two days later.

ACTIVE 40 MIN. - TOTAL 3 HOURS, 30 MIN.

MAKES ABOUT 3 CUPS

- 1 cup heavy whipping cream, plus more if needed
- 2 Tbsp. light corn syrup
- ½ tsp. table salt
- 3 cups granulated sugar, divided
- ¾ cup cold unsalted butter, cubed
- 1 Tbsp. vanilla extract

1. Place cream, corn syrup, salt, and 2⅓ cups granulated sugar in a medium Dutch oven; cook over medium, stirring often, until sugar is dissolved and mixture is boiling, 7 to 10 minutes. Reduce heat to low; cover and keep warm while caramelizing sugar.
2. Place remaining ⅔ cup granulated sugar in a medium stainless-steel skillet. Cook over medium, without stirring, until sugar starts to melt and begins to turn slightly golden, 4 to 6 minutes. Cook, stirring gently, until sugar dissolves, reaches a simmer, and becomes dark amber in color, 1 to 3 minutes. (Color change will happen rapidly.)
3. Carefully pour caramelized sugar into cream mixture in Dutch oven, stirring constantly until mixture comes together and is smooth. Cook over medium heat, stirring often and scraping bottom and sides of pot, until center of mixture registers 238°F on an instant-read thermometer, 2 to 6 minutes. Remove from heat, and immediately pour mixture into bowl of a stand mixer. Stir in butter and vanilla until smooth. Let stand at room temperature, stirring

Continued on page 185

The Six Commandments of Caramel

A few important rules to tackle this tricky frosting

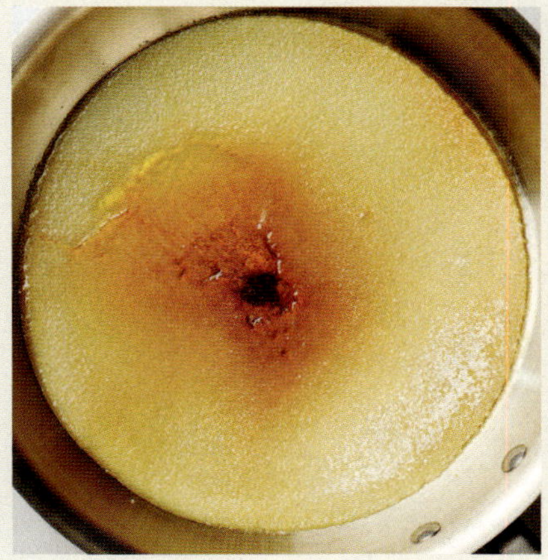

1. RESIST THE URGE TO STIR
Every pan and stove is different, so go slower than you normally would and don't crank up the heat. Once the sugar begins to melt and some areas take on a honey color, that is your cue to start stirring.

2. DON'T STRAY
Distraction is the downfall of caramel. Keep your eyes on the pan and a wooden spoon in hand. Stir often to cook the sugar evenly; when it reaches a dark amber hue, immediately remove from heat. (See our color guide on page 185.)

3. WATCH THE TEMPERATURE
To help the caramel meld into the mixture with ease, the cream must be warm—almost hot. Don't panic if the caramel clumps when you add it to the cream; exert your will, and stir with conviction. It'll come together.

4. STAY THE COURSE
You're almost there. Keep stirring as the caramel mixture simmers, being sure to scrape the bottom of the pan. Instead of aiming for a particular color, use a digital thermometer for a fast, accurate reading; 238°F is the target.

5. TAKE A BEAT
After the butter and vanilla extract are incorporated, you will finally get a chance to rest. Hold off on beating the caramel mixture until it's about 110°F. Then you can proceed until it's smooth, light, and thick.

6. PRACTICE PATIENCE
You'll be tempted to slather it on the cake now, but wait. This frosting will behave better when it drops below 75°F, which will take a couple of hours. But don't worry—you can store it at room temperature and use it the next day. (Yes, really!)

CLASSIC
YELLOW
CUPCAKES

Continued from page 182

occasionally, until just warm to the touch and an instant-read thermometer registers about 110°F, 45 minutes to 1 hour.

4. Beat mixture with a stand mixer fitted with a paddle attachment on medium speed until slightly lightened in color, thickened, and an instant-read thermometer registers below 90°F, 10 to 12 minutes. (If needed, beat in up to 1 tablespoon more cream, 1 teaspoon at a time, until smooth.)

5. Transfer mixture to a bowl, and let stand at room temperature, stirring occasionally, until thick, spreadable, and an instant-read thermometer registers below 75°F, about 2 hours. Use immediately, or store in an airtight container at room temperature up to 2 days. (If needed, stir in 1 teaspoon more cream at a time until frosting is thick but spreadable.)

Ultimate Caramel Frosting with Bourbon

Prepare as directed, substituting 2 Tbsp. **bourbon** for vanilla extract in Step 3.

Ultimate Salted-Caramel Frosting

Prepare as directed, substituting 1 Tbsp. **flaky sea salt** for table salt in Step 1. Garnish with more flaky sea salt.

Classic Yellow Cupcakes

This batter can also be used to make a two-layer cake. Prepare the recipe as directed, dividing the batter between two (8- or 9-inch) round cake pans coated with baking spray and lined with parchment. Bake at 350°F for 30 to 35 minutes for 8-inch cake layers or 25 to 30 minutes for 9-inch layers. Let cool in pans 10 minutes. Remove from pans; let cool completely on wire racks.

ACTIVE 45 MIN. - TOTAL 1 HOUR, 45 MIN.

MAKES 24 CUPCAKES OR 2 CAKE LAYERS

- **1½ cups granulated sugar**
- **1 cup unsalted butter, softened**
- **¼ cup packed light brown sugar**
- **4 large eggs, at room temperature**
- **2 tsp. vanilla extract**
- **2⅔ cups all-purpose flour**
- **1½ tsp. baking powder**
- **1 tsp. table salt**
- **½ tsp. baking soda**
- **¾ cup sour cream, at room temperature**
- **⅓ cup whole milk, at room temperature**
- **Ultimate Salted-Caramel Frosting (recipe left)**

1. Preheat oven to 350°F. Line 2 (12-cup) muffin trays with paper liners. Beat together granulated sugar, butter, and brown sugar in a stand mixer fitted with a paddle attachment on medium speed until light and fluffy, 3 to 4 minutes. Add eggs, 1 at a time, beating until combined after each addition. Beat in vanilla until just combined.

2. Whisk together flour, baking powder, salt, and baking soda in a bowl. Whisk together sour cream and milk in another bowl. Gradually add flour mixture to butter mixture, alternating with sour cream mixture; beat on low speed until combined, about 2 minutes.

3. Divide among prepared muffin wells (¼ cup each). Bake until a wooden pick inserted in centers comes out clean, 16 to 20 minutes. Let cool on wire racks 10 minutes. Remove from trays; let cool completely, 30 to 45 minutes. Top with Ultimate Salted-Caramel Frosting.

Cooking by Color

Too Light
The sugar has just melted but hasn't taken on any specific hue.

Time to Stir
When some of the sugar reaches this shade, it's okay to start stirring.

Stay Vigilant
The color can shift rapidly; watch closely, and stir often.

Almost There
Have the cream mixture warm and ready; go time is approaching.

Just Right
Take the caramel off the heat, and quickly add it to the cream mixture.

SUPPERTIME

Comfort with a Kick

Liven up dinner with flavorful recipes that don't require much effort.

SLOW-COOKER BARBECUE SPARERIBS

Slow-Cooker Barbecue Spareribs

ACTIVE 15 MIN. - TOTAL 3 HOURS, 20 MIN.
SERVES 4

- 1 slab St. Louis–style pork spareribs (about 3 lb.), halved crosswise
- 1 Tbsp. all-purpose barbecue rub
- 1½ tsp. smoked paprika
- 1 tsp. kosher salt
- ¾ tsp. black pepper
- 1¼ cups barbecue sauce, divided
- Dill pickle chips
- White bread slices

1. Remove and discard the thin outer membrane on back of ribs by loosening it with a sharp knife and pulling it off.
2. Stir together rub, smoked paprika, salt, and pepper in a small bowl; sprinkle mixture on both sides of ribs, patting to coat. Brush ¼ cup barbecue sauce over top of ribs.
3. Pour ¼ cup water into a 6-quart slow cooker. Place ribs, meat side up, in slow cooker, overlapping slightly if needed. Cover and cook until meat is tender but not falling off the bone, 3 hours on HIGH or 6 hours on LOW.
4. Preheat broiler with rack about 8 inches from heat source. Place ribs, meat side up, on a large rimmed baking sheet lined with aluminum foil. Brush ¼ cup barbecue sauce on top of ribs. Broil until sauce starts to caramelize, 6 to 8 minutes. Remove from oven. Brush top of ribs with ¼ cup barbecue sauce. Let rest 5 minutes.
5. Slice ribs between bones. Serve with remaining ½ cup barbecue sauce, pickle chips, and bread slices.

TIME-SAVER
Cut down on prep by asking the butcher to remove the membrane from the back of the slab of ribs for you.

Cowboy Chicken Spaghetti

(Photo, page 188)
ACTIVE 25 MIN. - TOTAL 45 MIN.
SERVES 6

- ¼ cup unsalted butter
- 1 small yellow onion, chopped (about 1 cup)
- 1 Tbsp. minced garlic (from 3 garlic cloves)
- 2 cups unsalted chicken stock
- 8 oz. processed cheese (such as Velveeta), cubed
- 3 cups shredded cooked chicken
- 8 oz. spaghetti, cooked according to pkg. directions
- 1 (10-oz.) can diced tomatoes and green chiles (such as Ro-Tel), drained
- 1 (4-oz.) can chopped green chiles
- ¼ tsp. black pepper
- 1 cup shredded sharp Cheddar cheese (about 4 oz.)
- Thinly sliced chives

1. Preheat oven to 350°F. Melt butter in a 12-inch cast-iron skillet or ovenproof skillet over medium-high. Add onion; cook, stirring often, until tender, about 5 minutes. Add garlic; cook, stirring often, until fragrant, about 1 minute. Stir in chicken stock; bring to a boil over medium-high. Add processed cheese; cook, stirring constantly, until cheese is melted and smooth, 2 to 3 minutes.
2. Add chicken, spaghetti, diced tomatoes, green chiles, and black pepper, folding until well combined and pasta is coated. Remove from heat, and top with Cheddar cheese.
3. Bake until sauce is bubbly, 15 to 20 minutes. Remove from oven, and let rest 5 minutes. Garnish with chives.

Hot Pants Chili

(Photo, page 189)
In 1974, Al'egani Jani Schofield became the first woman to win the annual World Championship Chili Cook-off, and this version is inspired by her famous recipe of the same name.
ACTIVE 30 MIN. - TOTAL 2 HOURS, 30 MIN.
SERVES 6

- 2 lb. 85/15 lean ground beef
- 2 white onions, diced (about 3 cups), plus more for garnish
- 2 large jalapeño chiles, seeded (if desired) and finely chopped (about ½ cup)
- 3 Tbsp. mole paste (such as Doña María Mole)
- 2 Tbsp. minced garlic (from 6 garlic cloves)
- 1½ tsp. ground cumin
- 4 cups unsalted beef stock
- 2 tsp. kosher salt
- 1 (15-oz.) can crushed tomatoes, undrained
- 1 (12-oz.) bottle lager beer
- 1 (1¼-oz.) envelope chili seasoning mix
- 3 Tbsp. masa flour (such as Maseca)
- Toppings: sour cream, shredded Cheddar cheese, and sliced scallions

1. Heat a large Dutch oven over medium-high. Add ground beef and onions; cook, stirring often, until crumbly and most of the liquid has evaporated, about 12 minutes.
2. Stir in jalapeños, mole, garlic, and cumin; cook, stirring constantly, about 2 minutes.
3. Stir in stock, salt, tomatoes, beer, and seasoning mix; bring to a boil over medium-high. Reduce heat to low; simmer, uncovered, until thickened, about 1 hour, 30 minutes, stirring occasionally.
4. Stir together ½ cup water and masa in a small bowl until smooth. Stir masa mixture into chili. Bring to a simmer over medium-low; cook, uncovered and stirring often, until slightly thickened, about 30 minutes.
5. Top servings with sour cream, cheese, scallions, and more diced white onion.

COWBOY CHICKEN SPAGHETTI
(PAGE 187)

HOT PANTS CHILI
(PAGE 187)

A Little Taste of Texas

Got an early tailgate? Serve up these Lone Star State favorites.

Skillet Huevos Rancheros

ACTIVE 30 MIN. - TOTAL 1 HOUR

SERVES 8

- 3 poblano chiles
- 2 Tbsp. canola oil
- 16 oz. fresh Mexican chorizo
- 1 white onion, thinly sliced (2 cups)
- 2 garlic cloves, minced (about 2 tsp.)
- 1 (28-oz.) can crushed tomatoes
- 1 (15.25-oz.) can black beans, drained and rinsed
- 2 tsp. kosher salt
- ½ tsp. dried oregano
- ¼ tsp. black pepper, plus more for garnish
- 8 large eggs
- Crumbled queso fresco
- Chopped fresh cilantro
- Texas toast, for serving

1. Preheat oven to broil with rack positioned 6 inches from heat source. Place poblanos on a baking sheet; broil until charred, about 6 minutes per side. Transfer to a large bowl, and cover with plastic wrap. Let stand 10 minutes. Using a paper towel, rub off skins from poblanos. Discard skins, stems, and seeds. Slice and set aside.

2. Heat oil in a 12-inch skillet over medium-high. Add chorizo; cook, stirring often, until crumbled and cooked through, about 6 minutes. Add onion; cook, stirring often, until softened, 4 to 6 minutes. Add garlic and poblanos; cook 2 minutes. Add tomatoes, beans, salt, oregano, and black pepper. Bring to a simmer over medium. Cook, stirring often, until thickened, about 10 minutes.

3. Decrease heat to medium-low. Crack eggs into mixture in skillet about 1 inch apart. Cover and cook until egg whites are set but yolks are still runny, about 8 minutes. Remove from heat. Garnish with additional black pepper, queso fresco, and cilantro. Serve with Texas toast.

The name "huevos rancheros" simply means ranch-style eggs in Spanish, named for the hearty, rustic meal eaten by farmers and ranchers in Mexico after rising early to work. The dish likely reaches back to the 16th century and came to this country through San Antonio.

ON THE SIDE
Enjoy this dish over warm corn tortillas for a Tex-Mex twist.

BAKE IT EASY
This Czech pastry was a big hit in our Test Kitchen; see "Cooking School" (page 200) for tips and step-by-step instructions.

Sausage Kolaches

ACTIVE 35 MIN. - TOTAL 2 HOURS, 20 MIN.

MAKES 12

- 3/4 cup whole milk
- 1/4 cup unsalted butter
- 1/4 cup warm water (100°F to 105°F)
- 2 1/4 tsp. active dry yeast
- 4 Tbsp. granulated sugar, divided
- 3 1/2 cups all-purpose flour, plus more for surface
- 2 Tbsp. canola oil, plus more for greasing bowl
- 1 tsp. kosher salt
- 3 large eggs
- 1 (16-oz.) pkg. smoked sausage (such as Conecuh), cut into 12 (4-inch) links, cooked and cooled
- 1 (8-oz.) block sharp Cheddar cheese, cut into 12 slices
- 2 jalapeños, thinly sliced
- Shredded Cheddar cheese

1. Stir together milk and butter in a small saucepan over medium until butter is melted. Remove from heat; let cool, 12 to 15 minutes.
2. Stir together warm water, yeast, and 1 tablespoon sugar in a small bowl. Let stand until foamy, about 5 minutes.
3. In the bowl of a stand mixer with a dough hook attachment, beat together milk mixture, yeast mixture, flour, oil, kosher salt, 2 of the eggs, and remaining 3 tablespoons sugar on medium speed until smooth and elastic, about 7 minutes (dough will stick to the bottom of bowl but pull away from sides). Transfer dough to a large bowl lightly greased with canola oil. Cover with plastic wrap or a clean kitchen towel, and let rise at room temperature until nearly doubled in size, about 1 hour. Preheat oven to 350°F.
4. Whisk together remaining egg and 1 tablespoon water in a small bowl until combined. Punch dough down; transfer to a lightly floured surface. Divide dough into 12 equal pieces. Form each piece into a 4-inch round. Brush edges with egg mixture. Place 1 piece of sausage in center of each round. Top each with 1 slice of cheese and 2 or 3 jalapeño slices. Lift sides of dough over sausage mixture, and pinch seam to seal. Place, seam side up, about 1 inch apart on a parchment-lined large baking sheet. Brush with remaining egg mixture. Top with more jalapeño slices and shredded Cheddar cheese.
5. Bake until golden brown, 20 to 25 minutes. Let cool 10 minutes before serving.

SNACK TIME

Happy Hour Hero

Bring out a crunchy mix starring bacon and nuts, and watch it disappear.

MIX IT UP
Use toasted peanuts, cashews, or pecans (or a combination of all three) instead of the smoked almonds.

Smoky Bacon Snack Mix

ACTIVE 30 MIN. - TOTAL 30 MIN.
SERVES 12

- 6 thick-cut bacon slices
- 1/4 cup unsalted butter, melted
- 1 Tbsp. smoked paprika
- 1 Tbsp. Worcestershire sauce
- 2 tsp. seasoned salt (such as Lawry's)
- 4 cups corn cereal squares (such as Corn Chex)
- 2 cups smoked almonds

1. Preheat oven to 350°F. Cook bacon slices in a large skillet over medium until crisp, about 8 minutes. Remove bacon to a paper towel–lined plate, and let cool until ready to use. Pour bacon drippings into a heatproof bowl, and set aside.

2. Whisk together melted butter, smoked paprika, Worcestershire sauce, seasoned salt, and 3 tablespoons of the warm bacon drippings in a large bowl. Add cereal, and toss until well coated. Pour onto a rimmed baking sheet, and spread in an even layer (do not rinse large bowl).

3. Bake cereal mixture until crispy and dry, about 15 minutes, stirring every 5 minutes. Remove from oven, and return cereal mixture to large bowl. Add smoked almonds, and crumble in reserved bacon; toss to combine.

Ready for Game Day

The *Today* anchor kicks off the season with this super-Southern dessert.

FOR CRAIG MELVIN, it's not a real tailgate without a little competition. "You need to have fans from both teams. There's got to be trash-talking," he says. "You can't engage in that if everyone's for the same squad." He roots for the Gamecocks. A native of Columbia, home to the University of South Carolina, his devotion only deepened when he returned to the area for his first postgrad news gig after attending Wofford College in Spartanburg. "My house was in the Rosewood neighborhood, within walking distance of Williams-Brice Stadium. I spent many Saturdays tailgating there," he says.

But whether you're celebrating on campus or watching in the living room, Craig maintains that a game-day gathering hinges on the menu. "You've got to have fried chicken from either Bojangles, Bojangles, or...Bojangles," he says. There should be plenty of libations, like beer and bourbon, plus nonalcoholic options too. "If my mom's there, you've got to have the kind of sweet tea where the sugar congeals at the bottom of the plastic container that's been in your family for roughly 40 years," he adds.

You can also count on desserts, like these pretzel-crust bourbon-pecan bites. "They combine my favorite pie with my favorite beverage," says Craig. And when it comes to his pronunciation of that ever-polarizing nut, the Palmetto State native remains loyal to the way he's always said it. "I say 'PEE-can.' Why do we have to conform?" he asks.

One-Bite Pretzel-Crust Bourbon-Pecan Pies

ACTIVE 30 MIN. - TOTAL 1 HOUR, 35 MIN.

MAKES 24

PRETZEL CRUST

- 1¼ cups finely crushed pretzel crumbs (from 4 cups pretzel twists)
- 6 Tbsp. unsalted butter, melted
- ¼ cup packed light brown sugar

FILLING

- ¼ cup unsalted butter
- 6 Tbsp. light brown sugar
- 2 Tbsp. light corn syrup
- 1 Tbsp. bourbon
- ½ tsp. vanilla extract
- 1 large egg
- 1 cup pecan halves, chopped

1. Prepare the Pretzel Crust: Preheat oven to 325°F. Line a 24-cup mini muffin tray using paper liners. Generously coat liners with cooking spray.

2. Stir together pretzel crumbs, melted butter, and brown sugar in a medium bowl until mixture is the consistency of wet sand.

3. Spoon a heaping tablespoon (not packed) of crust mixture into bottom of each paper liner. Using the bottom of a round teaspoon, create an indentation in center of crust mixture in each muffin tray well. Set aside.

4. Prepare the Filling: Cook butter in a small saucepan over medium, stirring often, until milk solids have browned, 3 to 5 minutes. Transfer brown butter to a medium-size heatproof bowl, and let cool slightly, about 2 minutes. Whisk in brown sugar, corn syrup, bourbon, and vanilla extract until smooth; whisk in egg until homogeneous. Stir in chopped pecans. Divide Filling evenly among prepared wells (about 1½ teaspoons in each).

5. Bake 12 to 15 minutes until edges are golden brown and Filling is set. Cool in tray about 5 minutes; remove pies from tray, and let cool completely on a wire rack, about 45 minutes.

Touchdown Dip for the Win

This warm and cheesy appetizer brings the heat no matter who's playing.

CERTAIN FOODS have the magical ability to transport you to a different place. When I was in college at the University of Georgia, our family tailgates were never complete without my mama's Dawg Food Dip, a nod to Uga, the team's bulldog mascot. One taste of this bubbling hot combo of Velveeta and Ro-Tel takes me back to a red-and-black tent on South Campus in Athens, where everyone crowded around a slow cooker for a last bite of the cheesy mixture before kickoff.

Back at home in Birmingham, I have re-created her recipe for game days—but with a twist I picked up from my travels. I visit New Mexico's Hatch Valley every fall to help family friends put up green chiles and then fly back with a cooler slam full of our efforts. Over time, I have found plenty of inventive ways to use up my stash (like my spicy lemonade recipe, at right), but the Touchdown Dip is easily the fan favorite.

My version takes a few creative liberties with my mom's classic queso (like using green chiles in place of Ro-Tel), but it's just familiar enough to make you dream of Saturdays in the South. Rivalries may be strong, but nothing brings us all together quite like hot, melty cheese.

Touchdown Dip

If you're not eating this right away, transfer it to a slow cooker set on low and garnish just before serving.

ACTIVE 25 MIN. - TOTAL 25 MIN.

SERVES 8

- 8 oz. fresh Mexican chorizo, casings removed
- 1 (12-oz.) can evaporated milk
- 1 lb. white American cheese, chopped or torn
- 1 cup shredded pepper Jack cheese (about 4 oz.)
- 3 (4-oz.) cans diced green chiles, drained
- Sliced jalapeño chile, fresh cilantro leaves, pickled red onions, and crumbled queso fresco, for garnish
- Tortilla chips and green hot sauce (such as El Yucateco), for serving

1. Heat a 10-inch cast-iron skillet over medium. Add chorizo; cook, stirring to crumble, until browned, about 8 minutes. Drain on a paper towel–lined plate; wipe skillet clean.

2. Add evaporated milk to the skillet; heat over medium until the edges begin to bubble, about 5 minutes. Reduce heat to medium-low. Add American and pepper Jack cheeses; cook, stirring constantly, until melted, 6 to 8 minutes. Stir in green chiles; cook until heated through, about 2 minutes. Remove skillet from heat. Top with cooked chorizo, jalapeño, cilantro, pickled red onions, and queso fresco. Serve with tortilla chips and hot sauce.

Green Chile Lemonade

ACTIVE 20 MIN. - TOTAL 20 MIN., PLUS 2 HOURS CH LLING

SERVES 6 TO 8

Stir together 3 cups water, 1½ cups each fresh lemon juice and simple syrup, and 2 (4-oz.) cans diced green chiles in a pitcher. Chill at least 2 hours or overnight. Pour through a fine mesh strainer into a large measuring cup or bowl, and discard green chiles. Return lemonade to pitcher. Serve over ice, and garnish with lemon wheels.

TOUCHDOWN DIP

PIECE OF CAKE

Turning into a Pumpkin

This seasonal spin on a Texas classic might be better than the original.

Pumpkin Spice Texas Sheet Cake

ACTIVE 25 MIN. - TOTAL 1 HOUR, 45 MIN.
SERVES 20

CAKE

- Baking spray
- 1 (15-oz.) can pumpkin puree
- 1 cup vegetable oil
- 1 cup packed light brown sugar
- ½ cup granulated sugar
- ½ cup whole buttermilk
- 2 tsp. vanilla extract
- 2 large eggs, at room temperature
- 2 cups all-purpose flour
- 2 tsp. pumpkin pie spice
- 1½ tsp. baking soda
- 1 tsp. kosher salt

FUDGE ICING

- ½ cup unsalted butter
- ½ (4-oz.) unsweetened chocolate baking bar, chopped
- 3 Tbsp. whole buttermilk, at room temperature
- 3 Tbsp. spicy, fruity cola soft drink (such as Dr Pepper), at room temperature
- ½ tsp. kosher salt
- 3 cups powdered sugar
- Chopped toasted pecans

1. Prepare the Cake: Preheat oven to 350°F. Coat a 17½- x 12½-inch rimmed baking sheet with baking spray; set aside.

2. Whisk together pumpkin, oil, brown sugar, granulated sugar, buttermilk, vanilla, and eggs in a large bowl. Sift together flour, pumpkin pie spice, baking soda, and salt over pumpkin mixture in bowl; whisk until just combined. Transfer batter to prepared baking sheet, spreading into an even layer.

3. Bake until a wooden pick inserted into center of Cake comes out clean, 20 to 22 minutes. Let cool in baking sheet on a wire rack while preparing Fudge Icing.

4. Prepare the Fudge Icing: Melt butter and chocolate in a medium saucepan over medium-low, whisking often, until smooth; remove from heat, and whisk in buttermilk, soft drink, and salt. Gradually sift in powdered sugar, about ½ cup at a time, whisking until fully combined after each addition. Immediately pour icing over warm Cake, spreading evenly using an offset spatula. Sprinkle with pecans. Cool completely in baking sheet until icing is set, about 1 hour.

The Texas Version of Pigs in a Blanket

Making Sausage Kolaches (page 193) is easier than learning the two-step.

1. PORTION THE DOUGH

Prepare the dough as directed, and cut into 12 equal pieces (about 2⅜ ounces each). A bench scraper or a pizza wheel will make this easy, or you can use any sharp knife. Shape dough into balls.

2. ROLL IT INTO ROUNDS

Flatten the dough balls into 12 (4-inch) rounds using a rolling pin or your hands. A ruler helps with precision, but you can eyeball it if you're comfortable with a little imperfection.

3. ADD FILLINGS

Brush the edges of each round with egg wash. Place a link of sausage in the center of each round, and then top with a piece of cheese and 2 or 3 jalapeño slices.

4. WRAP AND SEAL

Wrap the edges of dough around the filling, and pinch seam firmly. Brush with egg wash. Top with jalapeño slices and shredded cheese. Place 1 inch apart on a large baking sheet. Bake as directed.

October

STUFFED DELICATA SQUASH

Delicious Delicata

With nutty, sweet flesh and edible skin (no peeling required), this squash makes a simple side.

Stuffed Delicata Squash

ACTIVE 35 MIN. - TOTAL 45 MIN.
SERVES 6

Halve 3 **medium delicata squash** lengthwise, and scrape out seeds. Brush cut sides of squash with 1 Tbsp. **olive oil,** and sprinkle with 1 tsp. **kosher salt** and ½ tsp. **black pepper.** Place squash, cut sides down, on a large rimmed baking sheet. Bake at 425°F until squash are tender but still hold their shape, 22 to 30 minutes. Meanwhile, heat 3 Tbsp. **olive oil** in a large skillet over medium. Add ¾ cup each finely chopped **yellow onion** and finely chopped **fennel;** cook, stirring occasionally, until softened, 6 to 8 minutes. Stir in 2½ cups cooked **farro,** ½ cup chopped **dried tart cherries,** and ⅓ cup chopped **toasted pecans.** Cook, stirring occasionally, until warm, about 2 minutes. Remove from heat, and stir in ¼ cup crumbled **feta cheese;** 2 Tbsp. each chopped **parsley, fresh lemon juice,** and chopped **fennel fronds;** ¼ tsp. **black pepper;** and **salt** to taste. Turn squash cut sides up. Spoon farro mixture into squash halves (about ¾ cup each). Bake until heated through, 3 to 5 minutes. Garnish with chopped **parsley** and **fennel fronds.**

ROASTED DELICATA SQUASH

Roasted Delicata Squash

ACTIVE 20 MIN. - TOTAL 45 MIN.
SERVES 4

Trim about 1 inch off each end of 2 **large delicata squash**. Using a spoon, scrape out seeds. Slice into ½-inch-thick rings. Toss with 6 Tbsp. melted **butter**, 1 tsp. **smoked paprika,** ½ tsp. **kosher salt,** and ⅛ tsp. **cayenne pepper** in a large bowl until evenly coated. Arrange squash in a single layer on a large rimmed baking sheet, and drizzle with any butter mixture left in bowl. Bake at 450°F on lowest rack until undersides are browned, 18 to 20 minutes. Flip and bake until tender, about 5 minutes more. Transfer to a serving platter; drizzle with 1 Tbsp. **cane syrup,** and sprinkle with 3 Tbsp. chopped **smoked almonds.**

The Path to Perloo

This Lowcountry dish has roots well beyond the coastal South.

THE FIRE STARTS WITH PECAN WOOD burning down to glowing coals. Three cinder blocks hold up a well-worn cast-iron pot. Chef BJ Dennis crouches low to spread the coals just right to control the heat. He begins with the aromatics: onions, garlic, and herbs. Then come the meat and water, followed by the rice. It's an ancestral choreography, rooted in memory and muscle.

The result is perloo: a comforting one-pot Gullah Geechee dish that traces back to the days when rice was locally harvested rather than imported; when sweetgrass fanner baskets were made to separate rice grains from their husks rather than to hang on walls as art; when cookware was limited, seasonings were minimal, and cooking outdoors over coals was simply how it was done. Not many people are more qualified to talk about perloo than Dennis. The Charleston-reared Gullah Geechee chef has become one of the leading voices on the cuisine as he works to conserve his culture and honor those who shaped it.

Perloo is a nod to the Gullah Geechee people, whose tongue carried more African than English words, and to their ancestors before them, who brought the blueprint for this meal from Senegal, Guinea-Bissau, The Gambia, and Sierra Leone during the transatlantic slave trade. Sometimes spelled purloo, pirlou, pilau, or even preloo, it's a staple throughout the Gullah Geechee Cultural Heritage Corridor, a federally designated region stretching from North Carolina to Florida that recognizes the historic coastal communities of the descendants of enslaved West and Central Africans.

No two families make perloo the same, and that's kind of the point. As with its culinary cousins—jambalaya, red rice, and hoppin' John—the environment dictated what went into the pot. Those who lived near water leaned into seafood: shrimp, oysters, and crab. Inland folks turned to what they had: chicken, smoked sausage, rabbit, and squirrel. Today, perloo has migrated and evolved beyond its Lowcountry roots as home cooks and chefs have tailored it to suit regional tastes and modern pantries. It has become a template where rice remains the constant while the add-ins are the variables.

Dennis grew up eating versions made with chicken, okra, and seafood, but he didn't realize perloo's cultural significance until he got older and started exploring the foodways of his hometown. His research led him to old cookbooks and oral histories—and into the global communities holding on to these practices. It also brought him into the kitchens of Gullah matriarchs like Emily Meggett, famous for her chicken perloo, and introduced him to Sallie Ann Robinson's oyster rice with shrimp as well as Charlotte Jenkins' herring pilau.

Regardless of the name, if the rice is tender but dry and everything is cooked in one pot, then it's a perloo. However, if it sounds like macaroni and cheese when stirred, then it's a bog. "Bog is perloo, but it's wetter. Ms. Emily [Meggett] called chicken bog 'wet rice.' That's more from the Pee Dee region of South Carolina. On the coast—from Georgetown, South Carolina, down—that rice [is] dry," Dennis explains.

He has also experienced the culinary traditions of the African diaspora through travel, including a trip to Casamance, the southernmost region of Senegal, to observe its rice culture. There are striking similarities between the landscapes and foodways in Senegal and the Lowcountry. "Some people say that perloo comes from pilaf and point to the Middle East, but West Africa is home to some of the oldest rice-growing regions in the world outside of China," Dennis notes. "We saw with our own eyes how seafood and rice are still eaten together today. You've got one-pot rice dishes in Senegal, just like perloo here. A lot of what we [Gullah Geechee] did wasn't written down; it was passed on orally. But you still see things like smoked herring and rice in Charleston, just like you do in West Africa."

Senegal's national dish, thieboudienne, combines rice (thieb), fish (dienne), and vegetables. Variations include thiebou guinar (made with chicken) and thiebou yapp (made with meat). In Casamance, you'll still find women standing over fires, tending to enormous cast-aluminum pots and using long wooden paddles to stir and fluff their rice. While traditionally prepared outdoors like its foremother thieboudienne, perloo is more commonly cooked on indoor stoves these days. "I like to finish mine in the oven," Dennis says. "Gets it fluffy—not gummy. You don't have to stir and worry about it sticking."

This adaptability is part of why perloo has stood the test of time and why no two recipes look alike. Whether it's made in the Southeast or up North, it's not just food. It's culture. It's connection. "You make it when people come together," Dennis says. "It's for when you want to feed folks and make them feel at home."

(LEFT) BJ DENNIS HOSTED A DINNER AT THE CHARLESTON WINE + FOOD FESTIVAL IN COLLABORATION WITH ROLLEN'S RAW GRAINS, A NEARBY PRODUCER OF CAROLINA GOLD RICE.

ONE-POT
CHICKEN PERLOO
(PAGE 207)

Whether perloo is made in the Southeast or up North, it's not just food. It's culture. It's connection.

One-Pot Chicken Perloo

Test Kitchen Professional Jasmine Smith's perloo uses a whole chicken and smoked turkey neck pieces for depth. It's the type of meal you bring to a picnic or reunion, feeding many without breaking the bank.

ACTIVE 35 MIN. - TOTAL 1 HOUR, 40 MIN.

SERVES 8

- 1 (3-lb.) whole chicken, patted dry
- 1 tsp. black pepper, plus more for garnish
- 3½ tsp. kosher salt, divided
- 2 Tbsp. vegetable oil
- 1 medium-size yellow onion, chopped (about 1½ cups)
- 3 medium celery stalks, chopped (about 1 cup)
- 1 medium-size green bell pepper, chopped (1 cup)
- 1 (15-oz.) can diced tomatoes, undrained
- 2 Tbsp. minced garlic (from 6 cloves)
- 8 oz. smoked turkey neck pieces
- 5 (4-inch) thyme sprigs, plus fresh thyme leaves for garnish
- 2 fresh or dried bay leaves
- 1¼ cups uncooked jasmine rice, rinsed
- Thinly sliced scallions

1. Preheat oven to 375°F. Sprinkle chicken evenly with black pepper and 2½ teaspoons of the salt. Set aside at room temperature.

2. Heat vegetable oil in a large, heavy-bottomed pot over medium-high. Add onion, celery, green bell pepper, and remaining 1 teaspoon salt; cook, stirring occasionally, until vegetables soften, about 8 minutes. Add tomatoes with juices and garlic; cook, stirring occasionally, until all liquid is evaporated and mixture begins to caramelize, 10 to 12 minutes.

3. Pour 1¼ cups water into pot, scraping up any browned bits from bottom of pot. Nestle chicken, breast side up, into pot. Arrange smoked turkey neck, thyme sprigs, and bay leaves around chicken, making sure turkey pieces are fully submerged; bring to a simmer over high. Cover and transfer pot to oven. Roast until an instant-read thermometer inserted into inner thigh of chicken registers 160°F, about 40 minutes.

4. Remove pot from oven. Spoon jasmine rice around chicken, submerging in liquid and stirring as best you can in space around chicken. Cover pot, and return to oven. Bake until rice is tender and most of liquid is absorbed, about 15 minutes.

5. Uncover pot, and increase oven temperature to broil with pot still in oven. Broil until chicken skin is crisp, 8 to 10 minutes. Remove from oven, and let stand 15 minutes. Remove and discard thyme sprigs and bay leaves. Transfer chicken and turkey neck to a cutting board. Using 2 forks, gently shred meat, discarding any bones. Fluff rice, and return shredded meat to pot. Garnish with scallions, thyme leaves, and additional black pepper.

(RIGHT) BJ DENNIS LETS HIS PERLOO SIMMER IN A CAST-IRON POT OVER AN OPEN FIRE.

Lowcountry Perloo with Short Ribs, Shrimp, and Oysters

Chef BJ Dennis's perloo takes a bold surf and turf approach. The beef fat in the dish brings richness, the seafood adds brine, and the heat from a Scotch bonnet chile ties it all together.

ACTIVE 40 MIN. - TOTAL 3 HOURS

SERVES 8

- **4 garlic cloves**
- **1 fresh Scotch bonnet chile or habanero chile, seeded if desired**
- **1½ cups chopped yellow onion (from 1 large onion)**
- **2½ tsp. kosher salt, divided**
- **1¾ tsp. black pepper, divided**
- **1 lb. beef short ribs (about 2 short ribs), patted dry**
- **¼ cup canola oil**
- **8 oz. medium peeled, deveined raw shrimp (about 16 shrimp)**
- **2 tsp. tomato paste**
- **3 (4-inch) thyme sprigs, plus fresh thyme leaves for garnish**
- **1 fresh bay leaf**
- **¼ cup Worcestershire sauce**
- **2 cups uncooked Carolina Gold rice, rinsed**
- **6 oz. fresh shucked oysters (about ¾ cup or 12 oysters, such as East Coast oysters), patted dry**
- **Finely chopped fresh flat-leaf parsley**

1. Pulse garlic, chile, onion, and 1 teaspoon each salt and pepper in a food processor until very finely chopped, 8 to 10 pulses (makes 1 cup). Set aside.

2. Sprinkle short ribs evenly with ¾ teaspoon salt and ½ teaspoon pepper. Heat oil in a Dutch oven over medium-high. Add short ribs; cook, flipping occasionally, until browned on all sides, about 8 minutes. Transfer to a plate, reserving drippings in Dutch oven.

3. Sprinkle shrimp with ¼ teaspoon kosher salt and remaining ¼ teaspoon pepper. Add shrimp to drippings in Dutch oven; cook over medium-high, stirring often, until opaque, about 1 minute. Using a slotted spoon, transfer shrimp to a small plate; chill, uncovered, until ready to use.

4. Add ½ cup reserved onion mixture, tomato paste, thyme sprigs, and bay leaf to drippings in Dutch oven; cook over medium-high, stirring constantly, until fragrant, 2 to 3 minutes. Add 4 cups water, Worcestershire sauce, remaining ½ cup reserved onion mixture, and reserved short ribs. Bring to a boil over high. Cover, reduce heat to low, and cook until short ribs are very tender when pierced using a fork, 1 hour, 30 minutes to 2 hours. Uncover and increase heat to medium-high. Boil until liquid is reduced to 2½ cups, about 20 minutes. Remove Dutch oven from heat.

5. Preheat oven to 350°F. Stir rice, reserved shrimp, and remaining ½ teaspoon salt into mixture in Dutch oven. Cover and bake at 350°F until rice is tender, about 50 minutes, spooning oysters on top after 35 minutes of baking.

6. Remove and discard thyme sprigs and bay leaf. Transfer ribs to a cutting board. Using 2 forks, gently shred ribs into large pieces, discarding bones. Fluff rice, and return shredded ribs to Dutch oven. Garnish with fresh thyme leaves and parsley.

Regardless of the name, if the rice is tender but dry and everything is cooked in one pot, then it's a perloo.

BAKING

Dream Rolls

Build a better bread basket with store-bought shortcuts.

Herby Cloverleaf Rolls

Beer is the secret ingredient to making rolls from a mix taste homemade.

ACTIVE 30 MIN. - TOTAL 1 HOUR, 25 MIN.

MAKES 12

- 1 cup pilsner beer (from 1 [12-oz.] bottle)
- 1 (16-oz.) pkg. hot roll mix with yeast packet (such as Pillsbury)
- ½ tsp. kosher salt
- ⅓ cup chopped mixed fresh herbs (such as chives, thyme, and flat-leaf parsley), divided
- 1 large egg, at room temperature
- 8 Tbsp. melted salted butter, divided
- ⅓-½ cup all-purpose flour, as needed, plus more for work surface
- Flaky sea salt

1. Heat beer in a small saucepan over medium until temperature reaches 120°F to 130°F, about 1 minute, 30 seconds.
2. Whisk together roll mix, yeast packet from mix, salt, and ¼ cup herbs in a large bowl. Add beer, egg, and 2 tablespoons butter. Stir until a sticky dough forms.
3. Turn dough out onto a lightly floured surface. Knead gently (gradually adding flour, 1 tablespoon at a time, to dough, work surface, and hands, as needed, to prevent sticking); knead until dough is smooth and elastic, about 5 minutes. Cover loosely using plastic wrap; let rest 10 minutes.
4. Place 4 tablespoons butter in a small shallow bowl. Uncover dough, and divide into 12 equal portions. Working with 1 portion at a time (keeping remaining dough covered), divide each portion into 3 equal pieces. Roll each piece into a tight ball; dip into melted butter, turning to coat. Place 3 balls in each well of an ungreased 12-cup muffin tray.
5. Loosely cover tray using plastic wrap. Set aside in a warm place, and let rise until almost doubled and dough springs back slowly when gently pressed, about 20 minutes.
6. Meanwhile, preheat oven to 350°F. In a separate small bowl, stir the remaining 1 tablespoon herbs into the remaining 2 tablespoons melted butter; set aside.
7. Bake rolls until golden brown, 18 to 20 minutes. Remove from oven; brush rolls with reserved butter-herb mixture, and sprinkle with flaky salt. Serve warm.

Garlic-Brown Butter Crescent Rolls

A simple and savory topping transforms refrigerated crescent roll dough into a bread that's fit for company.

ACTIVE 25 MIN. - TOTAL 1 HOUR

MAKES 16

- ½ cup butter
- 2 garlic cloves, grated (about ¾ tsp.)
- 4 oz. Parmesan cheese, grated with a Microplane grater (about 2½ cups)
- ⅓ cup finely chopped salted roasted almonds
- 1 Tbsp. fresh thyme leaves
- ¼ tsp. black pepper, plus more for garnish (optional)
- 2 (8-oz.) cans refrigerated crescent rolls (such as Pillsbury)

1. Preheat oven to 375°F. Line a large baking sheet with parchment paper.
2. Heat butter in a small heavy-bottomed saucepan over medium, stirring often, until butter is golden brown in color and has a nutty aroma, 5 to 7 minutes. Remove from heat; transfer to a medium bowl, and stir in garlic. Let stand, uncovered, 15 minutes.
3. Meanwhile, stir together Parmesan cheese, almonds, thyme, and pepper in a small bowl. Set aside.
4. On a clean work surface, unroll and separate dough along perforations into triangles. Lightly brush each triangle with 1 teaspoon reserved garlic-butter mixture; top each with 1½ tablespoons cheese mixture. Roll up each triangle, starting at wide end, and curve edges slightly to form a crescent shape. Brush tops evenly with remaining garlic-butter mixture. Space evenly on prepared baking sheet.
5. Bake until golden brown, 15 to 17 minutes. Remove from oven; sprinkle with the remaining cheese mixture. Garnish with additional pepper, if desired. Serve warm.

Dressing Cornbread

Loaded with fresh herbs, celery, and poultry seasoning, this cornbread smells like Thanksgiving in a skillet.

ACTIVE 20 MIN. - TOTAL 50 MIN.

SERVES 8

- 7 Tbsp. unsalted butter
- 1 cup chopped yellow onion
- 1 cup chopped celery (from 2 large stalks)
- 1½ tsp. kosher salt
- 1 cup cornbread stuffing mix (such as Pepperidge Farm)
- 1 Tbsp. chopped fresh rosemary
- 1 Tbsp. chopped fresh sage
- 2 tsp. poultry seasoning (such as Bell's)
- 1½ cups buttermilk self-rising white cornmeal mix (such as White Lily)
- 1½ cups whole buttermilk, at room temperature
- 2 large eggs, at room temperature

1. Preheat oven to 425°F. Heat a 10-inch cast-iron skillet over medium-high. Add butter; cook, stirring constantly until melted, 1 minute. Pour 4 tablespoons of the melted butter into a small bowl; set aside.
2. Add onion, celery, and kosher salt to remaining butter in skillet; cook, stirring occasionally, until softened, 5 to 7 minutes. Add the cornbread stuffing, rosemary, sage, and poultry seasoning. Cook, stirring constantly, until cornbread stuffing mixture is toasted and fragrant, 1 to 2 minutes. Remove from heat, and set aside.
3. Stir together cornmeal mix, buttermilk, eggs, and reserved 4 tablespoons melted butter until just combined. Add 1 cup reserved onion mixture; fold to combine. Spread remaining onion mixture in skillet in an even layer; gently pour batter evenly over onion mixture.
4. Bake until golden brown and a toothpick inserted into center of cornbread comes out clean, 25 to 30 minutes. Let cool in skillet 5 minutes. Carefully invert onto a platter; serve warm.

Appalachian Apple Magic

Harvested from backyards and back roads, fall's most beloved fruit shines in these simple desserts that taste like home.

WHEN I THINK of apples in Appalachian cookery, the image starts in a house, usually in the kitchen but possibly on a porch or carport, where weathered metal dishpans, wooden crates, or peck baskets sit all around, brimming with fruit ready to be worked up. Some people use one of those peeler-corer contraptions that clamp onto a counter, but I put great store in cooks who skip the gadgets. In their knowing hands, a stubby paring knife, often with a blade worn into a thin scythe, can quickly spin the skin off an apple in one long ribbon. When I was little, my grandmother and aunts told me that if I dropped an unbroken one over my left shoulder, it would fall into the shape of the initial of someone who had a crush on me. Entranced by their mountain woman magic and playful augury, I must have studied yards of those curlicues while I was growing up. Let me tell you—anyone determined to see a letter, perhaps one that's already in mind, will.

What I didn't understand until later, after I started cooking, was that the real mountain magic lay in the apples and the recipes we made with them. My beloved Appalachia is home to hundreds of storied heirloom kinds, which once sprawled all over the South. We've lost many over time, but some are coming back into popularity thanks to orchardists and cooks who look out for them—and then look after them. Johnny Appleseed meant well, but only grafting can perpetuate a variety—something that humans have known how to do for over 2,000 years—and it's a skill I watched my granddaddy ply in our own backyard. We had three trees, but more than a dozen different apples grew on their branches, like a gallery of good flavors. As my friend Diane Flynt, a noted orchardist and author of *Wild, Tamed, Lost, Revived: The Surprising Story of Apples in the South*, puts it, "Every apple with a name has a human desire behind it. The flavor of an apple caused a human to pursue and preserve it. It reflects individuals, regions, and cultures."

The old-timey types are best eaten fresh, a seasonal delight, as anyone who's ever picked and munched on a juicy one on a crisp, clear day can attest. And by picking, I mean not only plucking them off trees but also seeking and selecting them from farmers' markets or roadside stands that offer local fruits not available in grocery stores. A drive along the winding mountain roads to explore orchards, along with a little leaf-peeping, is a lovely way to spend an autumn afternoon.

But the higher calling of most of these farmstead apples—way back when and now—is to be cooked, dried, stored, or pressed for cider (either for drinking or fermenting into vinegar for pickling and preserving other foods). I'm smitten by the folklore of Appalachian apples and pore over vintage cookbooks as though they were histories and novels, searching for old ways to make my new dishes more delicious. My favorites, like much of our cuisine, let the impeccable flavor of the main ingredient speak for itself. The desserts on these pages were inspired by the cooks in my life and what they made with the fruit from their backyards. The particular varieties didn't matter to them, and they don't in these recipes either. People used what they had on hand, and so should you. At the end of the day, simply pick good apples and then make good things with them. Maybe that's what those magical peels were trying to spell out all along.
—Sheri Castle

Apple Butter Pie

A jar of apple butter, either homemade or store-bought, delivers subtle sweetness and spice to this custard pie. Making apple butter is an Appalachian tradition. Cooks used to let it bubble outdoors in cast-iron cauldrons over open flames, stirring with a wooden paddle, to yield enough for their whole community. These days, it's often prepared in smaller, household-size batches in a slow cooker, in the oven, or on the stovetop. The hours of gentle simmering release aromas that perfume the whole home.

ACTIVE 20 MIN. - TOTAL 3 HOURS, 10 MIN., PLUS 4 HOURS CHILLING

SERVES 8

- **3 large eggs**
- **1½ cups apple butter (from 1 [18-oz.] jar)**
- **½ cup heavy whipping cream**
- **1 tsp. vanilla extract**
- **½ tsp. kosher salt**
- **1 (9-inch) frozen deep-dish piecrust shell, baked according to pkg. directions and cooled**
- **Tangy Whipped Cream (recipe opposite)**
- **Apple pie spice**

1. Preheat oven to 350°F. Whisk together eggs, apple butter, cream, vanilla, and salt in a large bowl until smooth. Pour filling into baked and cooled piecrust.

2. Bake until filling is nearly set, 50 minutes to 1 hour. (Center should jiggle but not slosh when pie is gently shaken.) Let cool on a wire rack until room temperature, about 2 hours. Cover loosely with plastic wrap, and refrigerate until pie is chilled, at least 4 hours or up to 12 hours.

3. Top pie with Tangy Whipped Cream, and dust with apple pie spice. Serve lightly chilled.

Tangy Whipped Cream

ACTIVE 10 MIN. - TOTAL 10 MIN.

MAKES ABOUT 2 CUPS

- 1 cup heavy whipping cream
- ¼ cup powdered sugar
- 1 tsp. vanilla extract
- ¼ cup sour cream

Whisk together cream and powdered sugar in a large chilled bowl until stiff peaks form, about 3 minutes. Whisk in vanilla; fold in sour cream until combined and smooth.

MINI APPLE
BISCUIT PUDDINGS
(PAGE 216)

SEARED APPLES WITH BRANDIED CIDER SYRUP (PAGE 216)

Seared Apples with Brandied Cider Syrup

(Photo, page 215)

Fried apples aren't actually fried at all but seared in a pan with butter (or bacon or sausage drippings) until the pieces are browned and glossy on the edges and then cooked gently over lower heat until tender. I've upgraded that idea into an elegant dessert with a syrup laced with brandy and lemon—it also makes good use of the peels. The trick to getting the texture right is to choose baking apples, which are varieties that hold their shape when cooked.

ACTIVE 55 MIN. - TOTAL 1 HOUR, 30 MIN.

SERVES 6

- **6 small Honeycrisp apples, unpeeled**
- **1 Tbsp. apple pie spice**
- **1/4 tsp. kosher salt**
- **3/4 cup granulated sugar, divided**
- **2 cups apple cider**
- **1 Tbsp. vegetable oil**
- **2 Tbsp. apple brandy (such as Calvados)**
- **1 Tbsp. fresh lemon juice (from 1 lemon)**
- **1 tsp. vanilla bean paste**
- **Chopped toasted pecans**
- **Vanilla ice cream**

1. Preheat oven to 350°F. Peel apples, and reserve peels. Cut apples in half lengthwise. Remove cores using a melon baller or round measuring spoon; reserve cores. Stir together apple pie spice, salt, and ½ cup sugar in a large bowl. Add halved apples, and toss to coat; set aside.
2. Bring apple cider and reserved apple peels and cores to a boil in a small saucepan over high. Reduce heat to medium-low; simmer, stirring occasionally, until reduced by about half, about 45 minutes.
3. During final 20 minutes of simmering, heat oil in a large cast-iron skillet over medium-high. Arrange sugar-coated apple halves, cut sides down, in skillet; discard excess sugar-spice mixture. Cook, undisturbed, until apples begin to caramelize, about 5 minutes. Transfer to oven, and bake until apples are tender when pierced with a wooden pick, about 25 minutes.
4. While apples are baking, drain cider mixture through a fine mesh strainer placed over a heatproof measuring cup with a spout, pressing firmly to extract as much juice as possible; discard solids. Return strained cider mixture to saucepan. Stir in remaining ¼ cup sugar; bring to a boil over high, stirring occasionally. Reduce heat to low; simmer, stirring often, until mixture thickens, 10 to 12 minutes. Remove from heat; stir in brandy, lemon juice, and vanilla paste. Turn apple halves cut sides up in skillet. Drizzle with syrup from saucepan; garnish with pecans. Serve with ice cream.

Mini Apple Biscuit Puddings

(Photo, page 214)

Most fans of Appalachian cuisine find the combination of cooked apples and hot biscuits irresistible. Sometimes the biscuits are fresh from the oven, but we also like to split and toast leftover ones the next morning. That's the inspiration for these bread puddings, which make great entrées for breakfast or brunch. Black walnuts are the local favorite, but hazelnuts, which also grow in the area, are a fine substitute. If you don't have ramekins, try our variation for an 8-inch square dish (recipe follows).

ACTIVE 40 MIN. - TOTAL 1 HOUR, 40 MIN.

SERVES 6

- **4 Tbsp. unsalted butter, divided, plus more for ramekins**
- **3 Tbsp. granulated sugar**
- **3½ cups cubed day-old biscuits (from 5 biscuits)**
- **2 small Honeycrisp apples, unpeeled and cut into ¾-inch cubes (about 2 cups)**
- **3/4 cup packed light brown sugar**
- **2 tsp. apple pie spice**
- **1/2 tsp. kosher salt**
- **1/2 cup chopped black walnuts or hazelnuts**
- **1/4 cup sweetened dried cherries**
- **4 large eggs**
- **1½ cups whole milk**
- **2 tsp. vanilla extract**
- **Powdered sugar**

1. Preheat oven to 350°F. Grease 6 (8-ounce) ramekins with butter. Pour granulated sugar into 1 buttered ramekin, turning until bottom and sides are lightly coated with sugar. Pour excess sugar into another buttered ramekin; repeat until all ramekins are coated with sugar. Discard excess sugar, and place ramekins on a large rimmed baking sheet.
2. Microwave 2 tablespoons butter in a small heatproof bowl on HIGH until melted, about 30 seconds. Toss together butter and biscuit pieces on a large rimmed baking sheet; spread in an even layer. Bake until lightly toasted, 10 to 15 minutes. Set aside, and let cool. Do not turn off oven.
3. Melt remaining 2 tablespoons butter in a medium skillet over medium-high. Stir in apples, brown sugar, apple pie spice, and salt; cook, stirring often, until apples are tender-crisp, about 8 minutes. Stir in black walnuts and dried cherries until combined. Remove from heat; let cool slightly, about 10 minutes.
4. Whisk together eggs, milk, and vanilla in a large bowl. Stir in biscuit pieces; let stand at room temperature, stirring occasionally, 5 to 8 minutes.
5. Stir cooled apple mixture into biscuit mixture until combined. Divide evenly among prepared ramekins. Bake until puffed and set, about 30 minutes. Let cool on a wire rack 5 minutes. Dust with powdered sugar, and serve warm.

Apple Biscuit Pudding

ACTIVE 40 MIN. - TOTAL 2 HOURS

SERVES 6

In Step 1, omit ramekins and grease an 8-inch square baking dish with butter. Add granulated sugar, and rotate dish until lightly coated with sugar; discard excess sugar. Proceed with recipe as directed, pouring all of biscuit-and-apple mixture into prepared baking dish. Bake at 350°F until puffed and set, about 50 minutes. Let cool in baking dish on a wire rack 5 minutes. Dust with powdered sugar, and serve warm.

Dried-Apple Hand Pies

(Photo, page 218)

These pies are as close as I've been able to come to replicating my grandmother's recipe, which always used dried apples. The pastry is like a combination of biscuit and pie doughs. The vinegar in the dough makes it easier to roll and keeps it from turning gray as it rests. These are pan-fried rather than deep-fried, so the crust stays tender. Old-fashioned Appalachian hand pie recipes called for using lard in the dough and in the skillet, but these days, I usually do a mix of shortening, oil, and butter, though if you can find leaf lard, it's delicious and works well too.

ACTIVE 1 HOUR, 5 MIN. - TOTAL 1 HOUR, 40 MIN., PLUS 4 HOURS CHILLING

MAKES 8

DOUGH

- 2 cups all-purpose flour, plus more for work surface
- 1 Tbsp. granulated sugar
- ¾ tsp. kosher salt
- ⅓ cup vegetable shortening
- 6 Tbsp. whole milk
- 1 Tbsp. apple cider vinegar or distilled white vinegar

FILLING

- 2 cups dried apples (about 6 oz.)
- ¼ cup packed light brown sugar

ADDITIONAL INGREDIENTS

- Vegetable oil
- 1 Tbsp. unsalted butter
- Powdered sugar (optional)

1. Prepare the Dough: Whisk together flour, granulated sugar, and salt in a large bowl. Using 2 forks or a pastry blender, cut in shortening until mixture is crumbly. Drizzle milk and vinegar over flour mixture; stir using a fork until large clumps form, about 30 seconds. Gently knead into a smooth, firm ball, about 1 minute. Transfer Dough to a sheet of plastic wrap; flatten into a disk, about 1 inch thick. Wrap tightly; refrigerate at least 4 hours or up to 12 hours.

2. Meanwhile, prepare the Filling: Bring apples and 2 cups water to a boil in a medium saucepan over high. Reduce heat to medium-low; simmer, stirring occasionally, until apples are softened and broken down, adding water as needed to keep moistened, 45 minutes to 1 hour. (After cooking, there should be no standing liquid in mixture.) Remove from heat, and mash apples using a potato masher until mixture resembles thick, slightly chunky applesauce, about 1 minute. Stir in brown sugar. Transfer to a medium-size heatproof bowl; refrigerate, uncovered, until chilled, about 1 hour or up to 24 hours.

3. Divide chilled Dough into 8 equal portions, about 1¾ ounces each; squeeze and shape each portion into a ball. Working with 1 ball at a time, roll into a 6-inch round on a floured work surface. (Dough should be as thin as possible without tearing or ripping.) Spoon about 3 tablespoons chilled Filling over lower half of Dough round. Using finger dipped in water, wet edges of round. Fold top half of Dough over to enclose Filling, pressing out any air bubbles; trim edges, if desired. Press together to seal; press fork tines around edge to seal and crimp. Repeat process with remaining 7 Dough balls and Filling. Dust off excess flour, and set aside.

4. Pour oil to a depth of ½ inch into a large skillet; heat over medium-high until a deep-fry thermometer registers 350°F, 10 to 15 minutes. Add butter, stirring until melted, about 30 seconds. Add 3 pies to skillet, leaving plenty of space between pies. Fry, flipping once halfway through cooking time, until golden brown, 5 to 6 minutes per batch, adjusting heat as needed to maintain temperature. Remove pies with a slotted spoon, and let drain on paper towels. Repeat process with remaining pies. Dust with powdered sugar, if using, and serve warm or at room temperature.

Apple Upside-Down Cake

(Photo, page 219)

Even though trusty cast-iron skillets are traditional in Southern cookery and with most upside-down cakes, this recipe turns out better in a cake pan. I love its unadorned simplicity, but adding a little whipped cream to the top is never a bad idea.

ACTIVE 35 MIN. - TOTAL 1 HOUR, 45 MIN.

SERVES 8

TOPPING

- ½ cup packed dark brown sugar
- ¼ cup unsalted butter
- 1 tsp. vanilla extract
- ¼ tsp. kosher salt
- 2 small Honeycrisp apples, unpeeled and sliced about ½ inch thick (3 cups)

CAKE

- 1½ cups all-purpose flour
- 2 tsp. apple pie spice
- 1½ tsp. baking powder
- ½ tsp. kosher salt
- 1 cup packed dark brown sugar
- ½ cup unsalted butter, softened
- 2 large eggs, at room temperature
- 1 tsp. vanilla extract
- ½ cup whole milk

1. Prepare the Topping: Preheat oven to 350°F. Coat a 9-inch round cake pan with cooking spray; line bottom with parchment paper. Set aside. Heat sugar and butter in a small saucepan over medium-high, stirring constantly, until mixture is smooth and thick, about 3 minutes. Remove from heat; stir in vanilla and salt. Immediately pour sugar mixture into prepared cake pan; tilt pan to spread evenly. Arrange apples in a single layer over sugar mixture; set aside.

2. Prepare the Cake: Whisk together flour, apple pie spice, baking powder, and salt in a small bowl; set aside. Beat together brown sugar and butter with a stand mixer fitted with a paddle attachment on high speed until light and creamy, about 2 minutes, scraping down sides of bowl as needed. With mixer on low speed, add eggs, 1 at a time, beating well after each addition. Beat in vanilla until just combined. With mixer on low speed, add flour mixture to butter mixture, alternating with milk and beating until just combined after each addition. Pour batter over apples in pan; spread evenly.

3. Bake until a wooden pick inserted in center of Cake comes out clean, about 50 minutes. Run a knife around Cake edges; let cool in pan on a wire rack 10 minutes. Invert onto a plate; remove and discard parchment. Let cool at least 10 minutes. Serve warm or at room temperature.

DRIED-APPLE HAND PIES (PAGE 217)

APPLE UPSIDE-DOWN CAKE (PAGE 217)

Good to the Last Crumb

Slice into this pecan-filled loaf with a decadent glaze.

Butter-Pecan Bread

ACTIVE 30 MIN. - TOTAL 2 HOURS, 45 MIN., PLUS 3 HOURS COOLING
SERVES 10

- 1 cup unsalted butter
- Baking spray
- 2 large eggs, at room temperature
- 1 large egg yolk, at room temperature
- ¾ cup sour cream, at room temperature
- ¾ cup packed dark brown sugar
- ⅓ cup granulated sugar
- 2 tsp. vanilla extract
- 1¼ tsp. kosher salt
- 1⅔ cups all-purpose flour
- 1½ tsp. baking powder
- ½ cup plus 3 Tbsp. chopped pecans, divided
- Brown Butter Glaze (recipe follows)

1. Cook butter in a light-colored skillet over medium, stirring constantly, until solids are caramel colored and butter has a nutty aroma, 7 to 9 minutes. Transfer to a heatproof bowl. Let stand until cool to the touch, about 1 hour, stirring occasionally. (For tips on making brown butter, turn to page 234.)
2. Preheat oven to 350°F. Coat an 8½- x 4½-inch loaf pan with baking spray; line bottom and sides with parchment paper, leaving a 2-inch overhang on long sides. Set aside prepared pan.
3. Place ¾ cup cooled brown butter in a large bowl; reserve 2 tablespoons in a small bowl for Brown Butter Glaze. Whisk eggs, egg yolk, sour cream, brown sugar, granulated sugar, vanilla, and salt into brown butter in large bowl until well combined. Gradually whisk in flour and baking powder until nearly combined. Fold in ½ cup pecans just until combined. Spread batter in prepared loaf pan; top with 1 tablespoon pecans.
4. Bake until a wooden pick inserted into center of bread comes out clean, 1 hour, 5 minutes to 1 hour, 10 minutes, loosely covering with aluminum foil to prevent overbrowning. Let cool in pan 10 minutes. Using parchment as handles, remove bread from pan; let cool completely on a wire rack, 2 to 3 hours. Discard parchment; transfer bread to a platter.
5. Drizzle Brown Butter Glaze evenly over cooled bread. Top with remaining 2 tablespoons pecans.

Brown Butter Glaze

Melt reserved 2 Tbsp. **brown butter**; add to a medium bowl. Whisk in 1 cup sifted **powdered sugar**, 1 Tbsp. **water**, and 1 Tbsp. **sour cream** until smooth. Whisk in up to 1 Tbsp. water, ½ tsp. at a time, until desired consistency is reached.

Layer Up!

Go big for game day with a dip that's delicious from top to bottom.

Southern Seven-Layer Dip

ACTIVE 30 MIN. - TOTAL 30 MIN.
SERVES 10

- 1 Tbsp. olive oil
- 1 (16-oz.) pkg. hickory-smoked sausage (such as Conecuh), chopped (about 3 cups)
- 1/3 cup red pepper jelly
- 1 (15½-oz.) can black-eyed peas, drained and rinsed
- 1 (11-oz.) can Mexican-style corn, drained
- 1/2 tsp. kosher salt, divided
- 1 (8-oz.) pkg. cream cheese, softened
- 1 cup chowchow, drained
- 2 small tomatoes, cored and chopped (about 1⅔ cups)
- 1 (11-oz.) container pimiento cheese
- Thinly sliced scallions
- Tortilla chips

1. Heat oil in a 10-inch cast-iron skillet over medium-high. Add sausage; cook, stirring occasionally, until browned, about 8 minutes. Remove from heat discard drippings. Set aside 1½ tablespoons cooked sausage for topping; leave remaining sausage in skillet.

2. Return skillet to stovetop over medium-high heat; add pepper jelly. Cook, stirring constantly, until jelly melts and coats sausage, about 25 seconds. Remove from heat; spread sausage mixture in an even layer in bottom of skillet.

3. Place black-eyed peas in a small bowl; mash with a fork until no whole peas remain. (If needed, add 1 tablespoon water to make peas easier to mash.) Spoon mashed black-eyed peas over sausage; spread in an even layer with the back of a spoon. Set aside 2 tablespoons corn; sprinkle remaining corn and ¼ teaspoon kosher salt over black-eyed pea layer. Spread cream cheese over corn; spread chowchow over cream cheese. Set aside 1 tablespoon tomatoes; sprinkle remaining tomatoes and ¼ teaspoon kosher salt over chowchow. Spread pimiento cheese over tomatoes. Top with reserved sausage, corn, and tomatoes. Garnish with scallions; serve with tortilla chips.

Helping Hands

Stash these puff pastry pies in your freezer for busy weeknights.

WHOEVER SAID "the road to hell is paved with good intentions" could have been talking about my freezer. When I store a container of leftover soup in there, I really do believe that, on some unknown day in the future, I will remember to defrost and reheat it for an effortless meal. Same with the mystery casserole with that layer of ice on top and the two-for-one packs of drumsticks that I purchased who knows how many months ago. The reality: Frozen chicken just won't cut it in a 6 p.m. pinch.

I finally had to be honest with myself. Despite even my very best plans, my freezer is often where food goes to die—with a few exceptions. I thought about the items that I actually do pull out and use: bags of parcooked rice, vegetables, dumplings (from potstickers to pierogi), tortellini, and breaded chicken cutlets. What do these things have in common? They're all flash frozen, they cook quickly, and I can make as many at a time as I need. They also act as building blocks for fuss-free meals, like pastas, tacos, and stir-fries.

As do the puff pastry hand pies you see here. Thanks to store-bought dough and simple fillings, they are so easy to assemble that you can make a double batch and freeze some for later. They take only 25 minutes to bake from frozen in the oven—no defrosting necessary. Use that time to rustle up a quick salad or a vegetable side, and then dinner is served. Best of all, you can fill the pies with just about anything that your family will eat, or use these three tasty ideas as starting points.
—Lisa Cericola

Ham-and-Pimiento Cheese Hand Pies

ACTIVE 35 MIN. - TOTAL 1 HOUR, 25 MIN.
MAKES 8

- 1 (17.3-oz.) pkg. frozen puff pastry sheets (such as Pepperidge Farm), thawed according to pkg. directions, divided
- All-purpose flour
- 1¼ cups pimiento cheese (from 1 [8-oz.] container)
- 1 cup diced ham (from 1 [8-oz.] pkg., such as Smithfield)
- ¼ cup chopped scallions (from 1 bunch)
- ½ cup red pepper jelly
- 1 large egg
- ½ cup shredded sharp Cheddar cheese (2 oz.), divided

1. Preheat oven to 400°F. Line 2 large rimmed baking sheets with parchment paper.
2. Roll 1 puff pastry sheet on a lightly floured work surface into a 12-inch square. Cut square into quarters.
3. Stir together pimiento cheese, ham, and scallions in a medium bowl. Spoon a scant 1 tablespoon pepper jelly in center of each pastry square; top each with ¼ cup ham mixture.
4. Whisk together egg and 1 tablespoon water in a small bowl. Brush egg mixture on edges of pastry squares. Fold squares in half diagonally over filling to create triangles. Press edges to seal, and crimp with a floured fork. Transfer pastries to 1 prepared baking sheet. Cut 3 (1-inch) slits in tops to vent.
5. Brush tops of pastries with egg mixture. Sprinkle ¼ cup Cheddar cheese evenly over pastries.
6. Bake until puffed and golden brown, 20 to 25 minutes. Let cool on baking sheet 5 minutes. While first batch bakes, repeat process with remaining pastry sheet, filling, egg mixture, and Cheddar cheese. Bake second batch as directed. Serve hot.

Barbecue Chicken Hand Pies

(Photo, page 224)

Prepare recipe as directed through Step 2. In Step 3, substitute 1¼ cups (5 oz.) shredded **smoked Cheddar cheese** for pimiento cheese, 1 cup chopped **cooked chicken** for ham, ¼ cup chopped **pickled jalapeños** for scallions, and ½ cup **barbecue sauce** for red pepper jelly. Proceed as directed, omitting adding Cheddar on top. Before serving, drizzle hand pies with more **barbecue sauce** and garnish with **chopped scallions.**

Pepperoni Pizza Hand Pies

(Photo, page 225)

Prepare recipe as directed through Step 2. In Step 3, substitute 1¼ cups (5 oz.) shredded **part-skim mozzarella cheese** for pimiento cheese, 1 cup **mini pepperoni slices** for ham, ¼ cup chopped **jarred roasted red bell peppers** for scallions, and ½ cup **marinara sauce** for red pepper jelly. Assemble and bake as directed, omitting adding Cheddar on top. In Step 6, brush pies with melted store-bought **garlic butter** after baking. Sprinkle with grated **Parmesan cheese** and fresh **basil.** Serve with **ranch dressing** for dipping, if desired.

MAKE THEM AHEAD
Prepare recipe as directed through Step 4. Freeze until firm, about 1 hour. Store in an airtight container in freezer up to 1 month. When ready to bake, brush pastries with egg mixture; sprinkle with Cheddar. Proceed as directed, baking pies without thawing.

HAM-AND-PIMIENTO
CHEESE HAND PIES

BARBECUE CHICKEN HAND PIES (PAGE 222)

PEPPERONI PIZZA HAND PIES
(PAGE 222)

You're Getting Warmer

Tuck into these four comforting dinners for cooler weather.

Pork Chops with Apples and Cider

ACTIVE 15 MIN. - TOTAL 25 MIN.
SERVES 4

- 2 Tbsp. canola oil
- 4 (1-inch-thick) bone-in rib-cut pork chops (about 3 lb. total)
- 1 tsp. black pepper
- 3¼ tsp. kosher salt, divided
- 3 small red apples, cut into ½-inch wedges (about 4 cups)
- 1 small yellow onion, sliced (1 cup)
- 2 Tbsp. chopped fresh sage, plus whole leaves for garnish
- 1½ Tbsp. all-purpose flour
- 1½ cups apple cider
- 2 Tbsp. Dijon mustard

1. Preheat oven to 400°F. Heat oil in a large ovenproof skillet over high. Sprinkle both sides of pork with pepper and 3 teaspoons salt. Add 2 pork chops to hot skillet; cook, undisturbed, until browned on 1 side, 4 to 5 minutes. Transfer to a plate; repeat cooking process with remaining pork chops. Cover with foil, and set aside.
2. Reduce heat to medium-high. Add apples, onion, and sage to skillet; cook until the apples are browned, about 4 minutes. Stir in flour; cook, stirring constantly, 1 minute. Add apple cider and mustard; cook, stirring constantly, until thickened, 1 to 2 minutes. Add remaining ¼ teaspoon salt. Remove from heat. Place all pork chops, browned sides up, in skillet.
3. Transfer skillet to oven; bake until a meat thermometer inserted into thickest portion of pork registers 140°F, about 10 minutes. Remove from oven, and garnish with sage leaves.

Beer-Braised Pot Roast

(Photo, page 229)
ACTIVE 20 MIN. - TOTAL 20 MIN., PLUS 4 HOURS SLOW-COOKING
SERVES 6

- 2 Tbsp. canola oil
- 1 (3½- to 4-lb.) boneless chuck roast, halved crosswise
- 1 tsp. black pepper
- 1 Tbsp. plus 2 tsp. kosher salt, divided
- 2 large yellow onions, sliced (about 4 cups)
- 6 garlic cloves, smashed
- 3 Tbsp. tomato paste
- 1 lb. carrots, peeled and cut into 2-inch pieces
- 1 (12-oz.) bottle beer (such as amber ale)
- 1 (1-oz.) pkg. onion soup and dip mix
- 1 bunch fresh thyme
- 1 Tbsp. light brown sugar
- 1½ Tbsp. apple cider vinegar
- Mashed potatoes, for serving

1. Heat oil in a large skillet or Dutch oven over medium-high. Sprinkle beef with pepper and 1 tablespoon salt. Add beef to skillet; cook, turning occasionally, until browned on all sides, about 12 minutes.
2. Transfer beef to a 6-quart slow cooker. Add sliced onions and garlic to skillet; cook, stirring occasionally, until onions are just softened, about 4 minutes. Stir in tomato paste; cook 1 minute. Stir in ½ cup water, scraping up browned bits from bottom of skillet. Pour onion mixture into slow cooker. Add carrots, beer, onion soup mix, thyme, and brown sugar.
3. Cover and cook until roast is fork-tender, 4 to 6 hours on HIGH or 8 to 10 hours on LOW. Stir in vinegar and the remaining 2 teaspoons salt. Transfer roast to a platter; shred into large chunks. Discard any large pieces of fat. Spoon vegetables onto platter around roast. Serve with mashed potatoes.

PORK CHOPS WITH APPLES AND CIDER

CHICKEN NO-POT PIE
(PAGE 230)

BEER-BRAISED POT ROAST (PAGE 226)

Chicken No-Pot Pie

(Photo, page 228)

ACTIVE 15 MIN. - TOTAL 1 HOUR, 5 MIN.

SERVES 6

- ½ (14.1-oz.) pkg. refrigerated piecrusts (1 piecrust)
- 2 Tbsp. unsalted butter
- 1 yellow onion, chopped (1½ cups)
- 2 garlic cloves, minced (1½ tsp.)
- 2 Tbsp. all-purpose flour
- 1¼ cups heavy whipping cream
- 2 cups shredded cooked chicken
- 1 cup frozen peas and carrots
- 2 tsp. fresh thyme leaves, plus more for garnish
- ¾ tsp. kosher salt
- ¼ tsp. black pepper
- 1 cup shredded sharp Cheddar cheese (about 4 oz.), divided
- 1 large egg, beaten

1. Preheat oven to 400°F. Line a large rimmed baking sheet with parchment paper. Roll piecrust into a 13-inch circle; place on prepared baking sheet. Chill while preparing filling.
2. Melt butter in a large skillet over medium-high. Add onion and garlic; cook, stirring often, until just tender, about 4 minutes. Add flour, and cook, stirring constantly, 1 minute. Stir in cream; bring to a simmer, whisking constantly, until slightly thickened, about 1 minute. Remove from heat; stir in chicken, frozen peas and carrots, thyme, salt, pepper, and ½ cup Cheddar cheese. Let cool 10 minutes.
3. Spoon chicken mixture into center of piecrust round, leaving a 1½-inch border. Fold edges up and over filling, overlapping edges as needed and pinching folds to help crust maintain its shape. Brush piecrust with beaten egg; sprinkle edges with remaining ½ cup cheese.
4. Bake until crust is browned and filling is bubbly, about 30 minutes. Remove from oven, and let cool 10 minutes before serving. Garnish with additional thyme.

Easy Pumpkin Soup with Chipotle Grilled Cheese

ACTIVE 15 MIN. - TOTAL 35 MIN.

SERVES 4

- 2 Tbsp. extra-virgin olive oil
- 1 yellow onion, finely chopped (1½ cups)
- 3 garlic cloves, minced (about 1 Tbsp.)
- 2 Tbsp. finely chopped cilantro stems, plus leaves for garnish
- 1 (15-oz.) can pumpkin puree
- 1-2 canned chipotle chiles in adobo sauce, finely chopped (about 1½ tsp. for 1 chile)
- 1 tsp. ground cumin
- 1 tsp. kosher salt
- ½ tsp. black pepper
- 4 cups chicken broth
- ¼ cup heavy whipping cream
- Roasted salted pumpkin seed kernels (pepitas)
- Chipotle Grilled Cheese (recipe follows)

1. Heat oil in a large Dutch oven over medium-high. Add onion, garlic, and cilantro stems; cook, stirring often, until lightly browned, about 6 minutes. Stir in pumpkin, chipotle chile, cumin, salt, and black pepper; cook, stirring often, until thickened and slightly darker in color, about 2 minutes. Stir in broth, and bring to a boil over medium-high. Reduce heat to medium-low; simmer until flavors meld, about 15 minutes.
2. Remove soup from heat; stir in heavy cream. Top with pepitas and cilantro leaves. Serve with Chipotle Grilled Cheese.

Chipotle Grilled Cheese

ACTIVE 15 MIN. - TOTAL 15 MIN.

SERVES 4

Stir together ½ cup **mayonnaise** and 1½ Tbsp. **adobo sauce** (from canned chipotle chiles in adobo sauce) in a small bowl until combined. Stir together ¼ cup mayonnaise mixture, 1 cup shredded **Monterey Jack cheese**, and 1 cup shredded **aged Cheddar cheese** in a bowl. Divide cheese mixture among 4 slices of **rye sandwich bread**; top with 4 more slices of rye bread. Spread the remaining mayonnaise mixture on tops and bottoms of sandwiches. Heat a large nonstick skillet over medium-high. Working in 2 batches, cook sandwiches until toasted and cheese is melted, 2 to 3 minutes per side.

EASY PUMPKIN SOUP
WITH CHIPOTLE
GRILLED CHEESE

BROWN BUTTER-
CHOCOLATE CHUNK
SKILLET COOKIE

Call the Cookie Monster!

Break out the skillet for an ooey-gooey, crowd-worthy dessert.

Brown Butter–Chocolate Chunk Skillet Cookie

New to browning butter? Turn to page 234 for pointers.

ACTIVE 20 MIN. - TOTAL 55 MIN., PLUS 1 HOUR COOLING

SERVES 8 TO 10

- ½ cup unsalted butter
- ½ cup granulated sugar
- ½ cup packed brown sugar
- 1 large egg, cold
- 1 Tbsp. vanilla extract
- 1¾ cups all-purpose flour
- 1 tsp. baking soda
- ½ tsp. baking powder
- ½ tsp. kosher salt
- 1 cup semisweet chocolate chunks
- ½ cup toasted pecan pieces
- ½ cup toffee bits (such as Heath Bits O'Brickle)
- Vanilla ice cream
- Flaky sea salt (optional)

1. Preheat oven to 350°F. Place butter in a 10-inch cast-iron skillet. Heat over medium, stirring constantly, until butter melts and browns, 8 to 13 minutes. Transfer to a large heatproof bowl. Let stand until cool to the touch, about 1 hour, stirring occasionally. Set aside skillet (do not wipe clean).

2. Stir granulated sugar and brown sugar into brown butter in bowl until incorporated. Add egg and vanilla, stirring until smooth. Stir in flour, baking soda, baking powder, and salt until just blended. Gently fold in chocolate, pecans, and toffee bits just until combined.

3. Carefully press dough evenly into bottom of skillet (it's okay that skillet is still warm). Bake until golden brown, 20 to 23 minutes. Let stand 15 minutes. Serve warm topped with ice cream and flaky sea salt (if desired).

ICED OATMEAL SKILLET COOKIE

S'MORES SKILLET COOKIE

Iced Oatmeal Skillet Cookie

Follow recipe as directed in Step 1. In Step 2, omit chocolate and pecans; fold in 1 cup **uncooked rolled oats** and 1 tsp. **ground cinnamon** with toffee bits. Proceed with recipe as directed, omitting ice cream and sea salt. While cookie cools, whisk together 1 cup **powdered sugar** and 4 to 5 Tbsp. **heavy whipping cream** in a small bowl until smooth. Drizzle over warm cookie; serve immediately.

S'Mores Skillet Cookie

Follow recipe as directed in Step 1. In Step 2, omit pecans and toffee bits; fold in 1 cup **mini marshmallows** with chocolate. Proceed with recipe as directed, sprinkling cookie with additional **marshmallows** when hot out of the oven in Step 3. Omit ice cream and sea salt, and serve warm.

COOKING SCHOOL

TIPS AND TRICKS FROM THE SOUTH'S MOST TRUSTED KITCHEN

A Southern Baker's Secret Ingredient

Enhance your favorite breads, cookies, and more with brown butter.

PICK THE RIGHT PAN
Place the butter in a light-colored skillet over medium heat. A dark pan will make it harder to see when the browning begins.

LET IT BUBBLE
While stirring constantly, let the butter begin to sizzle. You'll hear popping noises as the water evaporates.

STIR THE FOAM
As the popping quiets, a fine foam will appear on the surface. Keep stirring to reveal the browned bits underneath; those are the milk solids toasting in the butterfat.

WATCH IT CAREFULLY
The butter will turn a caramel color and have a nutty aroma. At that point, remove it from the heat and transfer it to a heatproof bowl to stop the cooking and prevent it from burning.

November

BOUNTY

Spud-tacular

Sweet potatoes go beyond the casserole.

KALE-SWEET POTATO SALAD

CROWD CONTROL
Divide the potatoes between two pans for maximum crispiness.

SWEET POTATO GNOCCHI

Kale–Sweet Potato Salad

ACTIVE 15 MIN. - TOTAL 40 MIN.
SERVES 6

Peel and cut 2 **large sweet potatoes** into ¾-inch wedges; toss with 1 Tbsp. **olive oil,** ½ tsp. **salt,** and ⅛ tsp. **ground cinnamon** in a large bowl. Divide between 2 large rimmed baking sheets. Bake at 450°F, turning potatoes after 15 minutes, until crisp and golden brown, about 25 minutes. Whisk together 3 Tbsp. **olive oil,** 2 Tbsp. **cider vinegar,** 1 tsp. **salt,** ¼ tsp. **cayenne pepper,** and ⅛ tsp. **ground cinnamon** in a small bowl. Gently toss cooked sweet potatoes, 1 thinly sliced **Honeycrisp apple,** 1 (4-oz.) pkg. **baby kale,** ½ cup **dried cranberries,** and dressing in a large bowl. Top with ½ cup toasted **sliced almonds.**

Sweet Potato Gnocchi

ACTIVE 35 MIN. - TOTAL 1 HOUR, 55 MIN.
SERVES 4

- 2 lb. sweet potatoes (about 3 medium), peeled and cut into 1-inch chunks (about 8 cups)
- ½ cup whole-milk ricotta cheese, patted dry (from 1 [15-oz.] container)
- 2 tsp. kosher salt, plus more for salting water
- 1¼ cups all-purpose flour, plus more for surface
- 3 Tbsp. unsalted butter, divided
- 1 Tbsp. olive oil, divided
- 16 fresh sage leaves, divided
- 2 garlic cloves, minced (about 2 tsp.)
- ¼ cup grated Parmesan cheese (about 1 oz.), plus more for serving
- Black pepper

1. Arrange half of sweet potatoes in an even layer in a shallow microwavable dish; drizzle with 2 tablespoons water. Cover with plastic wrap, and microwave until just tender when pierced with a fork, about 6 minutes. Drain, and repeat with remaining potatoes.
2. Place drained potatoes in a large bowl; mash with a fork until mostly smooth and no large chunks remain. Stir together mashed potatoes, ricotta, and salt in a large bowl; gradually add flour, stirring until a shaggy dough forms. Knead dough until smooth, 2 to 3 minutes (dough will still be soft and sticky).
3. Bring a large pot of salted water to a boil over high. Divide dough into 8 pieces. On a floured surface, use floured hands to roll each piece into a long rope (about ¾ inch in diameter). Cut ropes crosswise into 1-inch pieces; place on a paper towel–lined baking sheet.
4. Boil gnocchi in batches over medium-high until they puff and rise to the surface, 2 to 3 minutes; cook 30 seconds more. Transfer boiled gnocchi to a paper towel–lined baking sheet using a slotted spoon.
5. Melt 1½ tablespoons butter and 1½ teaspoons oil in a large nonstick skillet over medium. Add half of sage; cook until just starting to crisp, about 1 minute. Add half of gnocchi, and cook, undisturbed, until golden brown on the bottom, about 2 minutes. Add garlic; continue cooking, tossing occasionally, until gnocchi are golden all over, 1 to 2 more minutes. Transfer to a bowl; repeat with remaining 1½ tablespoons butter, 1½ teaspoons oil, sage, and gnocchi. Toss the entire browned gnocchi mixture with Parmesan, and sprinkle servings with pepper and additional Parmesan.

Lainey Wilson's Happy Place

The Louisiana country star has always known how to find her way home.

IN 2024, LAINEY WILSON won a Grammy for her album *Bell Bottom Country*, and a few months before that she won "Entertainer of the Year" at the 2023 Country Music Association Awards. Her most recent album is called *Whirlwind*, which says a lot about what her life looks like. She had a recurring role in season 5 of *Yellowstone*, her first acting gig, and in 2026 she'll make her film debut in *Reminders of Him*, adapted from the bestselling book by Colleen Hoover. She co-hosted the Country Music Awards in 2024, and was back in 2025 to co-host them again. Her dance card, as they say, is full.

In the midst of all this, Lainey invited *Southern Living* Editor-in-Chief Sid Evans to her home on the outskirts of Nashville for a recording of our podcast, *Biscuits & Jam*. They talked about a lot of things, but one of them was holidays in her hometown of Baskin, Louisiana. Here's a snippet:

Sid Evans: *How do you stay grounded when you have so much going on?*

Lainey Wilson: Oh my goodness. Well, I will tell you this. I think the thing that has helped me keep one foot on the ground is just keeping my people close. The ones that know Lainey and not Lainey Wilson. You know, I go home to Baskin and everybody's trying to stop by and see me, but it's not because of everything that's going on, it's just because they want to stop by and see me, you know? And just making sure that I'm taking the time to do the things that make me feel like Lainey, the sister and friend and daughter.

SE: Lainey, this story is gonna come out around Thanksgiving, which is such a busy time of year for you. When you go back and think about Thanksgiving at your house, what does that scene look like?

LW: Oh my gosh. Look, even if there are six people coming over, my mama's cooking for an army. That's how it feels. I'm like, Lord, we're gonna have leftovers for three years. But yeah, it's normally folks from my mama's side of the family and my daddy's side. My mama has a much larger family. And so it's all of her siblings, most of their kids, and then their kids now. And they like to have a good time too. Normally there's turkey, there's stuffing, and every now and then, we'll just do a steak and baked potatoes. And you're probably gonna hear my belly growl in a minute.

SE: (laughs)

LW: But yeah, they can whip it up for sure. I didn't get that gene. I could mess up a Hot Pocket. I mean, it's really that bad. My fiance [Devlin Hodges] definitely likes me for a lot of other reasons, because if he was dependent on my cooking, he'd be gone by now. So I feel like I can read directions and do it, but I don't have that little Louisiana touch like the rest of my folks.

Boudin Balls

"I'm gonna tell you right now, if you don't like boudin balls, I don't know if we can be friends," Lainey says, laughing. They're not always on her family's Thanksgiving menu, but "there were definitely years where we had boudin balls," she says. "I like a little kick in my food." She also serves them at her Nashville bar, Bell Bottoms Up, as a tribute to her Louisiana roots.

ACTIVE 1 HOUR - TOTAL 1 HOUR

MAKES 30

- 2½ lb. Cajun-style boudin sausage, casings removed
- 1¾ cups vegetable stock
- 1¼ cups cooked white long-grain rice
- 1 scallion, chopped (about ¼ cup)
- Canola oil, for frying
- 1½ cups all-purpose flour
- 1 Tbsp. Cajun seasoning
- ¾ tsp. kosher salt, plus more to taste
- ¾ tsp. black pepper
- 3 large eggs, beaten
- 3 cups panko breadcrumbs

1. Using clean hands, crumble sausage into small pieces in a large bowl. Add stock, rice, and scallions; toss until evenly combined (mixture should be damp, crumbly, and hold its shape when gently squeezed together). Using your hands, gently pat and form sausage mixture into 30 (¼-cup) balls, about 2 inches in diameter (do not roll); set aside.

2. Add oil to a large Dutch oven to a depth of 1½ inches; heat over medium-high to 350°F. Whisk together flour, Cajun seasoning, salt, and pepper in a large shallow bowl. Place eggs and panko in 2 separate large, shallow bowls. Working with 1 ball at a time, dredge in flour mixture, gently rolling to coat; shake off excess flour. Place in beaten eggs, rolling to coat; let excess drip off. Roll in panko until coated; place on a large parchment-lined baking sheet.

3. Working in batches of 10, carefully lower sausage balls into hot oil. Fry, stirring gently and occasionally, until golden brown, 4 to 5 minutes, adjusting heat as needed to maintain 350°F. Transfer to a paper towel–lined baking sheet; sprinkle with additional salt to taste. Repeat with remaining sausage balls, allowing oil to reach 350°F after each batch. Serve immediately.

Choose Your Side

Wherever Craig Melvin's crew celebrates Thanksgiving, you can count on a stellar spread.

CRAIG (FAR RIGHT) WITH HIS PARENTS AND BROTHER RYAN

CRAIG MELVIN rarely misses a Turkey Day dinner in Columbia, South Carolina; but given that this year is his first as cohost of *Today* (and that the holiday show is one of their biggest of the season), his plans aren't yet set in stone. "It's kind of up in the air in terms of what we're going to do," he explains. "If I can't leave, then we'll probably host the meal." No matter where they're spending the day, though, he's ready for good food.

"The menu doesn't change, which is one of the reasons I love Thanksgiving," says Craig. For the Melvins, the lineup includes two turkeys (one oven-roasted, one fried), green bean casserole, "never stuffing and always dressing," homemade cranberry sauce (his sole contribution), and his mother Betty Jo's trademark potato salad. "It's second only to her mac and cheese," he says. "If there's ever a family gathering, my mom makes it. I don't think I had anyone else's version until I was in my teenage years." Not that he felt like he was missing out. "Her potato salad is one of those dishes that people will try to make like her, and it's never the same. It's not as good—in part because I'm convinced that she deliberately never shares the accurate recipe," Craig says.

Betty Jo's Pimiento Potato Salad

ACTIVE 10 MIN. - TOTAL 1 HOUR, 40 MIN.
SERVES 8

- 5 russet potatoes (about 4 lb.), peeled and cut into 1/2-inch cubes
- 1/4 cup plus 1/2 tsp. kosher salt, divided
- Cold water
- 1 cup mayonnaise
- 1/2 cup finely chopped sweet onion
- 1 (4-oz.) jar sliced sweet pimientos, drained and roughly chopped
- 1/2 cup sweet pickle relish (from 1 [8-oz.] jar)
- 4 large hard-cooked eggs, roughly chopped
- 1 Tbsp. yellow mustard
- 1 Tbsp. celery seeds
- 1 tsp. dried dill weed
- Fresh dill

1. In a large pot, combine the cubed potatoes, a generous handful (about 1/4 cup) salt, and enough cold water to cover by 1 inch. Bring to a rolling boil over high heat, and cook until very fork-tender, about 30 minutes.

2. Drain potatoes, and transfer to a heatproof bowl. Refrigerate until chilled, about 1 hour. Add mayonnaise, onion, pimientos, relish, hard-cooked eggs, yellow mustard, celery seeds, dried dill weed, and 1/2 teaspoon salt; toss to combine. Garnish with fresh dill.

Quiche for a Crowd

This double-batch recipe makes enough for a full house.

GET AHEAD
To make quiches in advance, see note in Step 5. Then reheat at 325°F for about 10 minutes.

Quiche Lorraine

ACTIVE 20 MIN. - TOTAL 1 HOUR, 40 MIN.
MAKES 2 (9-INCH) QUICHES

- 1 (14.1-oz.) pkg. refrigerated piecrusts
- 1 Tbsp. olive oil
- 4 shallots, finely chopped (about 1 cup)
- 12 large eggs
- 2 cups heavy whipping cream
- 1 cup whole milk
- ½ tsp. dry mustard
- ½ tsp. kosher salt
- ¼ tsp. cayenne pepper
- 1½ cups shredded Gruyère cheese (6 oz.), divided
- 1¼ cups cooked and crumbled bacon (about 15 slices), divided
- Chopped fresh chives

1. Preheat oven to 400°F. Place 1 piecrust in a 9-inch pie plate; press into bottom and up sides. Fold edges under; crimp as desired. Lightly prick bottom and sides of dough with a fork. Repeat with remaining piecrust in another 9-inch pie plate. Freeze 10 minutes.
2. Line crusts with parchment; fill each with pie weights or dried beans. Bake until edges are dry, 10 to 12 minutes. Remove parchment and weights. Return to oven; bake until bottoms are light golden brown, about 5 minutes. Let cool 15 minutes.
3. Heat oil in a medium skillet over medium. Add shallots; cook, stirring often, until translucent, about 5 minutes. Remove from heat.
4. Reduce oven temperature to 350°F. Whisk together eggs, cream, milk, dry mustard, salt, and cayenne pepper until smooth. Stir in cooked shallots, 1 cup Gruyère cheese, and ¾ cup bacon. Divide mixture evenly between piecrusts. Sprinkle each with 2 tablespoons bacon and ¼ cup cheese.
5. Bake until lightly browned, 40 to 45 minutes, covering edges with foil to prevent overbrowning, if needed. Let stand 15 minutes. (If making ahead, let cool completely; cover and chill up to 3 days.) Garnish with chives and remaining ¼ cup bacon just before serving.

SUPPERTIME

Twice as Nice

This Cajun-style turkey shines on Thanksgiving and the day after.

HOLIDAY BONUS
Don't throw away those turkey bones. Save them to make a rich and flavorful stock for soup or gumbo.

FOR MANY SOUTHERNERS, Thanksgiving leftovers taste better than the feast itself. Nowhere is that more true than in Louisiana, where folks like cookbook author and New Orleans native Kevin Belton transform the last bits of their birds into gumbo—a dish that blows the socks off any sandwich.

"Around here, everyone saves their turkey carcass, and nine times out of ten it becomes a gumbo," he says. "The real magic is in the flavor of the stock that's made from the carcass. The taste is unlike any other."

Belton's love for this recipe came early at his family's dinner table. "My mom and grandmother would make a huge batch, and we'd eat on it for the first couple of weeks in December," he says. "It was the warm-up for the big Christmas gumbo."

Although this dish is commonly served with rice, there aren't many rules when it comes to fixing your perfect bowl. "I have a friend who adds cranberry sauce to his gumbo," says Belton. "I teased him, but he reminded me that I put potato salad in mine. That's the beauty of Louisiana cooking—everyone does it differently, but it all tastes good."

Cajun Turkey

A butter-bound mixture of lemon zest, fresh herbs, and Cajun seasoning gives this bird a rich, savory flavor with a subtly spicy kick.

ACTIVE 40 MIN. - TOTAL 5 HOURS, 40 MIN., PLUS 12 HOURS CHILLING

SERVES 8 TO 12

- **1 (12- to 14-lb.) fresh or frozen and thawed whole turkey, patted dry, giblets and neck removed**
- **¼ cup Cajun seasoning, divided**
- **2 Tbsp. kosher salt, divided**
- **1 cup unsalted butter, softened**
- **1 Tbsp. chopped fresh oregano, plus sprigs for garnish**
- **1 Tbsp. chopped fresh thyme, plus sprigs for garnish**
- **1½ tsp. black pepper**
- **½ tsp. cayenne pepper**
- **1 Tbsp. grated lemon zest (from 2 lemons)**
- **5 lemons, quartered**
- **4 celery stalks, cut into 4-inch pieces**
- **2 yellow onions, unpeeled and quartered**
- **2 Red Delicious apples, quartered**
- **½ cup chicken stock**
- **Lemon halves**

1. Set a roasting rack inside a large rimmed baking sheet. Sprinkle turkey with 2 tablespoons Cajun seasoning and 1½ tablespoons salt Place breast side up on rack. Chill, uncovered, 12 hours to 2 days.

2. Remove turkey from refrigerator. Let come to room temperature, about 1 hour. Preheat oven to 425°F with rack in lower third position. Line a large roasting pan with foil.

Continued on page 244

Continued from page 243

3. Stir together butter, oregano, thyme, black pepper, cayenne pepper, zest, 1 tablespoon Cajun seasoning, and remaining ½ tablespoon salt in a medium bowl until well combined. Rub ¼ cup butter mixture inside turkey cavity. Stuff turkey with half of the lemon quarters, celery, onions, and apples. Add chicken stock and remaining lemon quarters, celery, onions, and apples to bottom of roasting pan. Tie turkey legs together using kitchen twine; tuck wing tips under, if desired. Using your hands, spread remaining butter mixture all over turkey. Place turkey on rack in pan.
4. Roast until skin is light golden brown, about 45 minutes. Reduce oven temperature to 350°F, and bake until a thermometer inserted into thickest portion of thigh registers 165°F, 2 hours, 45 minutes to 3 hours, 45 minutes, basting with pan juices every 45 minutes. Tent with foil to prevent overbrowning, if needed.
5. Remove turkey from oven; let rest 30 minutes before slicing and serving. Add remaining 1 tablespoon Cajun seasoning to a small plate, and press lemon halves into seasoning until coated. Transfer to a serving platter; garnish with Cajun lemon halves, oregano sprigs, and thyme sprigs.

Day-After-Thanksgiving Turkey Gumbo

Tailor this stew to your family's tastes by using leftover white or dark meat and omitting the Scotch bonnet chile, if desired.
ACTIVE 1 HOUR, 10 MIN. - TOTAL 1 HOUR, 30 MIN.
SERVES 6

- ½ cup vegetable oil
- ½ cup all-purpose flour
- 4 celery stalks, finely chopped (about 1 cup)
- 1 green bell pepper, finely chopped (about 1¼ cups)
- 1 yellow onion, finely chopped (about 1¼ cups)
- 6 garlic cloves, minced (about 2 Tbsp.)
- ½ Scotch bonnet chile, seeded and finely chopped (about 1 tsp.)
- 1 Tbsp. Cajun seasoning
- 2 tsp. chopped fresh thyme
- ½ tsp. black pepper
- 6 cups chicken or turkey stock, warmed
- 1 lb. pork andouille sausage, sliced ¼ inch thick
- 2 cups sliced fresh or thawed frozen okra
- 1 dried bay leaf
- 1 lb. cooked Cajun Turkey (recipe page 243), coarsely shredded (about 4 cups)
- Hot cooked rice
- Sliced scallions
- Hot sauce

1. Heat vegetable oil in a large Dutch oven over high until almost smoking, 3 to 4 minutes. Whisk in flour, and cook over medium-high, whisking constantly, until deeply browned and nutty in aroma, 7 to 10 minutes. Reduce heat to medium. Stir in chopped celery, bell pepper, and onion; cook, stirring often, until softened, about 10 minutes. Stir in garlic, chile, Cajun seasoning, thyme, and black pepper; cook, stirring constantly, until fragrant, about 30 seconds.
2. Gradually whisk in warm chicken stock until no lumps remain; stir in andouille sausage, okra, and bay leaf. Bring to a boil over high; reduce heat to medium-low to maintain a simmer. Cook, stirring occasionally, until slightly thickened, 45 minutes to 1 hour, adding turkey during final 15 minutes of cooking.
3. Remove from heat; let stand, undisturbed, until thickened further, 10 to 15 minutes. Remove and discard bay leaf. Serve gumbo over rice with scallions and hot sauce.

Roux rules

The deeper the color, the richer the flavor. Keep your eyes on the pot and the whisk in your hand to ensure it doesn't burn.

STEP 1. Sprinkle the flour into the hot oil. Whisk constantly and vigorously, breaking up any lumps, until smooth.

STEP 2. With the heat on medium-high, continue whisking the roux constantly. It will gradually deepen in color as it cooks.

STEP 3. After 7 to 10 minutes, the roux should reach a deep chocolate brown color. Proceed with the recipe as directed.

DAY-AFTER-
THANKSGIVING
TURKEY GUMBO

The Only Piecrust You'll Ever Need

We've cracked the code on the most foolproof, fearproof dough.

CARAMEL-APPLE PIE
(PAGE 249)

FROM TOP LEFT: CARAMEL-APPLE PIE, SHORTCUT BROWNIE PIE, SALTED MAPLE-SWEET POTATO PIE

I LOVE EATING PIE, but baking one was never my strong suit—I'd rather tackle a layer cake any day. Pie dough has brought me to tears more than once, and not in a good way. I've splurged on fancy butter, only for the crust to taste like a cracker and crumble like one too. I've painstakingly crimped the edges to find that every careful pinch dissolved in the oven into a lumpy, uneven band. I finally mastered the technique the most expensive way possible: pastry school. During the first class, I learned to make pâte brisée, a French short-crust dough, which yielded the most crisp, flaky, and buttery results. No other kind I have tried since has come close. And no amount of apple cider vinegar, vodka, or other touted baking hacks have either.

That holy grail recipe is a little fussy, though, and I'm a little lazy. So over the years, I've simplified it. I was taught to use milk, not water, but truthfully both work—and one is free. The original formula called for an egg, which I now skip for a more tender result. In school, I was told to always incorporate the butter by hand, but I prefer to let my food processor do the hard part. All of this makes an easy pie dough that's rich and sturdy enough to withstand any filling you can dream up.

Occasionally, I'll still get anxious when I'm baking a pie—between tearing and slumping, a lot can go wrong—but I've also learned to trust this recipe, because as the name suggests, it's pretty damn near perfect. —Alana Al-Hatlani

Damn-Near-Perfect Pie Dough

ACTIVE 30 MIN. - TOTAL 2 HOURS

MAKES 2 (9-INCH) PIECRUSTS

- 2½ cups all-purpose flour, plus more for surface
- 1 Tbsp. granulated sugar
- 2 tsp. kosher salt
- 1 cup cold unsalted butter, cubed
- 6 Tbsp. cold water or whole milk, divided, plus more as needed

1. Place flour, sugar, and salt in bowl of a food processor; pulse until combined, 2 or 3 pulses. Add cold butter; pulse just until mixture resembles coarse meal (some pea-size pieces are fine), 12 to 15 pulses.

2. Transfer mixture to a bowl. (For best results, don't use the food processor for this next step, though you might be tempted.) Sprinkle 2 tablespoons of the water over mixture, gently tossing to evenly distribute. Repeat process twice with remaining 4 tablespoons water. A shaggy dough should begin to form. (Dough will look a little dry, but don't panic; add up to 1 tablespoon water, if needed.)

3. Turn mixture out onto a clean work surface. Using the heel of your palm, gently press and smear crumbly mixture into and across the work surface. Repeat process a few times, just until a cohesive dough forms.

4. Divide dough in half, and shape into 2 disks. Wrap in plastic, and chill for at least 1 hour, preferably overnight.

5. Roll out 1 dough disk on a lightly floured work surface to between ¼ and ⅛ inch thick, rolling in one direction, from center out, rotating dough a quarter turn every couple of rolls to prevent sticking. (This should yield a circle roughly 2 inches wider than a 9-inch pie plate all around. To check, place your pie plate upside down in center of dough.)

6. Gently roll dough onto rolling pin, and unroll over a tempered glass or metal pie plate; slide dough into bottom of pie plate. Tuck edges of dough under to form a lip; crimp as desired. Repeat process with other dough disk. Freeze for at least 30 minutes before baking or up to 1 month wrapped tightly in plastic wrap. Use dough as directed in desired pie recipes.

Find Your New Favorite Filling

These stir-together recipes call for a parbaked piecrust. *See page 251 for detailed instructions.*

Caramel-Apple Pie

Slice 3 **large apples** (a mix of green and red) into ¼-inch-thick half-moons. Spread ¼ cup **jarred caramel sauce** in bottom of a parbaked 9-inch **piecrust**. Cover with a layer of apple slices. Spread another ¼ cup **caramel sauce** over apples. Shingle remaining apples vertically, skin side up, in rows, alternating green and red, if desired, until full (some may be left over). Whisk together 3 Tbsp. melted **butter,** 2 tsp. each **water** and **cornstarch,** and ½ tsp. **cinnamon** in a small bowl until smooth; brush evenly over apples. Bake at 375°F until apples are tender and filling is bubbling, 45 to 50 minutes, covering edges with foil as needed to prevent overbrowning. Serve warm or at room temperature.

Shortcut Brownie Pie

Prepare 1 (18-oz.) pkg. **brownie mix** according to pkg. instructions, substituting an equal amount of brewed **coffee** for water and melted **butter** for oil. Fold in ½ cup **semisweet chocolate chips.** Pour into a parbaked 9-inch **piecrust.** Bake at 350°F until set and slightly puffed, 25 to 35 minutes. Serve warm or at room temperature.

Salted Maple-Sweet Potato Pie

In a large bowl, whisk together 1¾ cups **sweet potato puree,** ½ cup **pure maple syrup,** 3 **large eggs,** ¼ cup **heavy whipping cream,** 1½ tsp. **pumpkin pie spice,** and ½ tsp. **kosher salt** until smooth. Pour into a parbaked 9-inch **piecrust.** Bake at 350°F until center jiggles slightly but edges are set, about 50 minutes. Let cool completely, 2 hours. Top with **flaky sea salt.** Serve with **whipped cream.**

PIECRUST PERFECTION

Ten secrets for getting it right every time

1 Measure Carefully

Time to pull out your kitchen scale. For proper (not dry) pie dough, weigh out 10⅝ ounces of all-purpose flour. No scale? Use 2½ cups flour. Just remember to spoon it into the measuring cup (A); then level it with the back of a butter knife (B).

A

B

2 Keep Cool

The butter should be ice-cold. After cubing, return it to the fridge or freezer for at least 15 minutes. You can go the extra mile and chill the processor bowl and blade as well as the flour and salt, but the temperature of the water and fat is most important.

3 Watch the Water

It's extremely easy to overhydrate pie dough. This is why you should gradually incorporate the water using your hands instead of with a machine. That way, you can feel the mixture as you go and you're less likely to add too much, which can make the crust tough. You want your dough to barely hold together when squeezed. As it sits, the flour will continue to absorb liquid, making it pliable.

4 Give It a Rest

Let the dough hang out in the fridge to let the gluten (the protein that holds everything together) relax and give the butter time to resolidify. This will make it easier to roll out and reduce the chance of it retracting, tearing, or sticking. If the dough starts to give you trouble while rolling, return it to the fridge for 10 minutes.

5 Crimping Is Crucial

Achieving a perfectly even and sharp crimp is about more than just looks. It will anchor the crust to the dish, to help maintain its shape and to the dish to prevent it from sloping. Here are three different ways to go about it.

EASY
FORK CRIMP
Use your fingers to flatten dough onto the lip of the pie plate. Flour the tines of a fork; lightly press it into edge of the dough to create indentations. Repeat crimping, flouring fork as needed. You can also use the tip of a teaspoon to create a half-moon pattern.

INTERMEDIATE
CLASSIC CRIMP
Holding your thumb and index finger about 1 inch apart, pinch a section of the piecrust to form a V shape. Press the thumb and index finger of your other hand into the dough to crimp. Repeat, keeping your fingers the same distance apart for an even look.

EXPERT
PLEATED CRIMP
Use kitchen shears to make small diagonal snips in the dough edge. Gently fold the flaps over, toward the center, so that they slightly overlap each other. Continue folding them, following the angle of the cuts, until the crust is entirely pleated.

6

Freeze It

To ensure the crimped dough keeps its shape, freeze the piecrust for 30 minutes before parbaking. Since the crust goes straight from the freezer to the oven, avoid glass or ceramic plates that can't handle extreme temperature changes.

7

Material Matters

Not all pie plates are created equal. Take these tips into consideration before you roll out that dough.

METAL: The speedy heat conduction of metal will yield a flakier crust with better browning. Plus, it is lightweight and can safely go from the freezer to the oven.

GLASS: If you want to use an oven-safe glass dish, you should factor in a little extra baking time, as it will heat up more slowly than metal. Look for ones made with borosilicate or tempered glass that are designed to be sturdier and less prone to chipping or breaking.

CERAMIC: These plates warm up slowly and retain heat longer, so it's best to bake with them on a rack that's set in the lower third of the oven.

8

Fill with Weights

Parbaking is a technique that involves partially cooking the crust before adding a filling; it ensures that the pie shell bakes all the way through and stays crisp. Many kitchen stores sell pie weights, oven-safe ceramic or metal balls that are used for this purpose. Less-expensive dried beans are my go-to, but uncooked rice or lentils or even loose change (don't worry; it won't actually touch the crust, thanks to the parchment) will work just as well.

9

Bake It Once

To prep your pie shell for parbaking, line it with parchment or foil (it should come up over the edges). Fill the crust all the way up to the rim with your pie weights of choice. Bake at 400°F until the edges are light golden brown, about 20 minutes.

10

Bake It Again

Carefully remove the parchment and weights from the crust. Return it to the oven, and bake until the bottom of the shell is dry to the touch, about 5 minutes. (Pierce any large bubbles with a skewer or cake tester.) Set on a wire rack to cool slightly, about 30 minutes, before using.

Second Helpings

Make extra room on your menu for these standout sides from our recipe archives.

Texas Cornbread Dressing

Originally published in 1975, this recipe was sent to us by Mrs. Raymond F. Buck of College Station, Texas, and was dubbed "the ultimate" dressing by our Test Kitchen.

ACTIVE 40 MIN. - TOTAL 2 HOURS

SERVES 12

- 12 sweet cornbread muffins, torn into bite-size pieces (about 8 cups)
- 6 white bread slices, torn into bite-size pieces (about 6 cups)
- 1/4 cup unsalted butter
- 2 yellow onions, chopped (about 2 1/2 cups)
- 4 celery stalks, chopped (about 1 1/2 cups)
- 2 jalapeño chiles, finely chopped (about 1/4 cup)
- 2 tsp. poultry seasoning
- 1 tsp. granulated garlic
- 1 tsp. paprika
- 1 1/2 tsp. kosher salt, divided
- 1 tsp. black pepper, divided
- 1 lb. pkg. ground pork-and-sage sausage (such as Jimmy Dean)
- 3 1/2 cups chicken stock or turkey stock, plus more if needed
- 2 large eggs, beaten

1. Preheat oven to 350°F. Spread torn cornbread muffins and white bread on 2 large rimmed baking sheets. Bake until slightly dry, about 10 minutes, stirring occasionally. Let cool 15 minutes.

2. Meanwhile, melt butter in a large skillet over medium. Add onions, celery, and jalapeños; cook, stirring occasionally, until softened, 10 to 12 minutes. Stir in poultry seasoning, garlic, paprika, and 1/2 teaspoon each salt and pepper. Add sausage; cook, stirring often, until sausage is crumbly and no longer pink, about 5 minutes. Remove from heat; set aside, and let cool 5 minutes.

3. Transfer dried cornbread and bread to a large bowl; stir in stock. Let stand, stirring occasionally, until stock is absorbed, about 5 minutes.

4. Stir sausage mixture, eggs, and remaining 1 teaspoon salt and 1/2 teaspoon pepper into cornbread mixture until combined. If necessary, stir in up to 1/2 cup more stock until mixture is well moistened but not soggy. Spoon mixture evenly into a greased 13- x 9-inch baking dish. Bake at 350°F until set and top is toasted, 55 minutes to 1 hour. Let cool 10 minutes before serving.

KITCHEN TIP

If you can't find store-bought cornbread muffins, prepare two (7-ounce) packages Martha White Sweet Yellow Cornbread & Muffin Mix according to label directions.

EDNA'S
GREENS

Edna's Greens

Southern food icon Edna Lewis schooled our Test Kitchen in the mid-1990s with this recipe, garnering their highest praise. Instead of cooking everything together, Lewis simmered the pork low and slow before adding the greens, allowing them to retain their hearty texture.

ACTIVE 20 MIN. - TOTAL 2 HOURS, 20 MIN.

SERVES 12

- **1 (12-oz.) pkg. salt pork**
- **1 lb. smoked pork neck bones**
- **1 tsp. black pepper, divided, plus more for serving**
- **1 (32-oz.) bag chopped collard greens**
- **1 (16-oz.) bag chopped mustard greens**
- **2 tsp. kosher salt, plus more for serving**
- **Pepper-vinegar sauce (such as Texas Pete)**
- **Sliced scallions**

1. Slice salt pork at ¼-inch intervals, cutting to but not through the skin. Place salt pork, 12 cups water, pork neck bones, and ½ teaspoon pepper in a large Dutch oven; bring to a boil over high. Cover and reduce heat to low; simmer until broth is flavorful and meat is falling off the bones, 1 hour, 30 minutes to 2 hours. Remove pork from broth; set aside, and let cool slightly.

2. Bring broth in Dutch oven to a rapid boil over medium-high. Add collards; once wilted, add mustard greens. Bring to a simmer over medium-high; reduce heat to medium. Add salt and remaining ½ teaspoon pepper; simmer, uncovered, stirring occasionally, until greens are just tender but still bright green, about 17 minutes. If desired, pull off meat from pork bones; stir meat into greens. Discard bones.

3. Serve greens with a slotted spoon. Season with additional salt and pepper to taste along with pepper-vinegar sauce. Garnish with sliced scallions.

Butter-Steamed New Potatoes

(Photo, page 257)

When we set out to revamp this recipe from our 1980 book Cooking Across the South, *our team nicknamed these buttery spuds the "Bikini Potatoes" due to their peeled midsections.*

ACTIVE 40 MIN. - TOTAL 40 MIN.

SERVES 8

- **3 lb. baby red potatoes**
- **½ cup unsalted butter**
- **6 thyme sprigs, plus more for garnish**
- **1 Tbsp. finely chopped garlic (from 3 cloves)**
- **2 tsp. chicken bouillon granules or ½ chicken bouillon cube**
- **½ tsp. granulated garlic**
- **½ tsp. black pepper, plus more for garnish**
- **1½ tsp. kosher salt, divided**
- **½ tsp. grated lemon zest (from 1 lemon)**

1. If desired, peel off a strip around the middle of each potato using a vegetable peeler, leaving ends of potatoes unpeeled.

2. Melt butter in a large high-sided skillet over medium. Add thyme and chopped garlic; cook, stirring often, until fragrant, about 30 seconds. Stir in ¼ cup water, chicken bouillon, granulated garlic, pepper, and 1 teaspoon salt. Add potatoes, and stir until well coated.

3. Cover with a tight-fitting lid; cook over medium, swirling skillet every couple of minutes, until water is evaporated and potatoes are tender, about 25 minutes. Do not uncover skillet while cooking.

4. Remove skillet from heat; uncover and stir in lemon zest and remaining ½ teaspoon salt. Transfer potatoes to a platter, and drizzle with any butter remaining in skillet. Garnish with additional thyme sprigs and pepper.

Lowcountry Awendaw

(Photo, page 256)

Featured in The Southern Living Community Cookbook, *this cheesy side dish was pulled from* Charleston Receipts, *a classic cookbook published in 1950 by the Junior League of Charleston. The casserole reportedly takes its name from a town outside Charleston, South Carolina, which was originally inhabited by the Indigenous Sewee people.*

ACTIVE 30 MIN. - TOTAL 1 HOUR, 20 MIN.

SERVES 12

- **4 cups chicken broth**
- **1½ cups uncooked yellow grits**
- **2 Tbsp. unsalted butter, plus more for topping**
- **4 large eggs**
- **1½ cups whole milk**
- **¾ cup plain yellow cornmeal**
- **1½ tsp. kosher salt**
- **1 tsp. baking powder**
- **¼ tsp. cayenne pepper**
- **½ cup chopped fresh chives, plus more for garnish**
- **2 cups shredded smoked Cheddar cheese (8 oz.), divided**

1. Preheat oven to 375°F. Coat a 13- x 9-inch baking dish with cooking spray; set aside. Bring broth and 2 cups water to a boil in a large saucepan over high. Whisk in grits, and return to a boil, whisking constantly. Reduce heat to medium-low; cook, stirring occasionally, until thickened and grits are tender, 15 to 20 minutes. Remove from heat; stir in butter.

2. Whisk together eggs and milk in a medium bowl. Gradually ladle about 1 cup grits mixture into egg mixture, whisking constantly, until egg mixture feels warm to the touch. Add egg mixture to remaining grits mixture in saucepan, whisking constantly. Whisk in cornmeal, salt, baking powder, and cayenne pepper; fold in chives and 1½ cups cheese.

3. Transfer mixture to prepared baking dish; sprinkle with remaining ½ cup cheese. Bake until top is golden brown and feels set to the touch, 45 to 50 minutes.

4. Remove from oven; let cool slightly, about 5 minutes. Dot top with more butter; garnish with more chives.

LOWCOUNTRY AWENDAW
(PAGE 255)

BUTTER-STEAMED NEW POTATOES (PAGE 255)

TEXAS CORNBREAD DRESSING
(PAGE 252)

EDNA'S GREENS
(PAGE 255)

These timeless sides are the epitome of "oldies but goodies"—dishes that are part of our memories, our present, and future Thanksgiving celebrations too.

A Slice of Sunshine

In Florida and across the country, Key lime pie is upstaging classic flavors like apple and pecan.

IF YOU CAN smell a Key lime pie before you even set eyes on it, you know it's going to be good. This is especially true when walking into Fireman Derek's Bake Shop in Miami's Wynwood neighborhood, where the team is working at full tilt with pie orders two weeks ahead of Thanksgiving. But it's not the apple or pumpkin kind they're cranking out—it's Key lime.

The entire place, owned by former firefighter Derek Kaplan, smells of fresh zest. In a corner of the nearly 5,000-square-foot facility, two men are squeezing vats of Key limes as if they were born to juice. Across the room, bakers are molding the graham cracker crusts, adding a sweet, buttery scent to the wafting citrus.

Even though this beloved pie is believed to have originated over 100 miles south in Key West in the late 1800s, a handful of Miami bakeries are creating a new niche for it during the holiday season. The team at Fireman Derek's is working around the clock to pump out sweets for its three storefronts, plus Goldbelly orders that ship nationwide. Last year, 460 Key lime pies were preordered, and if the past numbers stay the course, they'll sell about 10,000 baked goods this November—with around 2,200 of those being Key lime pies.

Kaplan, who still uses the original recipe he came up with when he was just 15 years old, says that it's no surprise this dessert is becoming more popular. "I think one of the driving forces is that people are interested in branching out from the traditional apple and pumpkin pies," he says. "For my own family's Thanksgiving, we don't have turkey and warm pies anymore. Instead, it's stone crabs, Champagne, and ice-cold Key lime pie with whipped cream."

Data from Google Trends also shows spikes in searches for Key lime pie around Thanksgiving. Joshua Abril, owner of Fookem's Fabulous bakery in Coconut Grove, another Miami neighborhood, thinks it better suits the holiday anyway. "Key lime pie is the most American dish out there," he says, noting that apple pies can actually be traced back to Europe. "So the cliché 'as American as apple pie' isn't quite accurate."

The Miami native, who has both Cuban and Jewish roots, grew up eating lechón, or roasted pork, for Thanksgiving and believes holiday traditions are whatever families make them to be. And he's not alone. Last year, a line of customers about 50 people deep wrapped around the block of his shop, waiting to buy his signature Key lime pies with sea salt–graham cracker crusts before the bakery ran out.

Giancarlo and Christian Guevara, twin brothers and co-owners of Dbakers Sweet Studio in Miami, have witnessed this same craze, selling hundreds of Key lime pies from their two pastel-perfect shops. Giancarlo says this treat is like a taste of the tropics, offering an escape to one of his favorite destinations: the beach. Topped with a fluffy meringue that's as high as a skyscraper, the filling's sharp tartness is a nice counterbalance to the rich, carb-heavy foods typically found on the holiday table.

If you'd like to try something new this year but can't travel to Miami, check out our Cranberry–Key Lime Pie (recipe at right), which blends Florida flavors with a familiar Thanksgiving ingredient.

Cranberry–Key Lime Pie

ACTIVE 20 MIN. · TOTAL 35 MIN., PLUS 2 HOURS COOLING AND CHILLING
SERVES 8

- 6 oz. fresh or frozen cranberries (1½ cups)
- ½ cup granulated sugar
- 1 (14-oz.) can sweetened condensed milk
- 4 large egg yolks
- 6 Tbsp. Key lime juice
- ¼ tsp. red food coloring gel (optional)
- 1 (9-inch) ready-to-use graham cracker piecrust
- Whipped cream
- Lime wheels
- Sugared cranberries

1. Preheat oven to 350°F. Place cranberries, sugar, and ¼ cup water in a medium saucepan. Bring to a boil over medium, and cook, stirring often, until cranberries burst and mixture thickens, 6 to 8 minutes. Transfer to a blender, and secure lid. Remove center piece of blender lid to allow steam to escape; place a clean towel over opening. Process until smooth, about 1 minute. Set aside ⅓ cup of mixture, if desired.
2. Add sweetened condensed milk, egg yolks, Key lime juice, and food coloring gel (if using) to blender. Process until just smooth, 20 to 30 seconds, scraping down sides of blender as needed. Pour mixture into prepared crust.
3. Bake until center is set, about 15 minutes. Let cool completely on a wire rack, about 1 hour. Cover and chill at least 1 hour or up to 12 hours.
4. Spoon whipped cream over chilled pie. Garnish with lime wheels and sugared cranberries. Serve with reserved cranberry mixture, if desired.

IVY'S KITCHEN

Ready to Roll

I gave an old family recipe a fresh update—and the results are holiday-worthy.

WHEN MY FAMILY gathered for my grandmother's funeral earlier this year, my dad came across her recipe box. Inside, he found a splattered, handwritten index card for Pineapple Jelly Roll, one of his favorite desserts. He asked if I'd make it, so I took the recipe home and started poring over my grandmother's haphazard notes. Her measurements were clear, but the instructions were murky. I did my best to interpret her words, and a few hours later, my first attempt was ready. But there was one glaring issue: It was ugly, and not in an endearing way either. Even a generous dusting of powdered sugar didn't help. After making tiny tweaks to the filling (a tad less brown sugar, a splash of lemon juice) and adding pineapple whipped cream to cover up the craggy exterior, I finally felt like I had done Doris Odom justice. I'm baking it for my dad this Thanksgiving so that, for just a moment, we'll have my grandmother back at the table with us.

Pineapple Jelly Roll

ACTIVE 1 HOUR, 30 MIN. - TOTAL 2 HOURS, 30 MIN.

SERVES 12

- 2 (8-oz.) cans crushed pineapple in juice
- 2 Tbsp. cornstarch
- 2 Tbsp. light brown sugar
- 2 tsp. fresh lemon juice (from 1 lemon)
- 1/3 cup plus 3/4 cup granulated sugar, divided
- 1/2 tsp. kosher salt, divided
- 4 large eggs, separated
- 1/2 tsp. vanilla extract
- 3/4 cup all-purpose flour
- 1 tsp. baking powder
- 1 Tbsp. butter, melted
- 6 Tbsp. powdered sugar, divided
- 1 1/2 cups heavy whipping cream
- 2 Tbsp. pineapple-flavor gelatin (from 1 [3-oz.] pkg., such as Jell-O)
- Dried pineapple rings

1. Drain pineapple; reserve juice. Stir together pineapple, 1/3 cup reserved juice, cornstarch, brown sugar, lemon juice, 1/3 cup granulated sugar, and 1/4 teaspoon kosher salt in a saucepan. Cook over medium, stirring often, until very thick, 6 to 7 minutes. Transfer to a heatproof bowl, and chill, uncovered, 1 hour.

2. Preheat oven to 350°F. Coat a 7- x 12-inch rimmed baking sheet with cooking spray. Line with parchment paper; coat with cooking spray.

3. Beat egg whites and 1/2 cup granulated sugar in a large bowl with an electric mixer on medium speed until foamy. Increase mixer speed to high, and beat until stiff peaks form, 3 to 4 minutes.

4. Wipe beaters clean. Beat yolks, vanilla, and remaining 1/4 cup granulated sugar in a large bowl on high speed until pale and thick, about 2 minutes. Fold one-third of egg white mixture into yolk mixture until a few streaks of white remain; gently fold in remaining egg white mixture until just combined.

5. Sift flour, baking powder, and remaining 1/4 teaspoon salt into egg mixture; fold until combined. Drizzle in melted butter; fold in until combined. Pour batter into prepared baking sheet; spread in an even layer.

6. Bake until cake springs back when lightly touched, 10 to 11 minutes. Meanwhile, place a clean tea towel on a work surface. Sift 2 tablespoons powdered sugar over towel.

7. Remove cake from oven. Working quickly, run a knife around edges to loosen cake; invert onto prepared towel. Discard parchment. Starting from one short end, gently roll up warm cake with towel. Place seam side down on a wire rack; let cool 1 hour.

8. For frosting, beat heavy cream, pineapple gelatin, and remaining 4 tablespoons powdered sugar in a bowl on medium speed until stiff peaks form, 2 to 3 minutes. Cover; chill until ready to use.

9. Carefully unroll cooled cake. Spread chilled pineapple filling over cake, leaving a 1/2-inch border. Reroll, using the towel to gently lift cake. Place cake, seam side down, on a platter. Spread frosting over cake; garnish with dried pineapple rings.

Pineapple Jelly Roll my favorite #
Drain (1) Can crushed Pineapple;
Save the sauce. Sprinkle 2/3c brown
sugar. Beat 4 Egg Yolks w/ 1/4 c. sugar
1/2 tsp Vanilla. Beat 4 Egg Whites 1/2 cup
sugar beat till Stiff. Fold into Yolk
Mixture. Fold 2/3 c. Flour, 1 tsp baking
Powder + 1/4 tsp salt into mixture.
Bake 12 min. @ 375°.
Sauce – Pineapple Juice
+ 1 1/2 tbsp. Cornstarch
until thickened.

COOKING SCHOOL

TIPS AND TRICKS FROM THE SOUTH'S MOST TRUSTED KITCHEN

A First-Timer's Guide to Carving the Bird

Sharpen your knife, take a breath, and follow these easy steps.

1. START WITH THE LEGS
Place the turkey breast side up. Gently pull one leg away from the body; slice through the skin. Position the knife where the leg meets the body; slice through the joint. Repeat on the other side.

2. MOVE TO THE WINGS
Just like with the legs, gently pull one wing away from the body and slice through the joint, wiggling the knife to avoid cutting through the bone. Repeat on the other side.

3. CARVE THE BREAST
Position the knife on one side of the breast bone. Slice downward, staying close to the bone and curving as you move down, to remove the breast. Repeat on the other side.

4. TRANSFER TO A PLATTER
Separate the drumsticks from the thighs by cutting between the leg joints; place on a platter. Carve each breast into diagonal slices; fan out as desired. Tuck in the wings and desired garnishes.

December

BOUNTY

In a Nutshell

Chestnuts are a delight by the handful or the slice.

CHESTNUT CAKE WITH CHESTNUT WHIPPED CREAM

Chestnut Cake with Chestnut Whipped Cream

ACTIVE 30 MIN. - TOTAL 2 HOURS, 10 MIN.
SERVES 8 TO 10

- Baking spray
- 6 Tbsp. unsalted butter, melted and cooled
- Sweetened Chestnut Puree (recipe follows), divided
- 3 large eggs, at room temperature
- ½ cup granulated sugar
- 1 cup all-purpose flour
- 2½ tsp. baking powder
- ¾ tsp. ground cinnamon
- ½ tsp. kosher salt
- ¾ cup heavy whipping cream
- 1 Tbsp. powdered sugar, plus more for dusting

1. Preheat oven to 350°F. Coat a 9-inch round cake pan with baking spray, and line bottom with parchment paper; set aside.
2. Beat together butter and 1¼ cups Sweetened Chestnut Puree in a large bowl with an electric mixer on medium speed until incorporated, about 1 minute. Add eggs and sugar and beat on medium speed until smooth, about 30 seconds; set aside.
3. Whisk together flour, baking powder, cinnamon, and salt in a small bowl. Add flour mixture to chestnut mixture; beat on low speed until just combined, about 45 seconds. Transfer batter to prepared pan; spread in an even layer.
4. Bake until golden and a wooden pick inserted in center comes out clean, about 30 minutes. Let cool in pan on wire rack 10 minutes. Remove from pan, discard parchment, and let cool completely on wire rack, about 1 hour.
5. Whisk together cream, powdered sugar, and remaining ½ cup Sweetened Chestnut Puree in a large bowl until soft peaks form, 2 to 3 minutes. Transfer cake to a platter, dust with additional powdered sugar, and serve with chestnut whipped cream.

Sweetened Chestnut Puree

ACTIVE 10 MIN. - TOTAL 30 MIN.
MAKES 1¾ CUPS

Place 1½ cups **Sugar-and-Spice Roasted Chestnuts** in a saucepan; cover with water by 1 inch. Simmer over medium-high until soft, about 10 minutes. Remove from heat; drain. Return to pan; add ½ cup each water and **granulated sugar**. Cook over medium, stirring often, until sugar is dissolved. Transfer mixture to a food processor, add 2 teaspoons **vanilla extract**; process until smooth.

Sugar-and-Spice Roasted Chestnuts

ACTIVE 45 MIN. - TOTAL 2 HOURS, 15 MIN.
MAKES ABOUT 2 CUPS

- 1 lb. fresh whole chestnuts (about 30 large)
- 2 Tbsp. granulated sugar
- ½ tsp. ground cinnamon
- ⅛ tsp. ground nutmeg
- Pinch fine sea salt
- 2 Tbsp. unsalted butter, melted

1. Place chestnuts flat side down on a cutting board. Using a serrated knife, carefully score an X on rounded side of each chestnut, cutting through the hard outer shell and inner skin. Transfer scored chestnuts to a large bowl, add water to cover, and let soak at least 1 hour and up to 4 hours.
2. Preheat oven to 400°F. Drain chestnuts, and transfer to a large rimmed baking sheet, arranging scored side up. Bake until shells and skins peel back to reveal golden flesh, 25 to 30 minutes.
3. Immediately transfer hot chestnuts to a kitchen towel; wrap tightly, and let steam 5 to 10 minutes.
4. Working quickly with one chestnut at a time (leaving the rest covered), carefully peel off and discard the hard outer shell and paperlike inner skin.
5. Stir together sugar, cinnamon, nutmeg, and salt in a small bowl until evenly combined. Transfer peeled chestnuts to a serving bowl, drizzle with melted butter, and sprinkle with sugar mixture; toss to coat. Serve warm.

Pint-Sized Pies

Sometimes the smallest gestures make the biggest impression.

M Y GREAT-UNCLE JAMES WHIPPLE, known to our tight-knit community in Chattanooga as Uncle Jimmy, had a natural gift for making children feel at ease in his presence, likely because he himself was a kid at heart. A lovable troublemaker, he's the one who taught me and my brother, Jonathon, how to cheat at cards. (If we can see your hand in any sort of reflective surface, we will take advantage.) He rarely called me by my name—only by his own moniker, "GG" for Gorgeous Girl. And most of all, he always relied on his boyish, lopsided grin—plus good old-fashioned bribery—to get his way.

He was a fantastic cook and was often in charge of bringing the desserts, namely pies, for our family's holiday meals, where he still found a way to make me and Jonathon feel special. Since he had plenty of leftover dough and filling, he baked tiny, personalized pies just for us. While I always asked for apple, my brother was faithful to chocolate. Even with the miniatures, Uncle Jimmy put in the same amount of love and attention to detail, including generous dollops of homemade whipped cream and delicate chocolate shavings. You'd never know they were crafted from scraps.

When I was in third grade, he came to my school to talk about his job in the Navy. I was a very shy kid who dreaded public speaking, so the idea of introducing him to my peers turned my stomach. Without calling attention to my panic, he gathered me in a hug, shielding me from the class in his arms, and whispered in my ear, "GG, if you do this, I'll make you whatever pie you want. You can have a whole one to yourself—a big one." I snapped my head around to see if he was joking, and all he said in response was, "I know; it'll be apple."

A couple years back, when my sister-in-law was pregnant with her first child, I was struck with the overwhelming need to pass on this tradition. However, as a novice at best in the kitchen, I was sure I wouldn't be able to replicate his desserts. Uncle Jimmy used a heavy hand

KATHERINE AND HER UNCLE JIMMY

with practically everything, especially butter, so his crusts were flaky and full of flavor. His apple filling was a deep brown, saturated with cinnamon and other warm spices, and his chocolate pie was so thick it could stick to the roof of your mouth.

Uncle Jimmy once told me he didn't bake by taste but by smell, claiming his nose could detect if he needed to adjust a recipe as he went. I didn't discover that this was a lie until nearly a decade after his death. I think I accepted it for so long because I wanted to believe there was a certain magic to his dishes only he could access. It wasn't until I was working with the Test Kitchen to dream up an iteration of his chocolate pie that I realized I didn't need to mimic his recipes perfectly. The minis were special to me because of the love and effort he put into them, transforming otherwise forgotten scraps into beautiful gifts that communicated just how much he cherished me and my brother without him having to say a word.
—Katherine Polcari

Mini Chocolate Pies

In case you don't have any pie scraps, we created this recipe that uses store-bought piecrust.

ACTIVE 50 MIN. - TOTAL 3 HOURS, 20 MIN.
SERVES 12

- 1 (14.1-oz.) pkg. refrigerated piecrusts (2 crusts)
- 1 cup half-and-half
- 2 large egg yolks
- 1/4 cup packed light brown sugar
- 1 Tbsp. cornstarch
- 1 Tbsp. unsweetened cocoa
- 1/4 tsp. fine instant espresso powder (optional)
- 1/2 cup finely chopped semisweet chocolate
- 3 Tbsp. butter, cubed
- 1 tsp. vanilla extract
- Sweetened whipped cream
- Shaved semisweet chocolate

1. Preheat oven to 350°F. Unroll both piecrusts on a work surface; cut into 8 circles using a 4½-inch cutter. Reroll scraps; cut 4 more rounds. Discard remaining scraps.
2. Place dough rounds in the wells of a 12-cup muffin tray, pressing into the bottoms and up the sides, pleating edges as needed. Freeze until firm, about 10 minutes.
3. Place paper liners in wells; fill each to the top with pie weights or dried beans. Bake until edges of crusts are set, 10 minutes. Remove liners and weights; bake until golden, 10 to 12 minutes. Let cool 30 minutes in tray on a wire rack.
4. Heat half-and-half in a small saucepan over medium-low, whisking often, until steaming, 2 to 3 minutes. Stir together egg yolks, brown sugar, cornstarch, cocoa, and espresso powder (if using) in a medium bowl until well combined. Whisking constantly, gradually add warm half-and-half to egg yolk mixture until well combined.
5. Transfer egg mixture to saucepan; cook, whisking constantly, over medium-low until thickened and bubbles break the surface, 2 to 3 minutes. Remove from heat; whisk in chocolate, butter, and vanilla until smooth.
6. Spoon chocolate mixture into prepared crusts in muffin tray (about 2 tablespoons per crust). Cover and refrigerate until set, 1 hour, 30 minutes to 2 hours. Just before serving, garnish with whipped cream and shaved chocolate.

FAMILY FAVORITES

It's Not a Celebration Without "The Cake"

Atlanta chef Demetrius Brown shares his great-grandmother's recipe and the secret ingredient that makes it turn out just right.

CHEF DEMETRIUS BROWN literally outgrew his original dream job. "I always wanted to be a mechanic," he says. "The taller I got, though, the harder it was to work on cars." (Brown stands at six-foot-three, for reference.)

A steady diet of the Food Network, including Rachael Ray, Alton Brown, and Bobby Flay—who he would go on to beat on his eponymous competition show—helped foster his plan B career path. As much as Brown enjoyed the aspirational side of cooking, his interest in the craft was also practical; his mother worked two or three jobs to support him and his siblings growing up, which meant Brown prepared a lot of the family's meals. Spaghetti was one of his go-to dishes, and as a budding chef, of course he had to add his own twist—in this case, a squirt of Sriracha.

Television wasn't his only instructor in the kitchen. The matriarchs on both sides of his family guided him, including his great-grandmother Levinia Bright, whose legacy is remembered through a dessert his family lovingly calls "The Cake." At first glance, the spiced apple Bundt might seem like many others you've seen at potlucks, but this one has an unexpected component: mayonnaise. While the condiment is often used in Southern-style chocolate cakes, it's not typically found in other baked goods.

Brown's mother, Cotia Banson, discovered the recipe among her grandmother's belongings after Bright passed. Banson fondly remembers her mother making it during the holidays, so she decided to take up the tradition every Thanksgiving and Christmas, no matter what else is served. She faithfully prepares it to Bright's specifications, down to the Hellmann's, which is called out by name in the ingredient list. It's a quirky detail that the family never got a chance to ask Bright about, but it turns out that the brand makes a big difference.

Brown has tried the recipe with just about every alternative, from Duke's to Miracle Whip and even homemade mayonnaise—inexplicably, it just never turns out right. "I only buy Hellmann's for this cake," says Brown. You won't taste a hint of it in the Bundt, however, only the tender pieces of apples perfectly accented by cinnamon, nutmeg, and the sharpness of fresh ginger. Instead of flavor, the condiment gives the dessert a velvety, soft crumb the same way oil traditionally would.

CHEF DEMETRIUS BROWN OF BREAD & BUTTERFLY IN ATLANTA

This treasured recipe has even appeared on the menu at Bread & Butterfly, the Atlanta restaurant Brown took over in August 2023. The business remains a French-inspired bistro by day, and by night, it transitions to a menu that draws on his Caribbean heritage, with dishes such as Haitian beef patties with puff pastry, tamarind, and peppers or plantain buns with cane syrup butter.

"During the pandemic was really when I started to shift into making food from the African diaspora because I just missed my grandmother," says Brown. "And although the names may seem exotic, all the ingredients that we are using are mostly local, mostly easily accessible to anybody. Once you taste it, you can always draw a parallel to a childhood memory."

The Cake is also set to be featured in his forthcoming restaurant, Heritage Supper Club. It just won't look quite like his great-grandma's did. Instead, Brown will flex his Johnson & Wales University training and serve it with goat cheese and an agrodolce—because in some ways, he's still that kid experimenting in the kitchen.

"The Cake"

ACTIVE 25 MIN. - TOTAL 1 HOUR, 35 MIN., PLUS 2 HOURS COOLING

SERVES 10 TO 12

- Baking spray
- 2 large eggs
- 1¼ cups granulated sugar
- 1½ cups Hellmann's mayonnaise
- ¼ cup whole milk
- 1 tsp. freshly grated ginger
- 3½ cups all-purpose flour
- 1 Tbsp. baking soda
- ¾ tsp. ground cinnamon
- ½ tsp. ground nutmeg
- ½ tsp. kosher salt
- 3 cups chopped peeled apples (from 3 small Gala or Pink Lady apples)
- 2 cups toasted chopped walnuts
- ¾ cup raisins
- Powdered sugar

1. Preheat oven to 325°F. Generously coat a 12-cup Bundt pan with baking spray; set aside.

2. Beat together eggs and sugar with a stand mixer fitted with paddle attachment on medium speed until pale and fluffy, about 5 minutes. Add mayonnaise, milk, and ginger; beat on low speed until just combined, about 15 seconds.

3. Whisk together flour, baking soda, cinnamon, nutmeg, and salt in a medium bowl. Fold flour mixture into egg mixture until just combined. Fold in apples, walnuts, and raisins until evenly distributed (batter will be thick). Transfer batter to prepared pan; spread into an even layer with a small offset spatula.

4. Bake, rotating pan front to back halfway through, until a wooden pick inserted near center comes out with a few moist crumbs, 55 to 60 minutes. Let cake cool in pan on a wire rack 15 minutes. Invert cake onto wire rack; remove pan. Let cake cool completely, about 2 hours. Dust with powdered sugar. Slice and serve.

Holiday Greenery

'Tis time to let the winter veggies shine in these five delicious party appetizers.

SOUTHERN PESTO PULL-APART BREAD (PAGE 279)

HOPPIN' JOHN ROLLS
(PAGE 283)

SAUSAGE-AND-GREENS BALLS

Sausage-and-Greens Balls

ACTIVE 25 MIN. - TOTAL 45 MIN.

MAKES ABOUT 40 BALLS

- **10** cups chopped mustard greens
- **2** cups all-purpose baking mix (such as Bisquick)
- **1** lb. mild pork breakfast sausage
- **1** lb. sharp Cheddar cheese, shredded (4 cups)

1. Preheat oven to 350°F. Line a large rimmed baking sheet with parchment paper.
2. Place greens in a large microwavable bowl; cover using plastic wrap, and pierce wrap once to vent. Microwave on HIGH until wilted, about 3 minutes. Place greens on a double layer of paper towels. Let cool 5 minutes. Pat greens dry; finely chop.
3. Place baking mix in a large bowl; add sausage, and mix well using hands until thoroughly combined. Add cheese and chopped greens; knead until mixture holds together when squeezed.
4. Shape mixture into about 40 golf ball-size balls; space 1 inch apart on prepared baking sheet. Bake until lightly golden on top, 20 to 22 minutes.

Southern Pesto Pull-Apart Bread

(Photo, page 276)

ACTIVE 45 MIN. - TOTAL 1 HOUR, 15 MIN.

SERVES 16

- **5** cups loosely packed chopped mustard greens (from 1 bunch)
- **½** cup chopped toasted pecans
- **3** garlic cloves, chopped (about 1 Tbsp.)
- **½** tsp. crushed red pepper
- **¾** tsp. plus ⅛ tsp. kosher salt, divided
- **½** cup grated Parmesan cheese (2 oz.)
- **¾** tsp. grated lemon zest plus 1 Tbsp. fresh juice (from 1 lemon), divided
- **¾** cup extra-virgin olive oil, divided
- **4** (8-oz.) cans crescent roll dough, at room temperature
- All-purpose flour, for work surface
- **2** Tbsp. unsalted butter, melted
- Flaky sea salt

1. Preheat oven to 350°F. Line a large baking sheet with parchment paper. Cook greens in boiling salted water until just wilted and bright green, 30 seconds to 1 minute. Drain well. Arrange greens on a double layer of paper towels, and let cool slightly, about 2 minutes; squeeze greens to extract as much liquid as possible. Set aside.
2. Pulse together pecans and garlic in a food processor until finely chopped, about 10 pulses. Add greens, crushed red pepper, and ¾ teaspoon kosher salt; pulse until finely chopped. Add cheese and lemon zest; pulse until just combined. With processor running, gradually add ½ cup oil until combined, 15 to 20 seconds.
3. Form each can of dough into a ball; roll each ball into an 11-inch round on a lightly floured work surface. Place a 10-inch dinner plate on top of each dough round; trim each round into a perfect circle. Place 1 dough circle on prepared baking sheet; spread ⅓ cup pesto over dough, leaving a ¼-inch border. Repeat with pesto and dough circles 2 more times; place last dough circle on top. Reserve remaining pesto.
4. Place a 3-inch round ramekin or cup in center of dough stack. Cut dough into 4 equal quadrants, cutting from the ramekin outward, leaving center intact. Cut each quadrant into 4 equal pieces to yield 16 pieces. Pick up 2 adjacent dough pieces; twist 2 times in opposite directions (counterclockwise and clockwise). Pinch ends of the twisted pieces together to seal. Repeat with remaining dough pieces.
5. Bake until browned, about 30 minutes. While bread bakes, stir lemon juice and remaining ¼ cup olive oil and ⅛ teaspoon kosher salt into reserved pesto. Brush baked bread with melted butter; sprinkle with flaky sea salt. Serve with pesto mixture.

Do the Twist

Turn crescent roll dough into a festive appetizer in three easy steps.

Step 1 Place a 3-inch round ramekin or cup in center of dough stack. Cut dough into 4 equal quadrants, cutting from the ramekin outward and leaving center intact.

Step 2 Cut each quadrant into 4 equal pieces to yield 16 pieces.

Step 3 Pick up 2 adjacent dough pieces; twist each one 2 times in opposite directions (counterclockwise and clockwise). Pinch ends of twisted pieces together to seal. Repeat with remaining pieces.

COLLARD GREEN FRITTERS WITH SMOKY DIPPING SAUCE (PAGE 283)

WARM TURNIP GREENS-AND-COUNTRY HAM DIP (PAGE 283)

SAUSAGE-AND-GREENS BALLS (PAGE 279)

HOPPIN' JOHN ROLLS

Hoppin' John Rolls

This handheld twist on hoppin' John is a great appetizer for New Year's Eve.

ACTIVE 40 MIN. - TOTAL 55 MIN.

MAKES ABOUT 2 DOZEN ROLLS

- 24 large turnip green leaves (from 2 [1-lb.] bunches), rinsed (not patted dry)
- 2 oz. cream cheese, softened
- 8 thick-cut bacon slices, cooked and crumbled (about 3/4 cup)
- 1/3 cup thinly sliced scallions (from 3 scallions)
- 1/2 tsp. kosher salt
- 1/2 tsp. black pepper
- 1 (15-oz.) can seasoned black-eyed peas, drained
- 1 1/2 cups cooked long-grain white rice, warmed
- Toasted sesame seeds
- Hot sauce and lemon wedges, for serving

1. Trim stems from turnip green leaves; place stems in an even layer in the bottom of a large skillet with a lid. Stack trimmed leaves on a microwavable plate; cover loosely using plastic wrap. Microwave on HIGH until wilted, about 2 minutes. Uncover and set leaves aside.
2. Stir together cream cheese, bacon, scallions, salt, and pepper in a large bowl. Add peas and rice; stir well to combine.
3. Arrange 1 leaf on a work surface, vein side up. Spoon about 2 tablespoons rice mixture onto leaf, leaving a 1-inch border at bottom. Starting at the bottom, roll the end of the leaf so that it just overlaps the filling. Tuck in the sides of the leaf; roll tightly into a cigar shape. Place roll in prepared skillet, seam side down. Repeat with remaining leaves and filling.
4. Pour 2/3 cup water over rolls in skillet. Bring to a boil over medium-high. Cover and reduce heat to medium-low; let steam until heated through, 10 minutes. Uncover and let cool for 5 minutes. Sprinkle rolls with sesame seeds, and serve with hot sauce and lemon wedges.

Collard Green Fritters with Smoky Dipping Sauce

(Photo, page 280)

ACTIVE 50 MIN. - TOTAL 50 MIN.

SERVES 6

SMOKY DIPPING SAUCE

- 1/2 cup mayonnaise
- 2 Tbsp. sour cream
- 1 tsp. pepper vinegar
- 1/2 tsp. garlic powder
- 1/2 tsp. smoked paprika
- 1/8 tsp. cayenne pepper

COLLARD GREEN FRITTERS

- 1/2 cup all-purpose flour
- 1/2 cup cornstarch
- 3/4 tsp. kosher salt
- 1/2 tsp. baking powder
- 1/2 tsp. black pepper
- 1/2 cup shredded white Cheddar cheese
- 3 cups finely chopped collard greens with stems (about 5 large leaves)
- 1 cup thinly sliced sweet onion (from 1 onion)
- 2 cups canola oil or vegetable oil

1. Prepare the Smoky Dipping Sauce: Stir together all sauce ingredients in a small bowl until smooth. Cover and refrigerate until ready to serve.
2. Prepare the Collard Green Fritters: Whisk together flour, cornstarch, salt, baking powder, and black pepper in a large bowl. Whisk in 3/4 cup cold water until smooth; stir in cheese. Add collards and onion; toss gently to coat.
3. Heat oil in a large skillet over medium-high to 325°F. Working in batches, use a 1/4-cup measure to add 4 portions of greens mixture into hot oil; press to flatten slightly. Fry until lightly golden, about 3 minutes per side. Drain on paper towels. Repeat with remaining batter. Transfer fritters to a platter; serve hot with Smoky Dipping Sauce.

Warm Turnip Greens–and–Country Ham Dip

(Photo, page 281)

ACTIVE 25 MIN. - TOTAL 40 MIN.

SERVES 12

- 3 Tbsp. unsalted butter
- 4 garlic cloves, finely chopped (about 4 tsp.)
- 1/2 tsp. crushed red pepper
- 8 oz. coarsely chopped turnip greens with stems (about 8 cups)
- 1 cup finely chopped country ham (about 5 1/4 oz.)
- 8 oz. cream cheese, softened
- 1 cup mayonnaise
- 1/2 cup chopped scallions (from 3 scallions)
- 6 oz. Swiss cheese, shredded (1 1/2 cups)
- 12 round buttery crackers (such as Ritz), crushed (about 2/3 cup)
- Crackers and/or crostini, for serving

1. Preheat oven to 350°F. Melt butter in a 10-inch cast-iron skillet over medium. Add garlic and crushed red pepper to skillet; cook until fragrant, about 30 seconds. Gradually add greens, stirring until wilted, about 5 minutes. Spread greens mixture on a double layer of paper towels; let cool slightly, about 5 minutes. Do not wipe skillet clean.
2. While mixture is cooling, add ham to skillet; cook over medium, stirring often, until browned, 3 to 4 minutes. Add cream cheese; stir until melted, about 1 minute. Stir in mayonnaise, scallions, and Swiss cheese until just combined. Remove from heat.
3. Squeeze greens mixture to remove as much excess liquid as possible; finely chop. Stir greens into skillet. Sprinkle with crushed crackers.
4. Bake until just bubbly around edges, about 15 minutes. Serve with crackers and/or crostini.

All Wrapped Up

Our Test Kitchen's twist on an old-school favorite is fancy and foolproof.

Southern-Style Beef Wellington

ACTIVE 1 HOUR, 20 MIN. - TOTAL 3 HOURS, 30 MIN.

SERVES 6 TO 8

- 1 (2½-lb.) center-cut beef tenderloin, trimmed
- 1 Tbsp. plus ½ tsp. kosher salt, divided
- 3 Tbsp. canola oil, divided
- 3 Tbsp. country-style Dijon mustard
- 1 yellow onion, chopped (about 1¼ cups)
- 16 cups loosely packed stemmed, chopped fresh mustard greens (from 3 [8-oz.] bunches)
- 4 garlic cloves, finely chopped (about 2 Tbsp.)
- 1 Tbsp. Worcestershire sauce
- ½ tsp. crushed red pepper
- 8 slices prosciutto (about 4 oz.)
- 1 (17.3-oz.) pkg. frozen puff pastry, thawed (2 sheets) (such as Pepperidge Farm)
- All-purpose flour, for surface
- 1 large egg, beaten
- Flaky sea salt

1. Tie tenderloin crosswise at 2-inch intervals with kitchen twine. Sprinkle evenly with 1 tablespoon kosher salt. Place on a baking sheet, and let stand at room temperature for 30 minutes.

2. Heat 2 tablespoons oil in a 12-inch cast-iron skillet over medium-high. Pat tenderloin dry. Cook, turning occasionally, until browned on all sides, about 8 minutes. Return to baking sheet; let cool about 15 minutes. Remove and discard twine. Brush tenderloin with mustard. Refrigerate, uncovered, 30 minutes to 3 hours.

3. Wipe skillet clean. Heat 1 tablespoon oil in skillet over medium. Add onion; cook, stirring often, until browned, 8 to 10 minutes. Working in batches, add greens to skillet. Cook, stirring often, until moisture is evaporated, about 12 minutes. Add garlic, Worcestershire sauce, red pepper, and remaining ½ teaspoon kosher salt; cook, stirring constantly, about 2 minutes. Remove from heat; let cool 30 minutes. Pat greens mixture dry.

4. Preheat oven to 425°F. Overlap 2 sheets of plastic wrap on a work surface to make a large rectangle. Place prosciutto on plastic in 2 rows of 4 slices each, overlapping slightly to create a 12-inch square (see illustrations, right). Spread greens over prosciutto. Place tenderloin near center of square; use edges of plastic to tightly wrap prosciutto around tenderloin. Twist ends to tighten.

5. Roll out 1 sheet of puff pastry on a lightly floured work surface into a 15- x 12-inch rectangle. Brush top third of pastry with beaten egg. Remove plastic wrap from tenderloin; place lengthwise along opposite end of pastry. Roll pastry and tenderloin together until pastry overlaps and tenderloin is encased; pinch seam to seal. Turn seam side down; trim ends, leaving enough pastry to fold down and encase tenderloin. Pinch seams to seal. Roll out remaining pastry sheet; cut into desired shapes, such as bows, ribbons, or stars.

6. Transfer pastry-wrapped tenderloin to a parchment paper-lined baking sheet. Brush with beaten egg; top with pastry cutouts as desired. Using a knife, lightly score pastry around cutouts about ¼ inch deep. Sprinkle with flaky sea salt. Bake until pastry is browned and a thermometer inserted into center of tenderloin registers 120°F (for rare), 35 to 40 minutes, or until desired degree of doneness, covering with foil after 30 minutes if pastry becomes too dark. Transfer to a platter or cutting board; let rest 15 minutes. Using a serrated knife, cut into slices and serve.

Wrap and Roll Like a Pro

1. Place prosciutto on top of plastic wrap in rows, overlapping slightly to create a 12-inch square with no gaps. Spread mustard greens over prosciutto in an even layer.

2. Place tenderloin lengthwise near center of square. Using the edges of plastic wrap, tightly wrap prosciutto around tenderloin. Twist ends of plastic wrap to seal.

3. Brush top third of pastry with beaten egg. Remove and discard plastic wrap; place tenderloin lengthwise on opposite end of pastry. Roll together until encased.

4. Turn seam side down, and trim ends. Fold down excess pastry over ends of tenderloin, pinching seams to seal. Decorate exterior with pastry cutouts as desired.

A layer of garlicky mustard greens gives this elegant and classic special-occasion dish a distinctly Southern flavor.

Brown Butter Mashed Potatoes

ACTIVE 20 MIN. - TOTAL 45 MIN.

SERVES 6 TO 8

Melt 1 cup **unsalted butter** in a small saucepan over medium-low; cook, stirring often, until golden brown and nutty, 8 to 10 minutes. Pour into a heatproof bowl; set aside. Cook 4 lb. peeled and chopped **russet potatoes** in boiling salted water until tender when pierced with a fork, 15 to 20 minutes. Drain and return to hot pot. Stir and mash using a potato masher until most of the steam has escaped, about 1 minute. Gradually add ⅔ cup warm brown butter while mashing potatoes. Stir in 1½ cups warm **half-and-half,** 1½ tsp. **kosher salt,** 1 tsp. **garlic powder,** and ½ tsp. **black pepper** until smooth. Spoon potatoes into a bowl, and drizzle with remaining warm brown butter. Sprinkle with sliced **fresh chives, flaky salt,** and **black pepper.**

Maple-Dijon Roasted Carrots

ACTIVE 10 MIN. - TOTAL 40 MIN.

SERVES 6

Whisk together 3 Tbsp. each **olive oil** and **pure maple syrup**, 2 Tbsp. each **Dijon mustard** and **fresh orange juice**, 1 tsp. **kosher salt**, and ¾ tsp. **black pepper** in a small bowl. Place 2 lb. trimmed **multicolor carrots** in an even layer on a parchment paper-lined baking sheet; pour ½ cup of the maple syrup mixture over carrots. Add 1 tsp. **kosher salt**, and toss to coat. Bake at 425°F until tender and caramelized, about 30 minutes, tossing twice during baking. Transfer to a platter. Drizzle with remaining 2 Tbsp. maple syrup mixture; season to taste with additional **kosher salt**. Garnish with **fresh thyme** leaves and **orange zest**.

A Lowcountry Christmas

Sweeten the holidays with a cheerful cake inspired by the Holy City.

Holiday Mahogany Cake

ACTIVE 1 HOUR, 5 MIN. · TOTAL 3 HOURS, 5 MIN.
SERVES 12

- 3⅓ cups bleached cake flour
- 5 Tbsp. unsweetened cocoa powder
- 1½ tsp. baking soda
- 1 tsp. kosher salt
- ¾ cup unsalted butter, softened
- 2¼ cups granulated sugar
- ½ cup canola oil
- 2 tsp. vanilla extract
- 3 large eggs, at room temperature
- 1 large egg yolk, at room temperature
- 2 cups whole buttermilk, at room temperature
- Ermine Frosting (recipe, page 293)
- Decorated Sugar Cookies (recipe, page 294)

1. Preheat oven to 350°F. Coat 3 (8-inch) round cake pans with cooking spray; line bottoms of pans with parchment paper, and coat parchment with cooking spray.

2. Sift together flour, cocoa, and baking soda into a medium bowl; whisk in salt. Beat butter with a stand mixer fitted with a paddle attachment on medium speed until light and smooth, 2 to 3 minutes. Add sugar, oil, and vanilla; beat on medium speed until fluffy, about 2 minutes. Beat in eggs and egg yolk, 1 at a time, beating well after each addition.

3. With mixer on low speed, gradually add flour mixture to butter mixture alternately with buttermilk, beginning and ending with flour mixture. Divide batter among prepared cake pans (about 3¼ cups each); smooth tops. Tap cake pans on countertop several times to release any air bubbles.

4. Bake until a wooden pick inserted into centers comes out clean, about 30 minutes. Let cool in pans on wire racks about 10 minutes. Run a knife around edges to loosen. Invert cakes onto racks; remove and discard parchment. Let cool 1 hour. Trim cake layers flat with a serrated knife.

5. Place 1 cake layer on a plate; spread 1⅓ cups of the Ermine Frosting evenly on top. Repeat once. Top with remaining layer, trimmed side down. Spread a thin layer of frosting over top and sides of cake to create a crumb coat. Chill, uncovered, until firm, about 20 minutes.

6. Spread remaining frosting over top and sides of cake. Decorate sides and top of cake with Decorated Sugar Cookies as desired.

It's almost too pretty to eat—almost! Open these festive doors to a moist, tender, buttermilk-infused take on "velvet cake." Mahogany cake may not be as familiar as red velvet, but this spectacular cake gives it its due.

DECORATED SUGAR COOKIES

(PAGE 294)

The South's Original Chocolate Cake

Unlike the deep, dark crumb of devil's food, mahogany cake is a reddish-brown color reminiscent of its namesake wood. Often considered the original chocolate cake, the hallmark of this vintage recipe is its ultrasoft and tender crumb, a result of combining buttermilk and baking soda—a late Victorian-era trick for creating what were known as "velvet cakes." As the recipe evolved, red velvet was born. The earliest renditions of this Southern favorite were made with a standard mahogany cake batter tinted with either beet juice or food coloring.

The traditional pairing for both mahogany and early red velvet cakes is Ermine Frosting. Also known as "boiled-milk frosting," it is one of the lightest icings you'll find. Subtly sweet, with a silky whipped texture, it spreads like a dream. Before powdered sugar was widely available, clever cooks turned to milk and cooked flour as a base. When combined, the ingredients create a thick and luscious frosting with much less butter and sugar, which were both expensive and later rationed during wartime.

Ermine Frosting

ACTIVE 20 MIN. - TOTAL 1 HOUR, 20 MIN.

MAKES 6 TO 7 CUPS

- 2 cups granulated sugar
- 2/3 cup all-purpose flour
- 1/2 tsp. kosher salt
- 2 cups whole milk
- 2 cups unsalted butter, softened
- 2 tsp. vanilla extract

1. Whisk together sugar, flour, and salt in a medium saucepan. Gradually whisk in milk until no lumps remain. Cook, whisking constantly, over medium-high until mixture starts to bubble and is thicker than gravy but looser than pudding, 6 to 8 minutes.

2. Spread mixture into a 13- x 9-inch baking dish; press a piece of plastic wrap directly on surface to prevent a skin from forming. Refrigerate until cooled to room temperature, at least 1 hour or up to 24 hours.

3. Beat butter with a stand mixer fitted with a paddle attachment on medium speed until creamy, about 2 minutes. With mixer on medium speed, add cooled milk mixture in heaping spoonfuls, beating until smooth, 3 to 4 minutes. Beat in vanilla until combined.

4. Switch to a whisk attachment. Increase mixer speed to medium-high, and beat until light and fluffy, 2 to 4 minutes. Reduce mixer speed to low; beat for 5 minutes to remove excess air bubbles. Use immediately, or cover and refrigerate for up to 5 days. (Let frosting come back to room temperature and rewhip before using.)

Decorated Sugar Cookies

To help the cookies stand up on the top of the cake, press a 6-inch wooden skewer into each desired cutout before baking.

ACTIVE 45 MIN. - TOTAL 2 HOURS

MAKES 2½ TO 3 DOZEN

- 1 **cup powdered sugar, plus more as needed**
- ¾ **cup unsalted butter, softened**
- ¼ **cup granulated sugar**
- 1 **large egg, at room temperature**
- 1 **tsp. vanilla extract**
- 2½ **cups all-purpose flour, plus more as needed**
- ¼ **tsp. kosher salt**
- ¼ **tsp. baking soda**
- **Royal Icing (recipe below)**
- **Gold dragées (optional)**

1. Preheat oven to 375°F. Beat powdered sugar, butter, and granulated sugar with a stand mixer fitted with a paddle attachment on low speed just until combined. Increase mixer speed to medium-low; beat until light and fluffy, 2 to 3 minutes. Beat in egg and vanilla on medium-low speed until combined.
2. Whisk together flour, salt, and baking soda in a medium bowl. Reduce mixer speed to low; gradually add flour mixture to powdered sugar mixture, beating until dough just comes together, 1 to 2 minutes. Divide dough in half.
3. Working with 1 dough half at a time, roll out dough on lightly floured surface to ⅛-inch thickness. Using lightly floured cookie cutters, cut dough into desired shapes. Transfer to a parchment paper-lined baking sheet, spacing ¾ inch apart. Repeat process with remaining dough half.
4. Bake in batches until edges are lightly golden, 9 to 11 minutes. Remove from oven, and let cool on pan 5 minutes. Transfer cookies to wire racks, and let cool completely, about 30 minutes. Decorate with Royal Icing and dragées, if desired.

Royal Icing

ACTIVE 10 MIN. - TOTAL 10 MIN.

MAKES ABOUT 3 CUPS

Beat 6 cups powdered sugar, ½ cup water, ¼ cup meringue powder, and 2 tsp. vanilla extract with a stand mixer fitted with a paddle attachment on low speed just until combined. Increase mixer speed to medium, and beat until smooth and stiff, 30 seconds to 1 minute (mixture should hold stiff peaks). Use immediately, or store in an airtight container for up to 5 days.

Pipe delicate decor like garlands directly on the cookies.

For snowy trees, pipe a dot of white, then smudge downward with your fingertip.

Pipe elements like wreaths and topiaries onto parchment. Let dry, then peel off and apply to the doors with more icing.

Time to Decorate!

The secret to creating these festive cookies is to take your time. Follow the steps below to create your own signature designs.

1. Divide Royal Icing into bowls. Tint as desired (see right); thin with ¼ teaspoon water at a time as needed. Transfer to piping bags; snip a ⅛-inch hole in tips. If creating a window, pipe a rectangle of Haint Blue icing. Let set 1 hour. Pipe a thin border of desired icing color around cookie edge. Pipe window outline as desired.

2. Pipe same color icing to fill space within border, using a wooden pick to spread into an even layer, if needed. Add gold dragées for doorknobs. Repeat as needed with remaining cookies and various colors of Royal Icing. Let stand, uncovered, until icing is set, about 1 hour.

3. Use the same color icing to pipe additional details, like panels on doors and outlines for windows (see cookies at left). Let stand until icing is set, at least 6 hours.

4. To add details like topiaries, thicken icing gradually with powdered sugar until it holds soft peaks. Pipe directly onto cookies. (For more control, pipe onto parchment paper. Let dry 4 hours; peel and apply to cookies with more icing.)

The Lowcountry Palette

For the perfect hue, mix Wilton gel-base icing colors with ½ cup Royal Icing.

TOWN HOUSE TURQUOISE
2 drops Mint Green
+ 1 drop Turquoise

HAINT BLUE
1 drop Royal Blue

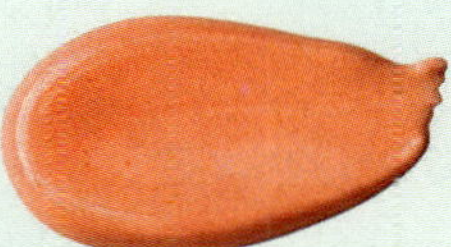

CREOLE PINK
1 drop Creamy Peach
+ 2 drops Pink

HOLLY BERRY RED
4 drops Red-Red

MAGNOLIA GREEN
3 drops Forest Green

GOLDENROD
3 drops Golden Yellow
+ 1 drop Brown

Candy Crush

Dress up your holiday cookies with a stocking's worth of sugary treats.

CHRISTMAS BLONDIES (PAGE 303)

STAINED GLASS STARS
(PAGE 302)

CHEWY PEANUT BUTTER-PISTACHIO COOKIES (PAGE 303)

Whether they're cutouts, dropped, shaped, rolled, or baked into a brownie or bar, cookies are the stars of the holiday dessert spread.

CINNAMON JELLY BEAN WREATHS (PAGE 302)

Make a Better Batch

Follow these tips for bakery-worthy results at home.

Mix Thoroughly
When stirring cookie dough, scrape down the sides of the bowl and fold in any unincorporated ingredients from the bottom with a spatula.

Rotate the Pans
When making more than one batch of cookies at a time, place racks in the top and bottom third positions of the oven. Rotate baking sheets from top to bottom and front to back halfway through the bake time.

Stay Cool
Cold cookie dough is easier to work with, so be sure to chill any scraps before rerolling.

Rest the Dough
If it has been refrigerated overnight, place it on the counter at room temperature for 15 minutes before rolling.

Top It Off
To easily and evenly crush candies for decorating, place individual flavors in separate ziplock plastic freezer bags; seal almost completely, and wrap each bag loosely in a kitchen towel. Using a rolling pin, smash candies into desired size. Transfer each flavor to its own small bowl.

PEPPERMINT DOUBLE-CHOCOLATE COOKIES (PAGE 303)

CARAMEL SNICKERDOODLES
(PAGE 302)

Stained Glass Stars

(Photo, page 297)

You'll find that many recipes for stained glass cookies use fruity candies for a vibrant look. We used butterscotch and cinnamon disks for more holiday flavor.

ACTIVE 45 MIN. - TOTAL 2 HOURS, 55 MIN.

MAKES ABOUT 2½ DOZEN

- 1 cup unsalted butter, softened
- 1 cup granulated sugar
- 2 large eggs, at room temperature
- 1 Tbsp. vanilla extract
- 3 cups all-purpose flour, plus more for dusting
- 2 tsp. baking powder
- 1 tsp. kosher salt
- ½ tsp. ground cardamom
- ½ cup finely crushed hard cinnamon candies or butterscotch disk candies (about 20 pieces)

1. Beat butter and sugar with a stand mixer fitted with a paddle attachment on medium speed until creamy, about 1 minute. Add eggs, 1 at a time, beating until incorporated. Beat in vanilla until combined.

2. Whisk together flour, baking powder, salt, and cardamom in a medium bowl; gradually add to butter mixture, beating on low speed just until combined. Divide dough in half; transfer each half to a sheet of plastic wrap, and shape each into a 6-inch disk. Wrap in plastic; refrigerate at least 1 hour or up to 1 week.

3. Preheat oven to 350°F. Working with 1 disk at a time, unwrap dough and roll on a lightly floured work surface to ¼-inch thickness. Cut dough using a 3-inch star cutter; place about 1 inch apart on large parchment paper-lined baking sheets (about 15 cookies per sheet). Cut centers from each large star using a 1¼- to 1½-inch star cutter. (Centers may be baked separately, according to instructions below, or reserved and rerolled with scraps to make additional large star cookies.)

4. Spoon about ¼ to ½ teaspoon of crushed candy in center opening of each star, using only 1 flavor per star. (Do not mix candies.) Bake, 1 pan at a time, until edges are lightly golden brown, 9 to 10 minutes. Let cool on pan on a wire rack about 10 minutes; transfer cookies to rack, and let cool 30 minutes. Repeat process with remaining dough disk.

Cinnamon Jelly Bean Wreaths

(Photo, page 299)

These festive desserts are dotted with cinnamon jelly beans for a cozy accent.

ACTIVE 30 MIN. - TOTAL 2 HOURS, 15 MIN.

MAKES ABOUT 2½ DOZEN

- 1 cup unsalted butter, softened
- ½ cup granulated sugar
- 1 large egg yolk
- 2 tsp. vanilla extract
- ⅛ tsp. green food coloring gel or paste
- 2¼ cups all-purpose flour, plus more for dusting
- ¼ cup cornstarch
- 1 tsp. kosher salt
- ½ tsp. ground cinnamon
- ½ cup cinnamon-flavor jelly beans, halved crosswise
- Powdered sugar

1. Beat butter and sugar with a stand mixer fitted with a paddle attachment on medium speed until smooth and creamy, about 1 minute. Add egg yolk, vanilla, and food coloring; beat just until combined, about 10 seconds. Whisk together flour, cornstarch, salt, and ground cinnamon in a medium bowl; gradually add to butter mixture, beating on low speed just until combined.

2. Divide dough in half; transfer each half to a sheet of plastic wrap, and shape each into a 1-inch-thick disk. Wrap in plastic; refrigerate at least 1 hour or up to 1 week.

3. Preheat oven to 350°F. Working with 1 disk at a time, unwrap dough and roll on a lightly floured work surface to ¼-inch thickness. Cut dough using a 2½- to 3-inch fluted round cutter; place about 1 inch apart on large parchment paper-lined baking sheets (about 16 cookies per sheet). Use a 1-inch fluted round cutter to cut out centers from wreaths. (Centers may be baked separately, according to instructions below, or reserved and rerolled with scraps to make more wreaths.)

4. Bake, 1 pan at a time, until cookies are just set, about 9 minutes. Remove from oven; carefully press 5 jelly bean halves, cut sides down, into each cookie. Return to oven, and bake 1 to 2 minutes more. Let cool on pan on a wire rack about 5 minutes; transfer cookies to rack, and let cool 20 minutes. Repeat with remaining dough disk. Dust cookies with powdered sugar before serving. Store cookies at room temperature in an airtight container up to 3 days.

Caramel Snickerdoodles

(Photo, page 301)

It's an unofficial rule that Southern grandmothers must keep a caramel hard candy tucked in their pocketbooks at all times. We use them to add richness to these classic cookies.

ACTIVE 20 MIN. - TOTAL 1 HOUR, 30 MIN.

MAKES ABOUT 3 DOZEN

- 1 cup unsalted butter, softened
- ½ cup packed light brown sugar
- 1¼ cups granulated sugar, divided
- 2 large eggs, at room temperature
- 3 cups all-purpose flour
- 2 tsp. cream of tartar
- 1½ tsp. baking soda
- ½ tsp. kosher salt
- 1 cup crushed hard caramel candies (such as Werther's Original) (about 40 pieces)
- 2 tsp. ground cinnamon

1. Preheat oven to 375°F. Beat butter, brown sugar, and ¾ cup granulated sugar with a stand mixer fitted with a paddle attachment on medium speed until light and fluffy, about 2 minutes. Add eggs, 1 at a time, beating just until combined, about 15 seconds.

2. Whisk together flour, cream of tartar, baking soda, and salt in a medium bowl. With mixer on low speed, gradually add to butter mixture, beating just until combined. Fold in caramel candies using a spatula, being sure to scrape down sides and bottom of bowl.

3. Stir together cinnamon and remaining ½ cup granulated sugar in a small bowl. Scoop dough using a 2-tablespoon scoop, and roll in cinnamon-sugar mixture. Place 3 inches apart on large baking sheets lined with parchment paper (about a dozen cookies per pan).

4. Bake, 1 pan at a time, until bottoms are light golden brown, about 10 minutes. Let cool on pan on a wire rack about 10 minutes; transfer cookies to rack, and let cool completely, about 30 minutes. Repeat process with remaining dough. Store at room temperature in an airtight container up to 3 days.

Peppermint Double-Chocolate Cookies

(Photo, page 300)

Unlike their hard candy cousins, soft peppermints dissolve on your tongue, making them the ideal stir-in for these deeply chocolate cookies.

ACTIVE 25 MIN. - TOTAL 2 HOURS, 35 MIN.

MAKES ABOUT 2 DOZEN

- 1½ cups unsalted butter, softened
- 1¼ cups packed light brown sugar
- 1 cup granulated sugar
- 2 large eggs, at room temperature
- 2 tsp. vanilla extract
- 3¼ cups all-purpose flour
- ¾ cup unsweetened cocoa powder
- 1½ tsp. baking powder
- 1½ tsp. kosher salt
- 1¼ tsp. baking soda
- 1 tsp. instant espresso powder
- 1 cup bittersweet chocolate chips (such as Ghirardelli), divided
- 1 cup crushed soft peppermint candies (such as Brach's) (about 30 candies), divided

1. Beat butter, brown sugar, and granulated sugar with a stand mixer fitted with a paddle attachment on medium-high speed until light and fluffy, about 2 minutes. Add eggs, 1 at a time, beating well after each addition. Beat in vanilla until combined.
2. Whisk together flour, cocoa powder, baking powder, salt, baking soda, and espresso powder in a medium bowl. With mixer on low speed, gradually add half of flour mixture to butter mixture, beating until just combined. Add ½ cup each of the chocolate chips and crushed peppermints; beat on low speed. Gradually add remaining flour mixture, beating until just combined. Using a rubber spatula, fold in remaining chocolate chips and peppermints. Cover using plastic wrap, and refrigerate at least 1 hour up or to 2 days.
3. Preheat oven to 375°F. Scoop dough using a 3-tablespoon scoop onto baking sheets lined with parchment, spacing 3 inches apart (about 9 cookies per pan).
4. Bake, 1 pan at a time, until cookies are set and tops begin to crack, 9 to 11 minutes. Cool on pan on a wire rack about 10 minutes; transfer cookies to rack, and let cool completely, about 30 minutes. Repeat process with remaining dough.

Christmas Blondies

(Photo, page 296)

These bars are wonderful any time of the year. Thanks to the plethora of colorways available, you can swap out the candy to match any season.

ACTIVE 20 MIN. - TOTAL 3 HOURS, 5 MIN.

MAKES 2 DOZEN

- Baking spray
- 3½ cups all-purpose flour
- 2 tsp. kosher salt
- 5 large eggs, at room temperature
- 2 cups granulated sugar
- ¾ cup packed light brown sugar
- 1 Tbsp. vanilla extract
- 2 cups unsalted butter, melted and cooled slightly
- 1 (10-oz.) bag red and green candy-coated chocolate pieces (such as M&M'S) (about 1½ cups), divided

1. Preheat oven to 325°F. Lightly coat a 13- x 9-inch baking pan with baking spray; line with parchment paper, leaving a 2-inch overhang on long sides. Spray parchment with baking spray; set aside.
2. Whisk together flour and salt in a medium bowl; set aside. Beat eggs and granulated sugar with a stand mixer fitted with a whisk attachment on medium-high speed until thick and pale yellow, about 4 minutes. Switch to a paddle attachment; add brown sugar and vanilla, and beat on low speed until combined, about 20 seconds. Gradually add cooled butter, beating on low speed until combined, about 1 minute total. Using a spatula, fold in flour mixture just until no streaks remain. Fold in 1¼ cups of the chocolate pieces. Pour batter into prepared pan, smoothing into an even layer. Sprinkle remaining ¼ cup chocolate pieces over top.
3. Bake until bars are set and a thermometer inserted into center registers 205°F, about 45 minutes. Cool completely in baking pan on a wire rack, about 2 hours. Using parchment as handles, transfer blondies from baking pan to a cutting board. Cut into 24 triangles.

Chewy Peanut Butter–Pistachio Cookies

(Photo, page 298)

The crushed treats that top these irresistibly chewy cookies are a Southern classic. The Atkinson family in Lufkin, Texas, has been making their Peanut Butter Bar candies for more than 90 years.

ACTIVE 30 MIN. - TOTAL 1 HOUR, 55 MIN.

MAKES ABOUT 3½ DOZEN

- 2 cups unsalted raw pistachios
- ½ cup packed light brown sugar
- ½ tsp. kosher salt
- ¾ cup powdered sugar
- ⅛ tsp. almond extract (optional)
- 2 large egg whites
- 2 dark chocolate bars (such as Ghirardelli), finely chopped (about 1⅓ cups)
- ¼ cup chopped peanut butter hard candy (such as Atkinson's) (about 5 pieces)

1. Preheat oven to 350°F. Process pistachios, brown sugar, and salt in a food processor until mixture resembles wet sand, 45 seconds to 1 minute. Transfer mixture to a large bowl, and add powdered sugar, almond extract (if using), and egg whites; stir until smooth. Scoop dough using a 2-teaspoon scoop onto large baking sheets lined with parchment paper, spacing about 2 inches apart (about 2 dozen cookies per baking sheet).
2. Bake, 1 pan at a time, until cookies are just set, about 12 minutes. Let cool on pan on a wire rack about 10 minutes; transfer cookies to rack, and let cool 30 minutes. Repeat process with remaining dough.
3. Microwave chocolate in a microwavable mug or small measuring cup on HIGH until mostly melted, 1 minute, 30 seconds to 2 minutes, stopping to stir every 20 seconds; continue stirring until smooth.
4. Dip half of each cooled cookie in melted chocolate; place on parchment. Sprinkle a pinch of chopped peanut butter candy on chocolate-dipped side of each cookie; let stand until set, about 20 minutes.

12 Days of Truffles

Surprise everyone on your gift list with the easiest homemade chocolates.

Classic Truffles

While these chocolates are perfectly decadent as is, they're easy to customize with a few substitutions and stir-ins.

ACTIVE 20 MIN. - TOTAL 2 HOURS, 50 MIN.

MAKES ABOUT 2½ DOZEN

- ¾ cup heavy whipping cream
- 1 Tbsp. unsalted butter
- 2 cups bittersweet (60% cacao) chocolate chips
- 1 cup cocoa powder

1. Heat cream and butter in a medium saucepan over medium until cream begins to simmer, about 2 minutes.
2. Place chocolate chips in a medium-size microwavable bowl. Pour cream mixture over chocolate, and let stand 1 minute; stir until smooth. If needed, microwave mixture on HIGH until completely melted, about 10 seconds. Cover and chill in refrigerator until solid, about 2 hours.
3. Let chocolate mixture stand at room temperature 30 minutes. Scoop into ¾-inch portions using a 1-inch diameter scoop or a tablespoon. Shape into round balls; place on a parchment paper-lined baking sheet. Roll in cocoa. (If dipping in melted coatings for variations at right, freeze truffles until firm before coating, about 15 minutes.)

A DOZEN FESTIVE FLAVORS

For a step-by-step tutorial on topping and coating, *see page 320.*

1. Ginger

In Step 1, add 1 tsp. **ground ginger** to cream mixture while heating. In Step 2, stir ½ cup finely chopped **candied ginger** into warm chocolate mixture. In Step 3, omit cocoa; dip frozen truffles in 2 cups melted **milk chocolate.** Garnish with chopped **candied ginger.**

2. Hazelnut

In Step 2, stir ¼ cup **chocolate hazelnut spread** (such as Nutella) and 2 Tbsp. **hazelnut liqueur** (such as Frangelico) into warm chocolate mixture. In Step 3, omit cocoa; roll truffles in 2 cups chopped toasted **hazelnuts.**

3. Dark Chocolate Orange

In Step 1, add 1 tsp. grated **orange zest** to cream mixture while heating. In Step 3, omit cocoa; roll truffles in 2 cups **chocolate sprinkles** to coat. Garnish truffles with chopped **candied orange peel** or **orange peel twists.**

4. Peppermint

In Step 2, stir ¼ tsp. **peppermint extract** into warm chocolate mixture. In Step 3, omit cocoa; dip frozen truffles in 2 cups melted **white chocolate.** Let truffles dry for 5 minutes. Drizzle with more melted white chocolate; sprinkle with chopped **hard peppermint candies.**

5. Mexican Hot Chocolate

In Step 1, add 1 tsp. **cinnamon** and a pinch of **cayenne pepper** to cream mixture while heating. In Step 3, garnish with a dusting of **chile powder** or **Aleppo pepper.**

6. Peanut Butter

In Step 2, stir ¼ cup **creamy peanut butter** into warm chocolate mixture. In Step 3, omit cocoa and dip frozen truffles in 2 cups melted **peanut butter chips** whisked together with 1 Tbsp. **whole milk.** Garnish with chopped roasted **salted peanuts.**

7. Sea Salt

In Step 1, add ½ tsp. **flaky sea salt** to cream mixture while heating. In Step 3, omit cocoa; dip frozen truffles in 2 cups melted **dark chocolate.** Garnish with **flaky sea salt.**

8. Coconut

In Step 1, substitute **canned coconut milk** for cream. In Step 2, stir ½ cup toasted **sweetened flaked coconut** and ½ tsp. **coconut extract** into warm chocolate mixture. In Step 3, omit cocoa; roll truffles in 2 cups toasted **sweetened flaked coconut.**

9. Pistachio Chai

In Step 1, add ¼ tsp. **ground cardamom** and 1 **chai tea bag** to cream mixture while heating. Let steep 5 minutes; discard tea bag. In Step 3, omit cocoa; roll truffles in 2 cups finely chopped **pistachios.**

10. Bourbon Pecan

In Step 2, stir 2 Tbsp. **bourbon** into warm chocolate mixture. In Step 3, omit cocoa; roll truffles in 2 cups chopped toasted **pecans.**

11. Milk Punch

In Step 1, reduce cream to ⅓ cup. In Step 2, substitute **white chocolate chips** for bittersweet chocolate chips. Stir 1 Tbsp. **bourbon,** 1 Tbsp. **rum,** 1 tsp. **vanilla extract,** and ¼ tsp. **ground nutmeg** into warm white chocolate mixture; whisk vigorously until smooth. In Step 3, omit cocoa and roll truffles in **sparkling sugar.**

12. Mocha

In Step 2, stir 1 tsp. **instant espresso granules** and 2 Tbsp. **coffee-flavor liqueur** (such as Kahlúa) into warm chocolate mixture. In Step 3, dip frozen truffles in 2 cups melted **dark chocolate.** Garnish each truffle with a **coffee bean.**

1
2
3
4
5
6
7
8
9
10
11
12

Remembering Gumbo Claus

Christmas is the perfect time to honor the memory of a true New Orleans original.

IT'S BEEN ALMOST a year since my friend Pableaux Johnson became an ancestor. My grief at his passing is lessening slightly. However, with the return of cooler weather and the year-end holidays, the loss barrels back in full force.

Pableaux loved Christmas almost as much as his grandmother's table—and he loved that table. That scarred and pitted piece of furniture became the locus of his art. "The table needs feeding," he would say. He used it to create a community that, after his death, revealed itself to be so far ranging that he had obituaries in *The New York Times, Los Angeles Times, Imbibe* magazine, this publication, and—much to everyone's surprise—*The Economist*.

A master photographer, his real fame came from his documentation of the African American parades and second lines that are so much a vital part of New Orleans. He loved the people who maintained this heartbeat of the city's culture, and they loved him back.

Pableaux would invite a small group of friends and their friends who were in town (10 people was the magic number) to join him around his old, stained wooden table each Monday for a home-cooked red bean supper accompanied by his rich skillet-made cornbread. An invitation to this standing meal became one of the city's most coveted. The guest list was stellar and included everyone from the second line members and Mardi Gras Indians that Pableaux photographed with affection and brilliance to award-winning chefs to journalists and visiting dignitaries. There were two rules: no cell phones and bring what you're drinking.

In the holiday season, he went into full-tilt-boogie mode. Every year, he sourced turkey carcasses from friends after Thanksgiving and stored them in a freezer on the porch of the shotgun house where he lived. Then, as Christmas was coming, he went into his kitchen and with a transformation as miraculous as that of Clark Kent morphing into Superman, emerged as Gumbo Claus.

As this alter ego, Pableaux made industrial amounts of the classic Louisiana dish, which he delivered to friends and relations. Then, to cap the season, he served the gumbo at an open house along with his melt-in-your-mouth smothered cabbage to honor the African American dictum to "eat something green for folding money" at the start of a new year. It was standing room-only with folks from uptown, downtown, and out of town—all greeting old friends and making new ones while savoring what someone once called "industrial quantities" of gumbo, cabbage, and cornbread.

This New Year's Day, Gumbo Claus will be serving his meal to the ancestors while I will be visiting friends away from home. But when I return, I will cook and savor some of Pableaux's cabbage, pour out some rum on the ground for his memory, and pray for folding money in 2026.
—Jessica B. Harris

Smothered Cabbage

ACTIVE 30 MIN. - TOTAL 1 HOUR, 15 MIN.
SERVES 6 TO 8

- **3 Tbsp. vegetable oil or olive oil**
- **1/2 lb. baked ham, chopped (about 3 cups), or smoked sausage, sliced 1/8 inch thick**
- **2 yellow onions, chopped (about 3 cups)**
- **1 (28-oz.) can whole peeled tomatoes in puree, undrained and crushed**
- **3/4 cup amber ale (such as Fairhope Brewing Co.)**
- **1/2 cup drained jarred olive salad or pitted green olives, finely chopped**
- **1 tsp. dried basil**
- **1 (2- to 3-lb.) head green cabbage, coarsely chopped (about 8 cups)**
- **1 tsp. kosher salt**
- **1 tsp. black pepper**
- **1 tsp. hot sauce (such as The Original Louisiana Hot Sauce)**

1. Heat oil in a large Dutch oven over medium until shimmering, about 1 minute. Add ham; cook, stirring occasionally, until browned and crisp, about 5 minutes. Add onions; cook, stirring occasionally, until onions are lightly browned, about 6 minutes. Stir in tomatoes, ale, olive salad, and basil; increase heat to medium-high, and bring to a simmer.

2. Add cabbage in 3 batches; cook, stirring often, until leaves are slightly wilted and coated in mixture after each addition. Reduce heat to medium-low; simmer, covered and undisturbed, until cabbage is tender, about 45 minutes. Stir in salt, pepper, and hot sauce.

The Gift of a Casserole

A make-ahead breakfast is the key to enjoying Christmas morning.

MORE THAN any other holiday, Christmas tends to inspire hopeful fantasies. Kids dream of finding a puppy under the tree; adults imagine the whole family miraculously getting along at the annual feast. My own daydream is more modest: It's the morning of the big day, and I'm sitting on the sofa in my pajamas, enjoying a warm mug of coffee, surrounded by family as presents are unwrapped. The best part is that breakfast is already made and the house smells like butter and cheese and heaven. And I am not in the kitchen.

This year, I'm determined to turn my fantasy into a reality. No more flipping pancakes while my coffee gets cold. No more standing at the stovetop while everyone else plays with their new toys. This is the year of the make-ahead breakfast casserole.

You probably already have a favorite recipe for one, and I do too. Let's be honest, though. Breakfast casseroles are delicious, but there's nothing festive about them. So we fancied up this dish with croissants so it's more special occasion worthy, even if you are still in your pj's.

One version has gooey fontina cheese, Dijon mustard, mushrooms, and fresh herbs (feel free to leave out the mushrooms if they make your kids scream in terror). The other one is heartier, with pimiento cheese and sausage. Either way, all you have to do on Christmas morning is pop it in the oven, and enjoy some family time. Sometimes dreams do come true.
–Lisa Cericola

Fontina-and-Herb Croissant Casserole

To make ahead, prepare recipe through Step 4; refrigerate up to 12 hours. Let stand at room temperature 30 minutes before baking.

ACTIVE 45 MIN. - TOTAL 2 HOURS, 45 MIN.
SERVES 8 TO 10

- 2 Tbsp. olive oil
- 1 lb. fresh cremini mushrooms, sliced (about 6 cups)
- 1 Tbsp. chopped fresh thyme
- 2 tsp. kosher salt, divided
- 1½ lb. day-old mini croissants (16 to 18), halved horizontally, divided
- 1 (5.3-oz.) pkg. garlic-and-herb spreadable cheese (such as Boursin)
- 8 oz. fontina cheese, shredded (about 2 cups), divided
- ½ cup finely chopped fresh tender herbs (such as chives, tarragon, and parsley), divided, plus more for garnish
- 2 cups half-and-half
- 1½ Tbsp. Dijon mustard
- ¾ tsp. black pepper, plus more for garnish
- ¾ tsp. granulated garlic
- 8 large eggs

1. Heat oil in a large skillet over medium-high. Add mushrooms, thyme, and ½ teaspoon salt; cook, stirring occasionally, until tender, about 10 minutes. Remove from heat.
2. Lightly coat a 13- x 9-inch baking dish with cooking spray. Set aside 12 croissant tops. Tear croissant bottom halves and remaining tops into bite-size pieces. Arrange two-thirds of torn croissants in an even layer in prepared dish.
3. Dollop spreadable cheese over torn croissants. Sprinkle with ½ cup fontina, ¼ cup herbs, and half of mushroom mixture. Top with remaining torn croissants; sprinkle with ½ cup fontina and remaining ¼ cup herbs and mushroom mixture.
4. Whisk together half-and-half, Dijon, pepper, garlic, eggs, and remaining 1½ teaspoons salt in a large bowl. Pour half of egg mixture over croissant mixture. Arrange croissant tops over mixture in dish; pour remaining egg mixture over top. Gently press croissant tops into egg mixture. Cover with foil; let stand at room temperature 1 hour.
5. Preheat oven to 350°F. Top casserole with remaining 1 cup fontina. Cover with foil, and bake 40 minutes. Uncover, and bake until set, about 10 minutes. Remove from oven, and let rest 10 minutes. Garnish with additional herbs and pepper.

Pimiento Cheese–and–Sausage Croissant Casserole

(Photo, page 314)

Omit Step 1. Cook 1 lb. **ground pork sausage** in a large skillet over medium until browned, 5 minutes. Add ½ cup sliced **scallions;** cook, stirring often, until softened, about 1 minute. Remove from heat. Proceed with Step 2 as directed. Omit Step 3; dollop 5- to 6-oz. **pimiento cheese** over torn croissants in dish. Sprinkle with ½ cup shredded **sharp Cheddar cheese** and half of sausage mixture. Top with remaining torn croissants; sprinkle with ½ cup shredded **sharp Cheddar** and remaining sausage mixture. Proceed with Step 4 as directed. In Step 5, omit fontina and replace with 1 cup shredded **sharp Cheddar;** bake as directed. Omit herb garnish and replace with additional sliced scallions.

FONTINA-AND-HERB CROISSANT CASSEROLE

PIMENTO CHEESE-AND-SAUSAGE CROISSANT CASSEROLE (PAGE 312)

Start with Seafood

Packed with shrimp and crab, this decadent casserole from chef Carla Hall is a brunch showstopper.

Lowcountry Breakfast Casserole

ACTIVE 1 HOUR - TOTAL 1 HOUR, 45 MIN.
SERVES 8

- 2 cups plus 3 Tbsp. all-purpose flour, divided
- 2¼ tsp. baking powder
- 2¼ tsp. granulated sugar
- ½ tsp. baking soda
- 1½ tsp. black pepper, divided
- 1 tsp. kosher salt, divided
- 1½ Tbsp. vegetable shortening
- 6 Tbsp. unsalted butter, frozen
- 2 large scallions, thinly sliced, plus more for garnish
- 1 cup whole buttermilk, chilled
- 2 medium-size red potatoes, cut into ½-inch pieces (about 1½ cups)
- 1 tsp. canola oil
- 8 oz. smoked sausage, cut into ½-inch pieces (about 1½ cups)
- 1 medium bell pepper, chopped (about 1 cup)
- 2 Tbsp. unsalted butter, at room temperature
- 2 cups seafood or chicken stock
- 1 cup whole milk, divided
- 1 tsp. Old Bay seasoning
- ¼ tsp. onion powder
- ¼ tsp. smoked paprika
- 6 large eggs
- 1 cup shredded sharp Cheddar cheese (4 oz.), divided
- 8 oz. medium-size peeled, deveined raw shrimp, cut into ½-inch pieces (about 1½ cups)
- 1 cup lump crabmeat (from 1 [8-oz.] pkg.), drained and picked over for shells

1. Whisk together 2 cups flour, the baking powder, sugar, baking soda, 1 teaspoon black pepper, and ¾ teaspoon salt in a large bowl. Pinch shortening into flour mixture until fully incorporated. Grate frozen butter into flour mixture, and toss to coat. Quickly pinch butter into flour mixture to create flattened pieces. Stir in scallions.
2. Add buttermilk to flour mixture, and stir lightly until no dry flour remains. Transfer dough to a lightly floured work surface; pat into a rectangle. Fold dough into thirds (like a letter). Repeat patting and folding twice. Roll dough into a ½-inch thickness, and cut into ¾-inch squares. Chill on a lightly floured baking sheet until ready to use.
3. Preheat oven to 350°F. Stir together potatoes, 1 tablespoon water, and remaining ¼ teaspoon salt in a medium microwavable bowl. Cover and microwave on HIGH until fork-tender, about 3 minutes. Drain and set aside.
4. Heat a large skillet over medium-high. Add oil and smoked sausage; cook, stirring occasionally, until browned, 4 to 5 minutes. Add bell pepper and potatoes; cook, stirring often, until vegetables are browned in spots, about 3 minutes. Transfer to a medium bowl using a slotted spoon.
5. Return skillet to medium heat; add room-temperature butter to drippings. Add remaining 3 tablespoons flour; cook, whisking constantly, until mixture smells nutty, 1 minute. Gradually whisk in stock and ½ cup milk, whisking constantly. Stir in Old Bay seasoning, onion powder, paprika, and remaining ½ teaspoon black pepper. Bring mixture to a boil over medium-high. Reduce heat to medium, and cook, whisking often, until mixture lightly coats the back of a spoon, about 5 minutes. Remove from heat. Stir cooked sausage, potatoes, and bell pepper into gravy mixture. Let cool 10 minutes.
6. Whisk together eggs, ½ cup of the cheese, and remaining ½ cup milk in a medium bowl. Coat a 13- x 9-inch baking dish with cooking spray; arrange dough pieces in a single layer. Gently fold shrimp and crabmeat into gravy mixture in skillet. Pour gravy mixture over dough pieces in baking dish. Pour egg mixture on top, and sprinkle with remaining ½ cup cheese. Bake, uncovered, until eggs are set and slightly puffed, 35 to 40 minutes.
7. Remove casserole from oven; let rest 5 minutes before serving. Garnish with scallions, if desired.

With a buttermilk-scallion biscuit base, Old Bay-spiced gravy, sausage, potatoes, and two kinds of seafood, this special-occasion dish is no ordinary strata.

A Knockout Punch

Spiked or not, this festive sipper will keep you cozy on winter nights.

THE CHRISTMAS punch bowls of my Southern childhood were filled with all sorts of delicious concoctions. There were melting scoops of pink sherbet floating in a cranberry-lemon-lime pool plus a crystal cauldron of brandy-laced milk punch that we kids knew better than to go near. I even occasionally got a sip of eggnog from my mom, giddy as I licked away the white mustache it left behind. As much as I loved all of these, I didn't find my absolute favorite holiday drink until I started dating my now-husband, Luis. One of the first times we visited his parents, who both grew up in Puerto Rico, his mom, Myriam, pulled a glass bottle of her homemade coquito from the fridge after dinner. Traditionally served at Christmastime, coquito, which translates to "little coconut" in Spanish, is made from both coconut milk and cream of coconut as well as evaporated milk, cinnamon, and occasionally other warm spices. It's thick, sweet, often spiked with rum, and—as I realized after my first sip—entirely irresistible. I asked my mother-in-law how to make it, and though my version differs ever so slightly from hers, I knew I'd done something right when Luis said, "This tastes like Christmas at home."

Coconut Milk Punch (Coquito)

ACTIVE 15 MIN. - TOTAL 1 HOUR, 15 MIN.
SERVES 6

- **2** (13½-oz.) cans coconut milk, well shaken and stirred
- **1** (15-oz.) can cream of coconut (such as Coco Lopez)
- **1** (12-oz.) can evaporated milk
- **1** (7.4-oz.) can sweetened condensed coconut milk
- **1** tsp. ground cinnamon, plus more for garnish
- **1** tsp. vanilla bean paste
- **½** cup dark rum (optional)
- **2** (4-inch) cinnamon sticks, plus more for garnish

Whisk together coconut milk, cream of coconut, evaporated milk, condensed coconut milk, ground cinnamon, and vanilla bean paste until very smooth. Transfer to a half-gallon pitcher; add rum (if using) and cinnamon sticks. Chill at least 1 hour before serving, or cover and refrigerate up to 10 days. Garnish with additional ground cinnamon and cinnamon sticks.

Coconut Milk Punch Rice Pudding

ACTIVE 1 HOUR - TOTAL 1 HOUR
SERVES 4

Place 1 Tbsp. **butter** in a medium saucepan; heat over medium until just melted, about 30 seconds. Add ½ cup **uncooked white medium-grain rice**; cook, stirring constantly, until rice is fragrant, about 2 minutes. Stir in 1 **cinnamon stick** and 5 cups **Coconut Milk Punch** (recipe left); bring to a rolling simmer over medium. Cover and reduce heat to low; cook, stirring often, until rice is tender and mixture is thick, 50 to 55 minutes. Discard cinnamon stick. Stir in ½ tsp. **vanilla bean paste** and ½ cup **Coconut Milk Punch.** Serve warm, or let cool completely before chilling overnight to serve cold. Garnish with **ground cinnamon** just before serving.

COCONUT MILK PUNCH RICE PUDDING

COCONUT MILK PUNCH (COQUITO)

BAKING SCHOOL

TIPS AND TRICKS FROM THE SOUTH'S MOST TRUSTED KITCHEN

Truffles for Gifting (or Keeping)

A custom box of homemade candies (recipes, page 306) is a few simple steps away.

1. PREPARE GANACHE
Heat cream and butter in a saucepan until cream begins to simmer and butter is melted. Pour mixture over chocolate chips, and let stand 1 minute. Whisk until mixture is smooth and glossy.

2. ROLL INTO BALLS
Cover and chill ganache until solid, about 2 hours. Bring to room temperature before scooping and rolling into ¾-inch balls. Place balls on a parchment paper–lined baking sheet.

3. ADD A COATING
Place desired ingredient on a plate or in a shallow bowl (pie pans work well for this). Gently roll each ball in the ingredient until completely covered. If truffles become too soft, chill in the freezer for a few minutes to firm up.

4. OR DIP IN CHOCOLATE
Freeze truffles for 15 minutes after rolling into balls. Using a fork, dip each into melted chocolate, and then place on a parchment-lined baking sheet. Garnish immediately.

Our Favorite Salads & Sides Recipes

When the weather is hot and you're craving something cool and crisp, tuck into a main-dish salad such as Fried Chicken Salad with Basil-Buttermilk Dressing (page 322), Southern Niçoise Salad (page 331), or Crunchy Chicken-Peanut Chopped Salad (page 322). Tote Tangy Tzatziki Pasta Salad (page 340) to a picnic. Round out a quick weeknight meal with Chipotle-Cilantro Slaw (page 340) or Cheesy Bread with Herbs (page 350), and a special occasion or holiday meal with Butternut Squash Spoonbread (page 349) or Pecan-Herb Cornbread Dressing (page 349).

MARINATED TOMATO-AND-HERB SALAD (PAGE 332)

Main-Dish Salads

Herbed Chicken-and-Rice Salad

(Photo, page 327)

ACTIVE 35 MIN. - TOTAL 45 MIN.

SERVES 8

- 2 (8½-oz.) pkg. microwavable basmati rice
- ½ cup loosely packed fresh tender herbs (such as dill, parsley, and chives), plus more for garnish
- ¼ cup plus 2 Tbsp. olive oil
- ¼ cup fresh lemon juice (from 2 large lemons)
- 2 Tbsp. chopped shallot (from 1 small shallot)
- ½ Tbsp. Dijon mustard
- 2 tsp. honey
- ½ tsp. kosher salt
- ¼ tsp. black pepper
- 2½ cups shredded cooked chicken breast (from 1 rotisserie chicken)
- 2 cups halved multicolor cherry tomatoes (from 1 [12-oz.] pkg.)
- 1¼ cups (¼-inch) diagonally sliced Persian or mini cucumbers (about 3 cucumbers)
- 1 cup sliced almonds, toasted
- 4 oz. feta cheese, crumbled (about 1 cup)
- ½ cup (¼-inch) sliced celery (from 1 large celery stalk)
- ¼ cup coarsely chopped celery leaves
- ¼ cup coarsely chopped fresh flat-leaf parsley

1. Microwave rice according to package directions; transfer to a large bowl, and cool completely, about 20 minutes.
2. Meanwhile, place herbs, olive oil, lemon juice, shallot, mustard, honey, salt, and pepper in a food processor or blender; process until smooth, about 30 seconds.
3. Add chicken, tomatoes, cucumbers, almonds, feta, celery, chopped celery leaves, and parsley to bowl with cooled rice; drizzle with dressing, and toss to coat. Transfer to a large serving platter or bowl, and garnish with additional herbs.

Crunchy Chicken-Peanut Chopped Salad

(Photo, page 324)

ACTIVE 15 MIN. - TOTAL 15 MIN.

SERVES 4

- 1 lb. fried chicken tenders (about 6 large tenders), chopped
- 3 cups shredded coleslaw mix (from 1 [10-oz.] pkg.)
- 2 cups shredded red cabbage (from 1 head cabbage)
- ½ cup thinly sliced scallions (from 4 scallions)
- ½ cup coarsely chopped fresh cilantro
- ¾ cup dry-roasted peanuts, coarsely chopped, divided
- 5 Tbsp. fresh lime juice (from 3 limes)
- 3 Tbsp. creamy peanut butter
- 3 Tbsp. toasted sesame oil
- 2 Tbsp. soy sauce
- 2 Tbsp. seasoned rice vinegar
- 2 Tbsp. light brown sugar
- Crushed red pepper

1. Toss together chopped chicken tenders, coleslaw mix, cabbage, scallions, cilantro, and ½ cup chopped peanuts in a large bowl.
2. Whisk together lime juice and peanut butter in a small bowl until smooth. Slowly whisk in oil, soy sauce, vinegar, brown sugar, and crushed red pepper to taste, whisking until creamy.
3. To serve, pour dressing over salad mixture; toss to coat evenly. Sprinkle with remaining ¼ cup peanuts.

Fried Chicken Salad with Basil-Buttermilk Dressing

(Photo, page 326)

ACTIVE 10 MIN. - TOTAL 10 MIN.

SERVES 4

- 1 cup chopped fresh basil
- ½ cup mayonnaise
- ⅓ cup whole buttermilk
- 1 medium garlic clove, coarsely chopped
- ½ tsp. granulated sugar
- ½ tsp. onion powder
- 1 tsp. kosher salt, divided
- 6 cups packed mixed greens (8 oz.)
- 8 oz. fried chicken tenders, cooled and cut into 1½-inch pieces (about 2½ cups)
- 2 oz. extra-sharp Cheddar cheese, shredded (about ½ cup)

1. Place basil, mayonnaise, buttermilk, garlic, sugar, onion powder, and ¾ teaspoon salt in a food processor. Process until completely combined and smooth, 15 to 30 seconds. Transfer to a small bowl.
2. Place greens, fried chicken, cheese, and remaining ¼ teaspoon salt in a large bowl. Drizzle ½ cup dressing over mixture; gently toss to coat. Divide evenly among 4 plates; drizzle with remaining ½ cup dressing.

Crispy Chicken-and-Broccoli Salad

(Photo, page 365)

ACTIVE 15 MIN. - TOTAL 15 MIN., PLUS 2 HOURS CHILLING

SERVES 4 TO 6

- 2 Tbsp. honey
- 2 Tbsp. apple cider vinegar
- 1 Tbsp. Dijon mustard
- 1 tsp. kosher salt
- ½ tsp. black pepper
- ⅔ cup olive oil
- 5 cups broccoli florets
- 1½ cups seedless grapes, halved
- 4 oz. sharp Cheddar cheese, grated (about 1 cup)
- ¾ cup sliced almonds, toasted
- ½ cup thinly sliced red onion (from 1 small red onion)
- 5 fried chicken tenders, coarsely chopped (about 4 cups)

Whisk together honey, vinegar, mustard, salt, and pepper in a large bowl until blended and smooth. Drizzle in oil, whisking until emulsified, 30 seconds. Stir in broccoli, grapes, cheese, almonds, and onion. Cover; chill at least 2 hours or up to overnight. Stir in chicken just before serving.

Clementine-and-Collard Salad

ACTIVE 20 MIN. - TOTAL 20 MIN.
SERVES 4

Squeeze juice from 1 **clementine** into a small bowl. (You should have about 2 Tbsp. juice.) Add 1 Tbsp. **apple cider vinegar**, 2 tsp. Dijon mustard, 1 tsp. **sorghum syrup** (or **honey**), ¼ tsp. **black pepper**, and ½ tsp. **kosher salt**. Slowly add ¼ cup **extra-virgin olive oil**, whisking to combine. Place 1 lb. **collard greens**, stemmed and cut into thin strips (8 cups), and 2 small sliced **shallots** (⅓ cup) in a large bowl. Add 2 Tbsp. dressing, and gently massage into greens mixture with hands until greens are wilted and tender, 1 minute. Reserve remaining dressing. Peel and slice 2 **clementines** into rings, and set aside. Place the greens mixture on a serving platter; top with 1½ cups shredded **cooked chicken** (about 6 oz.), ½ cup **chopped toasted pecans**, 3 oz. crumbled **goat cheese** (about ¾ cup), and sliced clementines. Drizzle reserved dressing over salad, and sprinkle with ¼ tsp. **kosher salt**.

Collard Salad with Chicken, Bell Pepper, and Roasted Squash

(Photo, page 328)
ACTIVE 20 MIN. - TOTAL 35 MIN.
SERVES 4

- 1 medium (2½-lb.) butternut squash, peeled, seeded, and cubed (7 cups)
- 1 medium red bell pepper, thinly sliced (1¼ cups)
- 2 medium shallots, sliced (½ cup)
- ¼ cup olive oil, divided
- 1½ tsp. kosher salt, divided
- 1 Tbsp. Champagne vinegar
- ¼ tsp. pure maple syrup
- 1 lb. fresh collard greens, stemmed and thinly sliced (about 9 cups)
- 2 cups coarsely shredded cooked chicken breast (from 1 rotisserie chicken)
- 2 oz. feta cheese, crumbled (about ½ cup)
- ⅓ cup roasted salted pumpkin seed kernels (pepitas)

1. Place 2 large rimmed baking sheets in oven; preheat oven to 425°F. (Do not remove baking sheets while oven preheats.) Toss butternut squash, bell pepper, and shallots with 2 tablespoons oil and 1 teaspoon salt in a large bowl. Spread evenly over preheated baking sheets. Bake until browned and tender, about 20 to 25 minutes, tossing halfway through baking time. Remove from oven; set aside to cool.
2. Whisk together vinegar, maple syrup, and remaining 2 tablespoons oil and ½ teaspoon salt in a small bowl.
3. Combine collards and 1 tablespoon dressing in a large bowl. Massage dressing into greens with hands until tender, about 30 seconds. Add chicken, squash-and-pepper mixture, feta, and pumpkin seed kernels to greens; toss gently to combine. Arrange on a serving platter; drizzle with remaining dressing.

Kale-and-Chicken Salad with Jalapeño-Lime Dressing

ACTIVE 20 MIN. - TOTAL 20 MIN.
SERVES 4

- 1 Tbsp. plus ¼ cup olive oil, divided
- 1 (5-oz.) bunch curly kale, stemmed and chopped (about 6 cups)
- 2 Tbsp. fresh lime juice (from 1 large lime)
- 2 Tbsp. chopped seeded jalapeño chile (from 1 medium-size chile)
- 1½ Tbsp. honey
- ¾ tsp. kosher salt
- ½ tsp. black pepper
- 2 cups sliced green cabbage (from 1 small cabbage)
- ½ cup packed fresh cilantro leaves
- ¼ cup packed fresh mint leaves
- 2 cups coarsely shredded cooked chicken (from 1 rotisserie chicken)
- ½ cup honey-roasted peanuts

1. Massage 1 tablespoon oil into kale in a bowl until kale softens, 30 seconds.
2. Process lime juice, jalapeño, honey, salt, black pepper, and remaining ¼ cup oil in a mini food processor until blended, 30 seconds.
3. Add lime dressing, cabbage, cilantro, and mint to kale in bowl; toss to coat. Stir in chicken. Arrange salad on a platter, and sprinkle with peanuts.

Chicken-Quinoa Salad with Green Goddess Dressing

ACTIVE 10 MIN. - TOTAL 30 MIN.
SERVES 4

- ⅔ cup mayonnaise
- 1 Tbsp. chopped fresh chives
- 1 tsp. white wine vinegar
- ½ tsp. anchovy paste
- 1 tsp. lemon zest plus 1 Tbsp. fresh juice (from 1 lemon)
- ¼ tsp. black pepper
- ½ cup loosely packed fresh parsley leaves, divided
- ⅓ cup loosely packed fresh tarragon leaves, divided
- ¾ tsp. kosher salt, divided
- ¾ cup water
- ½ cup uncooked quinoa
- 5 cups torn butter lettuce (from 1 head)
- 3 cups shredded cooked chicken (from 1 rotisserie chicken)
- ½ cup thinly sliced English cucumber (from 1 cucumber)
- ½ cup thinly sliced radishes (about 5 radishes)

1. Process mayonnaise, chives, vinegar, anchovy paste, lemon zest, lemon juice, black pepper, ¼ cup parsley leaves, 1 tablespoon tarragon leaves, and ¼ teaspoon salt in a food processor until smooth, about 1 to 2 minutes. Set aside.
2. Bring water, quinoa, and remaining ½ teaspoon salt to a boil in a medium saucepan over medium-high. Stir and cover. Reduce heat to low, and cook until quinoa is tender and liquid is absorbed, about 15 minutes. Remove from heat; let stand 5 minutes. Remove lid, and fluff with a fork.
3. Toss together butter lettuce and remaining ¼ cup each parsley and tarragon leaves. Toss lettuce mixture lightly with about ¼ cup dressing. Transfer to a serving platter. Sprinkle cooked quinoa over lettuce mixture; top with cooked chicken. Arrange cucumber and radish slices on top and around sides. Drizzle salad with an additional ¼ cup dressing, and serve remaining dressing on the side, if desired.

CRUNCHY CHICKEN-PEANUT CHOPPED SALAD (PAGE 322)

SOUTHERN NIÇOISE SALAD
(PAGE 331)

FRIED CHICKEN SALAD WITH BASIL-BUTTERMILK DRESSING (PAGE 322)

HERBED CHICKEN-AND-RICE SALAD (PAGE 322)

COLLARD SALAD WITH CHICKEN, BELL PEPPER, AND ROASTED SQUASH (PAGE 323)

CRUNCHY OKRA-AND-CORN SALAD WITH RANCH DRESSING (PAGE 331)

Greek Chicken Salad Wedges

ACTIVE 25 MIN. - TOTAL 25 MIN.
SERVES 4

- 2 cups shredded cooked chicken breast (from 1 rotisserie chicken)
- 1 cup chopped English cucumber (from 1 cucumber)
- 1 cup chopped tomato (from 1 tomato)
- 1/4 cup halved pitted Kalamata olives
- 1/4 cup finely chopped red onion (from 1 onion)
- 1/4 cup chopped fresh flat-leaf parsley
- 2 Tbsp. chopped fresh oregano
- 1 tsp. kosher salt
- 1 tsp. black pepper
- 6 Tbsp. red wine vinegar
- 2 Tbsp. Dijon mustard
- 4 tsp. honey
- 1/2 cup plus 2 Tbsp. olive oil
- 4 (5-oz.) baby romaine lettuce hearts, halved lengthwise
- 4 oz. crumbled feta cheese (1 cup)

1. Combine chicken, cucumber, tomato, olives, and onion in a medium bowl.
2. Whisk together parsley, oregano, salt, pepper, vinegar, mustard, and honey in a small bowl. Slowly whisk in oil in a steady stream until blended. Toss chicken mixture with ½ cup dressing.
3. Place 2 romaine lettuce heart halves on each of 4 plates, and top each evenly with chicken mixture. Drizzle plates evenly with remaining ½ cup dressing, and sprinkle with crumbled feta.

Southwestern Chopped Chicken Salad

ACTIVE 45 MIN. - TOTAL 1 HOUR, 30 MIN.
SERVES 4

- 2 (10-inch) flour tortillas
- 1 tsp. ground cumin
- 1/3 cup plus 1 Tbsp. olive oil, divided
- 1 tsp. kosher salt, divided
- 2 tsp. lime zest plus 1/2 cup fresh juice (from 6 limes)
- 1 shallot, minced (about 2 1/2 Tbsp.)
- 1 Tbsp. apple cider vinegar
- 1 tsp. Dijon mustard
- 1 tsp. honey
- 1/4 tsp. black pepper
- 4 cups chopped cooked chicken (1 large rotisserie chicken)
- 2 cups chopped ripe avocado (about 2 avocados)
- 2 romaine lettuce hearts, chopped
- 1/2 cup thinly sliced radishes (about 3 large radishes)
- 1/2 cup Pickled Red Onions (recipe follows)

1. Preheat oven to 425°F. Stack tortillas; cut in half, and cut crosswise into ½-inch strips. Place the tortilla strips on a rimmed baking sheet. Toss with cumin, 1 tablespoon olive oil, and ¼ teaspoon salt. Spread strips in a single layer; bake in preheated oven until golden brown and crisp, 10 to 12 minutes, turning halfway through baking. Cool strips to room temperature.
2. Meanwhile, whisk together lime zest and juice, shallot, vinegar, mustard, honey, pepper, and remaining ⅓ cup oil and ¾ teaspoon salt until well combined.
3. Toss together chopped chicken, avocado, romaine, sliced radishes, and Pickled Red Onions in a large bowl. Add 6 to 7 tablespoons vinaigrette; toss to coat. Place 2 cups salad on each of 4 plates; top with baked tortilla strips. Serve with remaining vinaigrette.

Pickled Red Onions

ACTIVE 5 MIN. - TOTAL 1 HOUR, 5 MIN.
MAKES 2 CUPS

- 1 cup hot water
- 1/2 cup red wine vinegar
- 1 Tbsp. granulated sugar
- 1 1/2 tsp. kosher salt
- 1 red onion, thinly sliced

Stir together hot water, red wine vinegar, sugar, and salt until sugar is completely dissolved. Place sliced onion in a medium bowl. Pour vinegar mixture over onion; let stand 1 hour. Store in an airtight container in refrigerator up to 1 month.

Chicken Taco Pasta Salad

ACTIVE 15 MIN. - TOTAL 25 MIN.
SERVES 6 TO 8

- 1 1/2 tsp. kosher salt, plus more for salting water
- 8 oz. uncooked small rigatoni pasta (about 2 cups)
- 2 ears fresh corn, shucked
- 1 small poblano chile, stemmed, seeded, and chopped (about 1/2 cup)
- 1 cup mayonnaise
- 1/2 cup loosely packed fresh cilantro leaves, plus more for garnish
- 1/3 cup chopped scallions (from 2 scallions)
- 2 Tbsp. fresh lime juice (from 1 lime)
- 1/2 tsp. smoked paprika
- 1/2 tsp. ground cumin
- 1/4 tsp. black pepper, plus more for serving
- 3 cups shredded cooked chicken (from 1 [2-lb.] rotisserie chicken)
- 2 cups shredded iceberg lettuce (from 1 small head)
- 2 cups cherry tomatoes, halved
- Blue corn tortilla chips, for serving

1. Bring a large pot of salted water to a boil over high. Add pasta; cook according to package directions for al dente. Add corn ears during final 5 minutes of cooking. Drain and rinse with cold water. Cut kernels from cobs, and set aside; discard cobs.
2. Process poblano, mayonnaise, cilantro, scallions, lime juice, 1½ teaspoons salt, paprika, cumin, and black pepper in a blender until smooth, about 1 minute.
3. Place cooked pasta, corn kernels, chicken, lettuce, and tomatoes in a large bowl. Drizzle with poblano mixture. Sprinkle with additional black pepper, and garnish with tortilla chips and additional cilantro.

Muffuletta Panzanella

ACTIVE 20 MIN. - TOTAL 45 MIN.
SERVES 4

- 1 (18-oz.) loaf ciabatta, cut into 1-inch cubes
- 1/4 cup plus 3 Tbsp. olive oil, divided
- 3/4 tsp. kosher salt, divided
- 2 large ripe tomatoes
- 1 cup chopped pitted marinated olives
- 1 cup chopped giardiniera (mixed pickled vegetables) plus 2 Tbsp. brine (from 1 [16-oz.] jar)
- 1/2 cup roasted red bell pepper strips (from 1 [16-oz.] jar)
- 2 Tbsp. red wine vinegar
- 3 garlic cloves, finely grated (about 1 1/2 tsp.)

- 1/3 lb. thinly sliced Italian deli meats (such as salami, hot capocollo, and mortadella), cut into bite-size pieces (about 1 cup packed)
- 4 oz. provolone cheese, cut into strips (about 1¼ cups)
- 2 cups packed baby arugula

1. Preheat oven to 350°F. Toss ciabatta with 3 tablespoons oil and ½ teaspoon salt on a large rimmed baking sheet; spread into an even layer. Bake until crisp, about 18 minutes, stirring halfway through baking time. Remove from oven. Let cool 15 minutes.
2. While bread bakes, cut 1 tomato in half. Place a box grater inside a large bowl. Grate tomato halves on largest holes of box grater; discard tomato skins. Stir in olives, giardiniera, brine, red bell pepper strips, vinegar, and remaining ¼ cup oil and ¼ teaspoon salt until combined.
3. Seed and roughly chop the remaining tomato. Add toasted ciabatta, chopped tomato, sliced meats, and cheese to grated tomato mixture in bowl; toss to coat. Let stand until bread absorbs most of dressing, about 10 minutes, tossing occasionally. Stir in arugula just before serving.

Southern Niçoise Salad

(Photo, page 325)

ACTIVE 20 MIN. - TOTAL 30 MIN.

SERVES 6

- 1 (8-oz.) pkg. microwavable haricots verts (slender French green beans)
- 1/3 cup finely chopped dill pickles plus 2 Tbsp. dill pickle juice (from 1 [16-oz.] jar)
- 4 tsp. Creole mustard
- 1 tsp. honey
- 3/4 tsp. kosher salt, divided
- 1/2 tsp. black pepper, divided
- 2/3 cup olive oil
- 1 small romaine lettuce heart, leaves separated
- 1 cup multicolor cherry tomatoes, halved
- 3 hard-cooked eggs, peeled and halved lengthwise
- 2 cups prepared potato salad
- 1 (8-oz.) pkg. hot-smoked trout fillets, broken into large pieces (skin discarded)

1. Microwave green beans according to package directions. Spread cooked beans in an even layer on a large plate lined with paper towels. Refrigerate, uncovered, until cooled, about 15 minutes.
2. Meanwhile, whisk together chopped pickles, pickle juice, mustard, honey, ½ teaspoon salt, and ¼ teaspoon pepper in a small bowl until combined. Gradually whisk in oil until dressing is creamy.
3. Toss together lettuce and ¼ cup dressing in a large bowl until coated; arrange on a large platter with cooked green beans, cherry tomatoes, eggs, potato salad, and trout. Sprinkle evenly with remaining ¼ teaspoon each salt and pepper. Drizzle assembled salad with remaining ¾ cup dressing. Serve immediately.

Side Salads

Crunchy Okra-and-Corn Salad with Ranch Dressing

(Photo, page 329)

ACTIVE 15 MIN. - TOTAL 15 MIN.

SERVES 4

- 1/3 cup mayonnaise
- 3 Tbsp. whole buttermilk
- 1 Tbsp. chopped fresh chives
- 1 Tbsp. chopped fresh dill
- 1 tsp. chopped fresh thyme
- 1 tsp. apple cider vinegar
- 1 medium garlic clove, grated
- 3/4 tsp. kosher salt, divided
- 1/2 tsp. black pepper, divided
- 1 Tbsp. canola oil, divided
- 8 oz. fresh purple okra pods, halved lengthwise
- 1 cup fresh corn kernels (from 1 ear)
- 8 cups torn iceberg lettuce (from 1 head)

1. Whisk together mayonnaise, buttermilk, chives, dill, thyme, vinegar, garlic, ¼ teaspoon salt, and ¼ teaspoon pepper in a medium bowl. Chill until ready to serve.
2. Heat a large cast-iron skillet over high. Add 1 teaspoon oil; swirl to coat. Add half of okra, cut side down. Cook just until cut side is lightly seared and purple color is still vibrant, 30 to 45 seconds. Remove from skillet. Repeat procedure with 1 teaspoon oil and remaining okra. Sprinkle okra with ¼ teaspoon salt.
3. Add remaining 1 teaspoon oil to skillet; swirl to coat. Add corn and remaining ¼ teaspoon each salt and pepper. Cook until lightly charred, stirring constantly, about 1 minute.
4. Arrange 2 cups torn lettuce on each of 4 plates; drizzle dressing evenly over salads. Top evenly with corn and okra.

Turnip Green Salad

(Photo, page 335)

ACTIVE 10 MIN. - TOTAL 25 MIN.

SERVES 6

- 1/4 cup Champagne vinegar
- 2 Tbsp. canned crushed tomatoes
- 1 Tbsp. finely chopped shallot (from 1 shallot)
- 1 tsp. chopped fresh sage
- 1 tsp. fresh lime juice (from 1 lime)
- 1 Tbsp. honey
- 1 tsp. kosher salt
- 1 tsp. Dijon mustard
- 1 tsp. hot sauce (such as Tabasco)
- 1/2 cup olive oil
- 5 cups chopped fresh turnip greens (from 1 [16-oz.] pkg. or 1 bunch greens)
- 4 cups purple cauliflower florets (from 1 head cauliflower)
- 2 cups baby kale (2 oz.)
- 1 cup watermelon radishes, cut into thin strips (from 2 medium radishes)
- 1 cup heirloom grape tomatoes, halved (from 1 pint)

1. Stir together vinegar, crushed tomatoes, shallot, sage, and lime juice in a medium bowl, and let stand 5 minutes. Whisk in honey, salt, Dijon mustard, and hot sauce. Add oil in a slow, steady stream, whisking constantly, until smooth.
2. Massage ¼ cup vinaigrette into turnip greens, cauliflower, baby kale, radishes, and tomatoes, and let stand 10 minutes (to help tenderize the greens). Serve salad with remaining vinaigrette.

Marinated Tomatoes

ACTIVE 10 MIN. - TOTAL 30 MIN.
SERVES 4

Whisk together ¼ cup **red wine vinegar**, ¼ cup **extra-virgin olive oil**, 1 Tbsp. minced **shallot** (from 1 small shallot), 1 tsp. **kosher salt**, ½ tsp. **black pepper**, and 3 minced **garlic cloves**. Gently stir in 1 lb. mixed **heirloom tomatoes**, cut into 1-inch-thick wedges; let stand 20 minutes. Serve as is, or use as directed in Marinated Tomato-and-Herb Salad (recipe follows).

Marinated Tomato-and-Herb Salad

(Photo, page 321)
ACTIVE 10 MIN. - TOTAL 10 MIN., PLUS 30 MIN. TO PREPARE MARINATED TOMATOES
SERVES 4

Gently remove **Marinated Tomatoes** from marinade, reserving marinade. Arrange Marinated Tomatoes on a serving platter with 1 large **beefsteak tomato** cut into ½-inch-thick slices, and 1 cup halved **heirloom cherry tomatoes**. Drizzle with reserved marinade, sprinkle with ½ tsp. **flaky sea salt**, and top with ½ cup loosely packed torn mixed **fresh herbs** (such as parsley, basil, dill, and chives).

Wedge Salad with Creamy Blue Cheese Dressing

(Photo, page 334)
ACTIVE 15 MIN. - TOTAL 15 MIN.
SERVES 8

- 1 cup whole buttermilk
- 2 garlic cloves, minced
- 6 Tbsp. mayonnaise
- 6 Tbsp. sour cream
- 4 Tbsp. chopped fresh chives
- 4 Tbsp. chopped fresh flat-leaf parsley
- 1 cup crumbled blue cheese (4 oz.), divided
- 2½ tsp. kosher salt
- 1 tsp. black pepper
- ½ tsp. paprika
- 2 iceberg lettuce heads
- 1 cup sweety drop peppers, drained and rinsed
- ¼ cup finely diced red onion
- ¼ cup flat-leaf parsley leaves

1. Whisk buttermilk, garlic, mayonnaise, sour cream, chives, and chopped parsley in a medium bowl. Stir in ¾ cup blue cheese and the salt, black pepper, and paprika.
2. Quarter each iceberg lettuce head, and divide among 8 plates. Spoon dressing evenly over lettuce. Divide sweety drop peppers, remaining ¼ cup blue cheese, red onion, and parsley leaves evenly on each plate.

Lettuce Wedge Salad

ACTIVE 30 MIN. - TOTAL 30 MIN.
SERVES 4

- 4 to 6 bacon slices
- 1 medium onion, sliced
- 1 cup buttermilk
- ½ cup sour cream
- 1 (1-oz.) envelope ranch-style dressing mix
- ¼ cup chopped fresh basil
- 2 garlic cloves
- 1 large head iceberg lettuce, cut into 4 wedges
- Shredded fresh basil, for garnish (optional)

1. Cook bacon in a large skillet over medium until crisp; remove bacon, and drain on paper towels, reserving 1 tablespoon drippings in skillet. Crumble bacon, and set aside.
2. Sauté onion in hot drippings in skillet over medium 10 minutes or until tender and lightly browned. Remove from heat; cool.
3. Process onion, buttermilk, sour cream, dressing mix, chopped basil, and garlic in a blender or food processor until smooth, stopping to scrape down sides.
4. Top each lettuce wedge with dressing; sprinkle with bacon, and top with shredded basil, if desired.

Pear-Green Bean Salad with Sorghum Vinaigrette

ACTIVE 15 MIN. - TOTAL 20 MIN., INCLUDING VINAIGRETTE
SERVES 8

- 8 oz. haricots verts (slender French green beans), trimmed
- 1 (5-oz.) pkg. mixed salad greens
- 2 red Bartlett pears, cut into thin strips
- ½ small red onion, sliced
- 4 oz. Gorgonzola cheese, crumbled
- 1 cup pecan halves, toasted
- Sorghum Vinaigrette (recipe follows)

Cook beans in boiling salted water to cover 3 to 4 minutes or until crisp-tender; drain. Plunge beans into ice water to stop the cooking process; drain. Toss together salad greens, pears, onion, cheese, pecans, and beans. Serve with Sorghum Vinaigrette.

Sorghum Vinaigrette

ACTIVE 15 MIN. - TOTAL 15 MIN.
MAKES ABOUT 2 CUPS

- ½ cup sorghum syrup
- ½ cup malt or apple cider vinegar
- 3 Tbsp. bourbon
- 2 tsp. grated onion
- 1 tsp. kosher salt
- 1 tsp. black pepper
- ½ tsp. hot sauce
- 1 cup olive oil

Whisk together sorghum syrup, vinegar, bourbon, onion, salt, pepper, and hot sauce until blended. Add oil in a slow, steady stream, whisking until smooth.

Shredded Rainbow Chard Salad with Pancetta & Dates

(Photo, page 339)
ACTIVE 15 MIN. - TOTAL 45 MIN.
SERVES 8

- 3 Tbsp. olive oil
- 2 Tbsp. red wine vinegar
- 1 tsp. Dijon mustard
- 1 tsp. fresh lemon juice
- ¼ tsp. kosher salt
- ¼ tsp. black pepper
- 1 small shallot, minced
- 3 cups shredded rainbow Swiss chard
- 11 pitted Medjool dates, thinly sliced
- 3 oz. cubed cooked pancetta

Whisk together olive oil, vinegar, mustard, lemon juice, salt, pepper, and shallot in a large serving bowl until emulsified. Add chard, and toss to coat. Cover and chill 30 minutes. Toss in dates and pancetta just before serving.

Beet, Fennel & Asian Pear Salad

ACTIVE 10 MIN. - TOTAL 55 MIN.
SERVES 6

- 2 medium beets (about 4 to 6 oz. each)
- 1 small fennel bulb, trimmed (about 5 oz.), halved lengthwise and cored (fronds reserved)
- 1 medium Asian pear (about 8 oz.), halved and cored
- 4 cups firmly packed arugula (about 5 oz.)
- 1/4 cup firmly packed fresh flat-leaf parsley or chervil leaves
- 1/4 cup firmly packed fresh mint leaves
- 1/4 cup extra-virgin olive oil
- 2 Tbsp. Champagne vinegar
- 1 tsp. orange zest plus 1 Tbsp. fresh juice (from 1 orange)
- 3/4 tsp. kosher salt
- 1/2 tsp. honey
- 1/4 tsp. black pepper

1. Place beets in a medium saucepan with cold water to cover. Bring to a boil over high; reduce heat to low, and simmer until beets are tender, 35 to 40 minutes. Drain and let stand until cool enough to handle, about 15 minutes. Peel beets, and cut into wedges.
2. While beets are cooling, use a mandoline or sharp knife to cut fennel bulb and Asian pear into very thin slices. Place in a large bowl with beet wedges, arugula, parsley or chervil, mint, and reserved fennel fronds.
3. Whisk together oil, vinegar, zest, juice, salt, honey, and pepper in a small bowl. Drizzle vinaigrette over beet mixture, and toss to coat. Serve immediately.

Fuyu Persimmon, Celery & Kale Salad with Bacon & Goat Cheese Crumbles

ACTIVE 15 MIN. - TOTAL 15 MIN.
SERVES 8

- 2 bunches Lacinato kale, stemmed and roughly chopped (6 cups)
- 8 celery stalks with leaves, thinly sliced (about 3 1/2 cups)
- 1 Fuyu persimmon, thinly sliced
- 4 cooked bacon slices, crumbled (reserve 1 1/2 Tbsp. bacon drippings)
- 2 oz. goat cheese, crumbled (about 1/2 cup)
- 3 Tbsp. fresh lemon juice (from 1 lemon)
- 2 Tbsp. finely chopped shallot
- 1 tsp. grainy Dijon mustard
- 3/4 tsp. freshly cracked black pepper, divided
- 1/2 tsp. flaky sea salt, divided
- 3 Tbsp. extra-virgin olive oil

1. Combine kale, celery, and persimmon in a large bowl. Reserve 3 tablespoons each of bacon and goat cheese. Add remaining bacon and goat cheese to kale mixture.
2. Combine lemon juice, shallot, mustard, reserved bacon drippings, 1/2 teaspoon black pepper, and 1/4 teaspoon salt in a small jar with a lid. Place lid on jar, and shake well to combine, about 30 seconds.
3. Add olive oil to jar. Place lid on jar, and shake until emulsified. Pour dressing over salad, and toss to combine. Sprinkle salad with reserved bacon and goat cheese and remaining 1/4 teaspoon each black pepper and salt. Serve immediately.

Marinated Vegetable Salad

ACTIVE 15 MIN. - TOTAL 15 MIN., PLUS 8 HOURS FOR CHILLING
SERVES 9

- 1/2 lb. fresh broccoli, trimmed
- 1/2 medium head cauliflower, trimmed
- 1/2 lb. carrots, diagonally cut into 1/4-inch pieces
- 3/4 lb. sliced fresh mushrooms
- 2 small green bell peppers, cut into 1-inch pieces
- 4 celery stalks, cut into 1/2-inch pieces
- 1 small zucchini, halved lengthwise and cut into 1/4-inch slices
- 1 medium cucumber, peeled, halved, seeded, and cut into 1/4-inch slices
- 1 1/2 cups tarragon vinegar
- 1/4 cup olive oil
- 1/4 cup vegetable oil
- 1/4 cup granulated sugar
- 1/2 Tbsp. yellow mustard
- 2 garlic cloves, minced
- 1 1/2 tsp. kosher salt
- 1 tsp. dried tarragon

1. Cut broccoli and cauliflower into bite-size pieces.
2. Combine broccoli, cauliflower, carrots, mushrooms, bell peppers, celery, zucchini, and cucumber in a large serving bowl; toss well.
3. Stir together vinegar, olive oil, sugar, mustard, garlic, salt, and tarragon. Pour over vegetables, and toss well. Cover and chill 8 hours or overnight.

Simple Beet Salad

ACTIVE 20 MIN. - TOTAL 2 HOURS, 5 MIN.
SERVES 6 TO 8

- 2 lb. assorted medium beets
- 1/3 cup bottled balsamic vinaigrette
- Kosher salt and black pepper
- 1/2 cup chopped walnuts, toasted
- Fresh parsley leaves, for garnish (optional)

1. Preheat oven to 400°F. Divide beets between 2 large pieces of heavy-duty aluminum foil; drizzle with vinaigrette, and sprinkle with salt and pepper to taste. Seal foil, making 2 loose packets.
2. Bake in preheated oven 45 to 55 minutes or until fork-tender. Let cool 1 hour in packets, reserving accumulated liquid.
3. Peel beets, and cut into slices or wedges. Arrange beets on a serving platter or in a bowl. Drizzle with reserved liquid, and sprinkle with walnuts. Garnish with fresh parsley, if desired.

WEDGE SALAD WITH CREAMY BLUE CHEESE DRESSING (PAGE 332)

TURNIP
GREEN SALAD
(PAGE 331)

WATERMELON SALAD
(PAGE 341)

MASHED POTATOES AND RUTABAGA WITH COLLARDS (PAGE 348)

SUMMER PASTA SALAD WITH LIME VINAIGRETTE (PAGE 340)

SHREDDED RAINBOW CHARD SALAD WITH PANCETTA & DATES (PAGE 332)

Feta-Stuffed Tomatoes

ACTIVE 15 MIN. - TOTAL 30 MIN.
SERVES 8

- 4 large tomatoes
- 4 oz. feta cheese, crumbled
- 1/4 cup fine dry breadcrumbs
- 2 Tbsp. chopped scallions
- 2 Tbsp. chopped fresh flat-leaf parsley
- 2 Tbsp. olive oil
- 1/4 tsp. kosher salt
- 1/4 tsp. black pepper
- Fresh flat-leaf parsley, for garnish (optional)

1. Preheat oven to 350°F. Cut tomatoes in half horizontally. Scoop out pulp from each tomato half, leaving shells intact; discard seeds, and coarsely chop pulp.
2. Stir together pulp, feta cheese, breadcrumbs, scallions, chopped parsley, olive oil, salt, and pepper in a bowl. Spoon mixture into tomato shells, and place in a 13- x 9-inch baking dish.
3. Bake in preheated oven 15 minutes or until tender. Garnish with parsley, if desired.

Tangy Tzatziki Pasta Salad

ACTIVE 35 MIN. - TOTAL 2 HOURS, 35 MIN.
SERVES 10

- 1 (16-oz.) container low-fat plain Greek yogurt
- 1/4 cup olive oil
- 1 Tbsp. chopped fresh dill
- 1 Tbsp. fresh lemon juice
- 1 tsp. kosher salt
- 1/2 tsp. black pepper
- 3 garlic cloves
- 1 (16-oz.) pkg. uncooked penne pasta
- 1 cup pitted Kalamata olives, sliced
- 2 cucumbers, peeled, seeded, and diced
- 3/4 cup sun-dried tomatoes in oil, drained and chopped
- 1 (9.9-oz.) jar marinated artichoke hearts, drained and chopped
- 1 1/2 cups crumbled feta cheese

1. Process yogurt, olive oil, dill, lemon juice, salt, pepper, and garlic in a food processor 30 seconds or until thoroughly blended. Transfer to a bowl, and cover and chill 1 to 24 hours.
2. Cook pasta according to package directions; drain and rinse with cold water.
3. Place cooled pasta in a large bowl. Stir in olives, cucumbers, sun-dried tomatoes, and artichokes until well blended. Add yogurt mixture, and stir just until well coated. Gently stir in feta cheese. Cover and chill 1 hour.

Summer Pasta Salad with Lime Vinaigrette

(Photo, page 338)
ACTIVE 30 MIN. - TOTAL 40 MIN., INCLUDING VINAIGRETTE
SERVES 6

- 8 oz. uncooked farfalle pasta, prepared according to pkg. directions for al dente
- 1 (1 1/2- to 2 1/2-lb.) whole cooked chicken, skin removed and meat shredded
- 1 medium zucchini (about 5 oz.), thinly sliced
- 2 small yellow squash (about 5 oz.), thinly sliced
- 2 nectarines, coarsely chopped
- 1/3 cup coarsely chopped fresh flat-leaf parsley
- Lime Vinaigrette (recipe follows)
- Kosher salt and black pepper
- 1/4 cup sliced almonds, toasted

Rinse prepared pasta with cold water, and drain well. Gently stir together pasta, chicken, zucchini, yellow squash, nectarines, parsley, and Lime Vinaigrette in a large bowl. Add salt and pepper to taste. Sprinkle salad with sliced almonds, and serve immediately.

Lime Vinaigrette

ACTIVE 10 MIN. - TOTAL 10 MIN.
MAKES ABOUT 3/4 CUP

Whisk together 1 Tbsp. **lime zest**; 2 Tbsp. fresh **lime juice**; 2 Tbsp. **white balsamic vinegar**; 1 Tbsp. **Creole mustard**; 1 1/2 tsp. **honey**; 1 small **garlic** clove, minced; and 1/2 tsp. each **kosher salt** and **black pepper** in a small bowl. Add 1/2 cup **olive oil** in a slow, steady stream, whisking mixture constantly until smooth.

Picnic Potato Salad

ACTIVE 20 MIN. - TOTAL 1 HOUR, 15 MIN.
SERVES 10 TO 12

- 4 lb. Yukon Gold potatoes
- 3 hard-cooked eggs, peeled and grated
- 1 cup mayonnaise
- 1/2 cup diced celery
- 1/2 cup sour cream
- 1/3 cup finely chopped sweet onion
- 1/4 cup sweet pickle relish
- 1 Tbsp. spicy brown mustard
- 1 tsp. kosher salt
- 3/4 tsp. black pepper
- Fresh parsley leaves, for garnish (optional)

1. Cook potatoes in boiling water to cover 40 minutes or until tender; drain and cool 15 minutes. Peel potatoes, and cut into 1-inch cubes.
2. Combine potatoes and eggs in a large bowl.
3. Stir together mayonnaise, celery, sour cream, onion relish, mustard, salt, and pepper in a small bowl; gently stir into potato mixture. Serve immediately, or cover and chill 12 hours. Garnish with fresh parsley, if desired.

Chipotle-Cilantro Slaw

ACTIVE 15 MIN. - TOTAL 15 MIN.
SERVES 6 TO 8

- 1/4 cup mayonnaise
- 1 Tbsp. granulated sugar
- 2 Tbsp. sour cream
- 1 tsp. lime zest plus 2 Tbsp. fresh juice (from 1 lime)
- 2 tsp. red wine vinegar
- 1/2 tsp. kosher salt
- 1/2 tsp. black pepper
- 1 (16-oz.) pkg. shredded coleslaw mix
- 1 carrot, shredded
- 2 canned chipotle chile peppers in adobo sauce, finely chopped
- 1/2 cup chopped fresh cilantro

Whisk together mayonnaise, sugar, sour cream, lime zest and juice, vinegar, salt, and black pepper in a large bowl. Add coleslaw mix, carrot, chipotle chiles, and cilantro, and stir until well combined. Serve immediately, or cover and chill up to 1 hour.

Watermelon Salad

(Photo, page 336)

ACTIVE 20 MIN. - TOTAL 25 MIN.

SERVES 6

- 8 cups seedless watermelon, cut into 1-inch cubes (from 1 watermelon)
- 3 lb. heirloom tomatoes, cored and cut into 1-inch wedges
- 1 tsp. kosher salt
- 4 cups arugula (4 oz.)
- 2 satsumas (4 oz. each), peeled and cut into segments
- 5 Tbsp. extra-virgin olive oil, divided
- 2 Tbsp. chopped fresh mint
- 1½ Tbsp. red wine vinegar
- ½ tsp. black pepper
- 2 oz. goat cheese, crumbled (about ½ cup)
- ½ cup chopped pecans, toasted

1. Combine watermelon and tomatoes in a large bowl. Sprinkle with salt, and toss gently to combine; let stand 10 minutes.
2. Combine arugula, satsumas, and 1 tablespoon oil in a medium bowl, tossing to coat. Add to watermelon mixture, and toss gently to coat. Whisk together mint, vinegar, pepper, and remaining 4 tablespoons oil in a small bowl. Drizzle over watermelon mixture. Sprinkle with goat cheese and toasted pecans, and serve.

Summer Fruit Salad

ACTIVE 20 MIN. - TOTAL 20 MIN.

SERVES 8 TO 10

- ½ cup bottled poppy-seed dressing
- 2 tsp. grated fresh ginger
- 2 avocados, thinly sliced
- 4 cups loosely packed arugula
- 2 cups halved seedless green grapes
- 1 mango, julienned
- 1 cup sliced fresh strawberries
- ¼ cup thinly sliced green onions
- ¼ cup fresh cilantro leaves

Whisk together dressing and grated ginger in a large bowl. Cut avocado slices in half crosswise; gently toss with dressing mixture. Add arugula, grapes, mango, strawberries, green onions, and cilantro; gently toss to coat. Serve immediately.

SUNSHINE FRUIT SALAD

Sunshine Fruit Salad

ACTIVE 25 MIN. - TOTAL 25 MIN.

SERVES 6

- 1 cup orange sections (from about 3 oranges)
- 1 cup grapefruit sections (from about 2 grapefruits)
- ½ cup pomegranate arils
- 4 kiwifruits, peeled and sliced
- 1 (4-lb.) pineapple, peeled and cut into 1-inch cubes
- 1 tsp. lemon zest plus 1 Tbsp. fresh juice (from 1 lemon)
- 1 Tbsp. fresh orange juice
- ½ cup sliced almonds, toasted and divided
- Greek yogurt (optional)

1. Combine orange sections, grapefruit sections, pomegranate arils, kiwi, and pineapple in a medium bowl. Combine lemon zest and citrus juices in a small bowl. Gently stir lemon mixture into fruit; cover and chill.
2. Just before serving, stir ¼ cup almonds into the fruit mixture. Serve with a dollop of yogurt, if desired, and sprinkle remaining almonds on each serving.

Best Waldorf Salad

ACTIVE 15 MIN. - TOTAL 15 MIN.

SERVES 6 TO 8

- 2 large Gala apples, diced
- 1 large Granny Smith apple, diced
- 1½ cups halved seedless green grapes
- ½ cup coarsely chopped pecans
- ½ cup diced celery
- ⅓ cup raisins
- ⅓ cup mayonnaise

Stir together Gala apples, Granny Smith apple, grapes, pecans, celery, raisins, and mayonnaise.

Vegetables & Breads

Blistered Brussels Sprouts

ACTIVE 15 MIN. - TOTAL 15 MIN.
SERVES 4

Heat a 12-inch cast-iron skillet over medium-high 5 minutes. Trim 1 lb. fresh **Brussels sprouts,** and cut in half lengthwise. Add 3 Tbsp. **canola oil** to skillet, and tilt skillet to coat bottom evenly. Place Brussels sprouts, cut side down, in a single layer in skillet. Cook, without stirring, 4 minutes or until browned. Sprinkle with ¾ tsp. **kosher salt**; stir and cook 2 more minutes. Stir together 1 Tbsp. **honey** and 1 Tbsp. hot water. Stir 2 cloves minced **garlic**, 1 Tbsp. **soy sauce**, ¼ tsp. **crushed red pepper**, and honey mixture into Brussels sprouts. Stir in ½ cup torn **fresh mint leaves**, and serve immediately.

Brussels Sprouts with Crunchy Croutons

ACTIVE 5 MIN. - TOTAL 40 MIN.
SERVES 8 TO 10

- 2 lb. Brussels sprouts, trimmed and halved
- 1½ Tbsp. olive oil
- 1 tsp. kosher salt
- ¼ tsp. black pepper
- 2 cups cubed day-old French bread (½-inch cubes)
- ¼ cup salted butter
- 1 shallot, minced
- 1 Tbsp. fresh thyme leaves

1. Preheat oven to 425°F. Toss together Brussels sprouts, olive oil, salt, and pepper in a large bowl; divide evenly between 2 rimmed baking sheets. Bake until golden brown, about 20 minutes. Reduce oven heat to 350°F.
2. Spread bread cubes evenly on a baking sheet; bake at 350°F until browned and crispy, about 15 minutes.
3. Cook butter, stirring constantly, in a medium skillet over medium until foaming. Add shallot and thyme; cook, stirring often, 1 minute. Drizzle butter mixture over toasted bread. Arrange sprouts in a serving dish; top with crouton mixture.

Fresh Green Beans Amandine

ACTIVE 20 MIN. - TOTAL 45 MIN.
SERVES 4 TO 6

- 2 lb. fresh green beans, rinsed, trimmed, strings removed and cut in half diagonally
- 4 thick hickory-smoked bacon slices, cooked and crumbled
- 2 Tbsp. butter
- ⅓ cup finely chopped onion
- ½ tsp. kosher salt
- ⅔ cup slivered almonds, toasted

1. Place beans in a 5-qt. Dutch oven; add bacon and 1 cup water. Bring to a boil over medium-high; cover, reduce heat, and simmer 15 minutes. Drain.
2. Melt butter in a medium skillet over medium. Add onion; sauté over medium-high 3 minutes or until tender. Add salt and toss well to coat.
3. Add almonds to skillet; toss well to combine. Serve immediately.

Fried Okra

ACTIVE 10 MIN. - TOTAL 55 MIN.
SERVES 8 TO 10

- 2 lb. fresh okra
- ¾ cup kosher salt
- 2 cups plain yellow or white cornmeal
- Canola oil

1. Cut off and discard tip and stem ends of okra; cut okra crosswise into ½-inch-thick slices. Place in a large bowl.
2. Combine 3 qt. water and the salt; pour over okra. Soak 30 minutes; drain, rinse well, and drain again. Dredge okra, in batches, in cornmeal.
3. Pour oil to a depth of 2 inches into a Dutch oven; heat to 375°F. Fry okra, in batches, 4 minutes or until golden. Drain on paper towels. Serve immediately.

Fried Green Tomatoes

ACTIVE 15 MIN. - TOTAL 15 MIN., PLUS 6 MIN. PER BATCH COOK TIME
SERVES 4 TO 6

- 4 large green tomatoes
- 1½ cups buttermilk
- 1 Tbsp. kosher salt
- 1 tsp. black pepper
- 1 cup all-purpose flour
- 1 cup self-rising cornmeal
- 3 cups vegetable oil
- Kosher salt

1. Cut tomatoes into ¼- to ⅓-inch-thick slices; place in a shallow dish. Pour buttermilk over tomatoes. Sprinkle with salt and pepper.
2. Combine flour and cornmeal in a shallow dish or pie plate. Dredge tomato slices in flour mixture.
3. Fry tomatoes, in batches, in hot oil in a large cast-iron skillet over medium 3 minutes on each side or until golden. Drain tomatoes on paper towels. Sprinkle with additional salt to taste. Serve immediately.

Old-Fashioned Succotash

(Photo, page 344)
ACTIVE 35 MIN. - TOTAL 1 HOUR
SERVES 6

- 2 cups fresh lima beans
- 4 fresh thyme sprigs
- ½ small onion
- 1 garlic clove
- 1½ cups diced sweet onion
- 2 Tbsp. olive oil
- 4 cups fresh corn kernels (about 6 ears)
- 1 tsp. honey
- 2 Tbsp. unsalted butter
- Kosher salt and black pepper
- 3 Tbsp. chopped fresh chives

1. Place lima beans, thyme sprigs, onion half, and garlic in a medium saucepan, and cover with water. Bring mixture to a boil over medium-high; reduce heat to medium, and simmer, stirring occasionally, 20 minutes or until beans are tender. Drain beans, reserving ½ cup cooking liquid. Discard thyme sprigs, onion, and garlic.

2. Sauté diced sweet onion in hot oil in a large skillet over medium-high 5 minutes. Stir in corn and honey; cook, stirring often, 6 minutes or until corn is tender. Stir in beans and ½ cup reserved cooking liquid; cook, stirring occasionally, 5 minutes. Stir in butter, and add salt and pepper to taste. Sprinkle with chives.

Southern-Style Creamed Corn

ACTIVE 15 MIN. - TOTAL 30 MIN.
SERVES 4 TO 6

- 6 ears fresh corn, husks removed
- ¼ cup butter
- ½ cup half-and-half or whole milk
- 2 tsp. cornstarch
- ½ tsp. kosher salt
- ¼ tsp. black pepper

1. Cut tips of corn kernels into a large bowl; scrape milk and remaining pulp from cobs into bowl.*
2. Combine corn, butter, and ¼ cup water in a large skillet or saucepan. Cover and cook over medium, stirring occasionally, 10 minutes.
3. Combine half-and-half, cornstarch, salt, and pepper in a small bowl, whisking until blended. Gradually add cream mixture to corn, stirring well. Cover and cook 3 minutes or until thickened, stirring often.
***Note:** Puree half of the corn for even creamier results.

Creamed Greens

ACTIVE 1 HOUR, 10 MIN. - TOTAL 1 HOUR, 30 MIN., INCLUDING SAUCE
SERVES 8 TO 10

- 4½ lb. fresh Lacinato kale*
- 1 lb. bacon slices, chopped
- ¼ cup butter
- 2 large onions, diced
- 3 cups chicken broth
- ½ cup apple cider vinegar
- 1 tsp. kosher salt
- ½ tsp. black pepper
- Béchamel Sauce (recipe follows)

1. Rinse greens. Trim and discard thick stems from bottom of kale leaves (about 2 inches); coarsely chop kale.
2. Cook bacon, in batches, in an 8-qt. stockpot over medium 10 to 12 minutes or until crisp. Remove bacon, and drain on paper towels, reserving drippings in stockpot. Reserve ¼ cup cooked bacon.
3. Add butter and onions to hot drippings in stockpot. Cook onions, stirring often, 8 minutes or until tender. Add kale, in batches, and cook, stirring occasionally, 5 minutes or until wilted. Stir in chicken broth, vinegar, salt, and pepper. Add remaining bacon.
4. Bring to a boil. Reduce heat to low, and cook, stirring occasionally, 15 minutes or to desired degree of tenderness. Drain kale, reserving 1 cup liquid.
5. Stir in Béchamel Sauce. Stir in reserved cooking liquid, ¼ cup at a time, to desired consistency. Transfer to a serving dish, and sprinkle with reserved ¼ cup bacon.
***Note:** 2 (1-lb.) packages fresh kale, trimmed and chopped, may be substituted.

Béchamel Sauce

ACTIVE 15 MIN. - TOTAL 15 MIN.
MAKES ABOUT 4½ CUPS

- ½ cup butter
- 2 medium shallots, minced
- 2 garlic cloves, minced
- ¾ cup all-purpose flour
- 4 cups whole milk
- ½ tsp. kosher salt
- ½ tsp. black pepper
- ¼ tsp. ground nutmeg

1. Melt butter in a heavy saucepan over low; add shallots and garlic, and cook 1 minute. Whisk in flour until smooth. Cook, whisking constantly, 1 minute.
2. Increase heat to medium. Gradually whisk in milk; cook, whisking constantly, 5 to 7 minutes or until sauce mixture is thickened and bubbly. Stir in salt, pepper, and nutmeg.
Note: Sauce can be made ahead and stored in an airtight container in the refrigerator up to 2 days; warm over low before using.

Creamed Spinach

ACTIVE 35 MIN. - TOTAL 45 MIN.
SERVES 4

- 2 cups heavy whipping cream
- ½ cup butter
- ⅔ cup grated Parmesan cheese
- ½ tsp. kosher salt
- ½ tsp. freshly grated nutmeg
- ½ tsp. black pepper
- 2 (9-oz.) pkg. fresh spinach, thinly sliced
- Hot cooked grits (optional)
- ¼ cup pine nuts, toasted

1. Combine whipping cream and butter in a large saucepan. Bring to a boil over medium-high; reduce heat to medium, and cook, stirring often, 15 minutes or until thickened.
2. Stir in cheese, salt, nutmeg, and pepper. Add spinach; cook over low, stirring often, 3 minutes or until spinach has wilted. Serve over grits, if desired; sprinkle with pine nuts.

Radishes in Warm Herb Butter

ACTIVE 10 MIN. - TOTAL 15 MIN.
SERVES 8

- 1 tsp. fennel seeds
- 5 Tbsp. cold unsalted butter, diced, divided
- 1 garlic clove, finely grated
- 1¾ lb. assorted radishes, trimmed and quartered (about 4 cups)
- 2 Tbsp. thinly sliced fresh chives
- 2 Tbsp. finely chopped fresh basil
- 1½ tsp. coarse grey sea salt
- ¼ tsp. black pepper

Crush fennel seeds with a rolling pin or heavy skillet. Heat 1 tablespoon butter in a large, deep skillet over medium until melted. Stir in crushed fennel seeds and grated garlic cook, stirring often, until fragrant, about 1 minute. Stir in radishes; cook, stirring constantly, until radishes are warmed through, 2 to 3 minutes. Remove from heat. Add chives, basil, and remaining 4 tablespoons butter; stir until butter is melted. Sprinkle with salt and pepper.

OLD-FASHIONED
SUCCOTASH
(PAGE 342)

TWICE-BAKED POTATOES (PAGE 348)

BUTTERNUT SQUASH SPOONBREAD (PAGE 349)

CHEDDAR-CARAMELIZED ONION BREAD WITH WH PPED SWEET POTATO BUTTER (PAGE 350)

Twice-Baked Potatoes

(Photo, page 345)

ACTIVE 30 MIN. - TOTAL 1 HOUR, 45 MIN.

SERVES 16

- 8 medium baking potatoes (about 4 lb.)
- Canola oil
- ½ cup butter, cut into slices
- 1 (8-oz.) container sour cream
- 8 thick-cut apple-smoked bacon slices, cooked and crumbled
- ½ cup whole milk
- ½ tsp. seasoned salt
- ½ tsp. black pepper
- 4 oz. white Cheddar cheese, grated (about 1 cup)
- ¼ cup sliced fresh chives, plus additional for garnish
- 4 oz. blue cheese, crumbled (about 1 cup)

1. Preheat oven to 400°F. Rub potatoes with oil. Bake on a baking sheet 45 to 50 minutes or until potatoes are tender and skins are crisp.
2. Meanwhile, stir together butter, sour cream, bacon, milk, salt, and pepper in a large bowl.
3. Remove potatoes from oven, and let cool 15 minutes. Reduce oven temperature to 300°F. Cut warm potatoes in half lengthwise, and carefully scoop out pulp into bowl with butter mixture, leaving potato shells intact.
4. Mash pulp and butter mixture together using a potato masher. Stir in Cheddar cheese, chives, ½ cup blue cheese, and additional seasoned salt and black pepper to taste. Spoon mixture into potato shells; place on baking sheet. Sprinkle with remaining ½ cup blue cheese.
5. Bake at 300°F until cheese is melted and potatoes are thoroughly heated, 15 to 20 minutes. Garnish with additional fresh chives.

Cheesy Scalloped Potatoes

ACTIVE 25 MIN. - TOTAL 1 HOUR, 10 MIN.

SERVES 8

- 3 Tbsp. butter
- ⅓ cup chopped scallions
- ⅓ cup chopped red bell pepper
- 1 garlic clove, minced
- ¼ tsp. cayenne pepper
- 2 cups heavy whipping cream
- ¾ cup whole milk
- ¾ tsp. kosher salt
- ¼ tsp. black pepper
- 2½ lb. red potatoes, peeled and cut into ⅛-inch-thick slices
- 1 cup shredded Swiss cheese (4 oz.)
- ¼ cup freshly grated Parmesan cheese (1 oz.)

1. Preheat oven to 350°F. Lightly grease an 11- x 7-inch baking dish.
2. Melt butter in a Dutch oven over medium-high; add scallions, bell pepper, garlic, and cayenne. Cook, stirring constantly, 2 minutes. Stir in whipping cream, milk, salt, and black pepper.
3. Add potato slices; bring to a boil over medium, and cook, stirring gently, 10 minutes or until potato slices are tender. Spoon potatoes and sauce into prepared dish; sprinkle with Swiss and Parmesan cheeses.
4. Bake in preheated oven 25 minutes or until bubbly and golden. Let stand 15 minutes before serving.

Mashed Potatoes and Rutabaga with Collards

(Photo, page 337)

ACTIVE 30 MIN. - TOTAL 50 MIN.

SERVES 12

- 2 lb. Yukon Gold potatoes, peeled and cut into 1-inch pieces (about 5 cups)
- 3 cups chopped (½-inch pieces) peeled rutabaga (from 1 [1½-lb.] rutabaga)
- 1 Tbsp. plus 1¼ tsp. kosher salt, divided
- ½ cup unsalted butter, cut into 1-Tbsp. pats, softened, divided
- 1 cup chopped scallions (white and light green parts only, from 1 [6-oz.] bunch)
- 6 cups coarsely chopped stemmed collard greens (from 1 [1-lb.] bunch)
- 1 cup whole milk, warmed
- 4 oz. white Cheddar cheese, shredded (about 1 cup)

1. Place potatoes and rutabaga in a large Dutch oven or heavy-bottomed saucepan, and cover with 9 cups cool water. Stir in 1 tablespoon salt. Bring mixture to a boil over high. Reduce heat to medium-high, and simmer until vegetables are very tender, about 20 minutes. Remove from heat. Drain; return cooked vegetables to Dutch oven. Let stand 5 minutes or until they are dry and have a slightly chalky appearance.
2. Meanwhile, heat 3 tablespoons butter in a large skillet over medium until foamy. Add chopped scallions. Cook, stirring often, until scallion greens are slightly wilted, about 1 minute. Add collards and ½ teaspoon salt. Cover; cook, stirring occasionally, until collards are just tender-crisp, 7 to 8 minutes. Remove skillet from heat.
3. Add warm milk, 2 tablespoons butter, and remaining ¾ teaspoon salt to drained potato-rutabaga mixture. Mash to desired consistency using a potato masher. Stir in cheese and collard mixture until cheese is melted. Spoon into a serving bowl; top with remaining 3 tablespoons butter.

Goat Cheese Grits

ACTIVE 10 MIN. - TOTAL 30 MIN.

SERVES 8

- 9 cups low-sodium chicken broth
- 3 cups uncooked quick-cooking grits
- 8 oz. soft goat cheese, crumbled (about 2 cups)
- 8 scallions, white and light green parts only, chopped (about 1 cup)
- Kosher salt (optional)
- Chopped fresh flat-leaf parsley
- Crushed red pepper

In a medium saucepan, bring chicken broth to a boil over high. Gradually whisk in grits; reduce heat to low, and cook, whisking, until very thick, 4 to 5 minutes. Whisk in cheese and scallions until well combined. Taste and season with salt, if desired. Remove from heat, and cover to keep warm. Top with chopped parsley and crushed red pepper to serve.

Baked Cheese Grits

ACTIVE 10 MIN. - TOTAL 1 HOUR, 20 MIN.
SERVES 6 TO 8

- 1 tsp. kosher salt
- 1½ cups uncooked regular grits
- ½ cup butter, cut up
- 4 cups shredded sharp Cheddar cheese (16 oz.)
- 3 large eggs, lightly beaten
- Smoked paprika (optional)

1. Preheat oven to 350°F. Lightly grease a 2½-qt. baking dish.
2. Bring salt and 6 cups water to a boil. Stir in grits, and reduce heat to low. Cover and cook, stirring occasionally, 15 to 20 minutes or until thickened. Remove from heat.
3. Add butter and cheese, stirring until blended. Gradually stir about one-fourth of hot grits into eggs; add egg mixture to remaining hot grits, stirring constantly. Pour grits into prepared baking dish.
4. Bake in preheated oven 45 minutes or until slightly firm. Sprinkle with paprika, if desired.

Butternut Squash Spoonbread

(Photo, page 346)
ACTIVE 25 MIN. - TOTAL 1 HOUR, 10 MIN.
SERVES 8

- 2 cups buttermilk
- 4 large eggs, separated
- 2 cups thawed, frozen unseasoned, pureed butternut squash
- 1½ oz. Parmesan cheese, freshly grated (about ⅓ cup)
- 1 cup stoneground white cornmeal
- 1 tsp. baking powder
- 1 tsp. chopped fresh rosemary, plus more for garnish
- ½ tsp. baking soda
- ½ tsp. kosher salt
- ¼ cup butter, melted

1. Preheat oven to 350°F. Cook buttermilk in a heavy saucepan over medium-high, stirring often, 4 to 6 minutes or until bubbles appear around edges (do not boil); remove from heat. (Mixture may curdle.)
2. Lightly beat egg yolks in a large bowl; stir in squash and cheese. Combine cornmeal, baking powder, rosemary, baking soda, and salt in a small bowl. Stir cornmeal mixture into squash mixture. Pour warm buttermilk over squash mixture; whisk until smooth. Let stand 15 minutes or until lukewarm.
3. Brush a 2½- to 3-qt. baking dish or 12-inch cast-iron skillet with 1 Tbsp. melted butter; stir remaining melted butter into squash mixture.
4. Beat egg whites with an electric mixer on high speed until stiff peaks form. Carefully fold into squash mixture. Pour mixture into prepared baking dish.
5. Bake in preheated oven 30 to 35 minutes or until top is golden and a wooden pick inserted in center comes out clean. Garnish with additional rosemary.

Pecan-Herb Cornbread Dressing

ACTIVE 40 MIN. - TOTAL 3 HOURS
SERVES 15

CORNBREAD

- 2 cups self-rising white cornmeal mix
- 1 tsp. granulated sugar (optional)
- 2 large eggs
- 2 cups buttermilk
- 3 Tbsp. butter

DRESSING

- ½ cup butter
- 2 large sweet onions, chopped (3 cups)
- 6 stalks celery, chopped (2 cups)
- 2 Tbsp. chopped fresh sage
- 2 tsp. chopped fresh thyme
- 2 tsp. chopped fresh rosemary
- 6 large eggs
- 1 (14-oz.) pkg. herb-seasoned stuffing mix
- 1½ cups chopped toasted pecans
- ½ cup chopped fresh flat-leaf parsley
- 10 cups chicken broth
- 2 tsp. black pepper
- 1 tsp. kosher salt
- Fresh herb leaves (such as sage, thyme, and rosemary)

1. Prepare the Cornbread: Preheat oven to 425°F. Combine self-rising cornmeal mix and, if desired, sugar in a large bowl. Stir together eggs and buttermilk in a medium bowl; add to cornmeal mixture, stirring just until moistened.
2. Place butter in a 10-inch cast-iron skillet; place skillet in the oven for 5 minutes. Stir melted butter into batter. Pour batter into hot skillet.
3. Bake in preheated oven until cornbread is golden, about 25 minutes; cool in skillet 20 minutes. Remove from skillet to a wire rack, and cool completely, 20 to 30 more minutes. Crumble cornbread. Reduce oven heat to 350°F. (If desired, freeze cornbread in a large heavy-duty zip-top plastic bag up to 1 month. Thaw in refrigerator.)
4. Prepare the Dressing: Melt butter in a large skillet over medium-high; add onion and celery, and cook, stirring often, until tender, 10 to 12 minutes. Add chopped sage, thyme, and rosemary, and cook, stirring often, 1 minute.
5. Stir together eggs in a very large bowl; stir in crumbled cornbread, onion mixture, stuffing mix, pecans, parsley, chicken broth, black pepper, and kosher salt until blended.
6. Spoon mixture into 2 lightly greased 13- x 9-inch (3-qt.) baking dishes. Cover and freeze up to 3 months, if desired; thaw in refrigerator 24 hours. (Uncover and let stand at room temperature 30 minutes before baking.)
7. Bake, uncovered, until lightly browned and cooked through, 1 hour to 1 hour and 15 minutes. Garnish with fresh herb leaves.

Spicy Cheese Twists

ACTIVE 20 MIN. - TOTAL 55 MIN.
SERVES 12

- 6 oz. aged Gouda cheese, grated (about 1 cup)
- 1 Tbsp. fresh thyme leaves
- ½ (17.3-oz.) pkg. frozen puff pastry sheets (1 sheet), thawed
- All-purpose flour, for work surface
- 1 large egg, beaten
- ½ tsp. kosher salt
- ½ tsp. garlic powder
- ½ tsp. cayenne pepper

1. Preheat oven to 425°F. Line 2 baking sheets with parchment paper, and set aside. Mix together Gouda and thyme in a small bowl.
2. Roll puff pastry sheet into a 14-inch square on a lightly floured work surface. Thoroughly prick all over with a fork. Whisk together egg and 1 tablespoon water in a small bowl. Brush pastry lightly with egg mixture. Sprinkle evenly with salt, garlic powder, and cayenne pepper. Cut pastry in half

Continued on page 350

Continued from page 349

lengthwise to form 2 (14- x 7-inch) rectangles. Spread about ¾ cup of the Gouda mixture evenly over one of the rectangles, and press with palms of hands to bind cheese to pastry. Place remaining pastry sheet, egg wash side up, directly onto pastry sheet with cheese. Sprinkle remaining ⅓ cup Gouda mixture evenly over top pastry, pressing with palms of hands to bind cheese to pastry. (Alternatively, gently roll a rolling pin over both sheets to bind cheese.) Cut pastry stack lengthwise into 2 (14- x 3½-inch) rectangles. Cut each rectangle into 12 (about 3½- x 1-inch) strips.

3. Working with 1 strip at a time, twist the ends in opposite directions so that each end is cheese side up, resembling a bow tie. Arrange twists on prepared baking sheets, at least ½ inch apart. Press ends down gently to adhere to parchment. Pinch middle of each strip with fingers to create center of twist. Bake in preheated oven, 1 baking sheet at a time, until crispy and golden brown, about 12 to 16 minutes. Cool on baking sheet at least 5 minutes. Serve warm or at room temperature.

Cheesy Bread with Herbs

ACTIVE 10 MIN. - TOTAL 20 MIN.
SERVES 6

- Cooking spray
- 8 day-old rolls
- ⅓ cup butter, melted
- 3 garlic cloves, minced
- 1 Tbsp. chopped fresh flat-leaf parsley
- ½ tsp. crushed red pepper
- 1½ oz. mozzarella cheese, shredded (about ⅓ cup)
- 1 oz. Parmesan cheese, grated (about ¼ cup)

1. Preheat oven to 350°F. Lightly coat an 8- x 4-inch loaf pan with cooking spray.
2. Cut an X in the top of each roll, and arrange them cut-side up in the loaf pan.
3. Mix together butter, garlic, parsley, and red pepper flakes, and drizzle the mixture over slits in rolls. Sprinkle mozzarella and Parmesan evenly over surface. Cover with foil. Bake in preheated oven 15 minutes. Remove foil, and bake 5 minutes more or until cheese is melted and tops of rolls are lightly browned. Serve immediately.

Cheddar-Caramelized Onion Bread

(Photo, page 347)
ACTIVE 35 MIN. - TOTAL 1 HOUR, 30 MIN.
SERVES 8

- ½ cup plus 2 Tbsp. unsalted butter, divided
- 2 tsp. caraway seeds
- 1 Tbsp. extra-virgin olive oil
- 1 large red onion, thinly sliced
- 1 tsp. kosher salt, divided
- 1 cup almond flour
- 1 cup all-purpose flour
- 1 tsp. baking powder
- ¼ tsp. baking soda
- ½ cup heavy whipping cream
- 1 large egg
- 2 tsp. honey
- 4 oz. Cheddar cheese, shredded (about 1 cup)
- Whipped Sweet Potato Butter (recipe follows)
- Chopped fresh thyme (optional)

1. Place ½ cup butter in freezer until solid, at least 30 minutes.
2. Preheat oven to 350°F. Heat a medium skillet over medium. Add caraway seeds, and cook, stirring constantly, until lightly toasted, about 1 minute. Remove seeds from skillet, and set aside.
3. Add oil to skillet, and heat over medium-high. Add onion, and cook, stirring often, until starting to soften, about 3 minutes. Reduce heat to medium-low, and cook, stirring occasionally, until tender and browned, about 15 minutes. Season with ¼ teaspoon salt. Remove onion from skillet, and let cool 10 minutes.
4. Place a 9-inch cast-iron skillet in preheated oven. Stir together almond flour, all-purpose flour, baking powder, baking soda, ½ teaspoon salt, and toasted caraway seeds in a medium bowl. Whisk together cream, egg, and honey in a separate bowl.
5. Remove butter from freezer. Using the large holes on a box grater, grate frozen butter into coarse shreds. Add shredded butter to flour mixture, stirring to combine. Add cream mixture, cheese, and caramelized onion to flour mixture; stir just until dough comes together. Turn dough out onto a lightly floured surface; pat into an 8-inch circle. Add remaining 2 tablespoons butter to hot cast-iron skillet, swirling to melt. Gently place dough in skillet; sprinkle with remaining ¼ teaspoon salt.
6. Bake bread in preheated oven until sides and top are golden brown, 20 to 25 minutes. Remove from oven, and let cool in skillet 5 minutes. Remove bread from skillet, and place on a wire rack to cool to room temperature, about 30 minutes. Serve with Whipped Sweet Potato Butter, and sprinkle with thyme, if desired.

Whipped Sweet Potato Butter

ACTIVE 15 MIN. - TOTAL 1 HOUR, 5 MIN.
SERVES 20

- 1 lb. sweet potatoes, peeled and cut into 2-inch chunks
- 2 tsp. white vinegar
- 2½ tsp. kosher salt, divided
- 1 cup unsalted butter, softened
- ¼ cup honey
- ¾ tsp. ground cinnamon
- ¼ tsp. black pepper

1. Place potatoes in a medium saucepan, and cover with cold water by 1 inch. Add vinegar and 2 teaspoons salt. Bring to a boil over high. Reduce heat to medium, and cook until tender, about 20 minutes.
2. Drain potatoes, and transfer to a large bowl; cool completely, about 20 minutes. Add butter, honey, cinnamon, pepper, and remaining ½ teaspoon salt to potatoes. Beat with an electric mixer or process in a mini food processor until smooth, about 45 seconds. Chill until ready to serve.

Baking at High Altitudes

Liquids boil at lower temperatures (below 212°F) and moisture evaporates more quickly at high altitudes. Both of these factors significantly impact the quality of baked goods. Also, leavening gases (air, carbon dioxide, water vapor) expand faster. If you live at 3,000 feet or below, first try a recipe as is. Sometimes few, if any, changes are needed. But the higher you go, the more you'll have to adjust your ingredients and cooking times.

A Few Overall Tips

- Use shiny new baking pans. This seems to help mixtures rise, especially cake batters.
- Use butter, flour, and parchment paper to prep your baking pans for nonstick cooking. At high altitudes, baked goods tend to stick more to pans.
- Be exact in your measurements (once you've figured out what they should be). This is always important in baking, but especially so when you're up so high. Tiny variations in ingredients make a bigger difference at high altitudes than at sea level.
- Boost flavor. Seasonings and extracts tend to be more muted at higher altitudes, so increase them slightly.
- Have patience. You may have to bake your favorite sea-level recipe a few times, making slight adjustments each time, until it's worked out to suit your particular altitude.

Ingredient/Temperature Adjustments

CHANGE	AT 3,000 FEET	AT 5,000 FEET	AT 7,000 FEET
Baking powder or baking soda	Reduce each tsp. called for by up to ⅛ tsp.	Reduce each tsp. called for by ⅛ to ¼ tsp.	Reduce each tsp. called for by ¼ to ½ tsp.
Sugar	Reduce each cup called for by up to 1 Tbsp.	Reduce each cup called for by up to 2 Tbsp.	Reduce each cup called for by 2 to 3 Tbsp.
Liquid	Increase each cup called for by up to 2 Tbsp.	Increase each cup called for by 2 to 4 Tbsp.	Increase each cup called for by to 3 to 4 Tbsp.
Oven temperature	Increase 3°F to 5°F	Increase 15°F	Increase 21°F to 25°F

Metric Equivalents

The recipes that appear in this cookbook use the standard United States method for measuring liquid and dry or solid ingredients (teaspoons, tablespoons, and cups). The information on this chart is provided to help cooks outside the U.S. successfully use these recipes. All equivalents are approximate.

METRIC EQUIVALENTS FOR DIFFERENT TYPES OF INGREDIENTS

A standard cup measure of a dry or solid ingredient will vary in weight depending on the type of ingredient. A standard cup of liquid is the same volume for any type of liquid. Use the following chart when converting standard cup measures to grams (weight) or milliliters (volume).

Standard Cup	Fine Powder (ex. flour)	Grain (ex. rice)	Granular (ex. sugar)	Liquid Solids (ex. butter)	Liquid (ex. milk)
1	140 g	150 g	190 g	200 g	240 ml
3/4	105 g	113 g	143 g	150 g	180 ml
2/3	93 g	100 g	125 g	133 g	160 ml
1/2	70 g	75 g	95 g	100 g	120 ml
1/3	47 g	50 g	63 g	67 g	80 ml
1/4	35 g	38 g	48 g	50 g	60 ml
1/8	18 g	19 g	24 g	25 g	30 ml

USEFUL EQUIVALENTS FOR LIQUID INGREDIENTS BY VOLUME

1/4 tsp.								=	1 ml		
1/2 tsp.								=	2 ml		
1 tsp.								=	5 ml		
3 tsp.	=	1 Tbsp.			=	1/2 fl oz.		=	15 ml		
		2 Tbsp.	=	1/8 cup	=	1 fl oz.		=	30 ml		
		4 Tbsp.	=	1/4 cup	=	2 fl oz.		=	60 ml		
		5 1/3 Tbsp.	=	1/3 cup	=	3 fl oz.		=	80 ml		
		8 Tbsp.	=	1/2 cup	=	4 fl oz.		=	120 ml		
		10 2/3 Tbsp.	=	2/3 cup	=	5 fl oz.		=	160 ml		
		12 Tbsp.	=	3/4 cup	=	6 fl oz.		=	180 ml		
		16 Tbsp.	=	1 cup	=	8 fl oz.		=	240 ml		
		1 pt.	=	2 cups	=	16 fl oz.		=	480 ml		
		1 qt.	=	4 cups	=	32 fl oz.		=	960 ml		
						33 fl oz.		=	1000 ml	=	1l

USEFUL EQUIVALENTS FOR DRY INGREDIENTS BY WEIGHT

(To convert ounces to grams, multiply the number of ounces by 30.)

1 oz.	=	1/16 lb.	=	30 g
4 oz.	=	1/4 lb.	=	120 g
8 oz.	=	1/2 lb.	=	240 g
12 oz.	=	3/4 lb.	=	360 g
16 oz.	=	1 lb.	=	480 g

USEFUL EQUIVALENTS FOR LENGTH

(To convert inches to centimeters, multiply the number of inches by 2.5.)

1 in.					=	2.5 cm
6 in.	=	1/2 ft.			=	15 cm
12 in.	=	1 ft.			=	30 cm
36 in.	=	3 ft.	=	1 yd.	=	90 cm

USEFUL EQUIVALENTS FOR COOKING/OVEN TEMPERATURES

	Fahrenheit	Celsius	Gas Mark
Freeze Water	32°F	0°C	
Room Temperature	68°F	20°C	
Boil Water	212°F	100°C	
Bake	325°F	160°C	3
	350°F	180°C	4
	375°F	190°C	5
	400°F	200°C	6
	425°F	220°C	7
	450°F	230°C	8
Broil			Grill

Recipe Title Index

This index alphabetically lists every recipe by exact title.

G

H

I

K

L

M

N

O

P

Q

R

S

P

BOOKS CONSUMER MARKETING
Director, Direct Marketing-Books: Daniel Fagan
Marketing Operations Manager: Max Daily
Marketing Manager: Kylie Dazzo
Senior Marketing Coordinator: Elizabeth Niwamanya
Content Manager: Julie Doll
Senior Production Manager: Liza Ward

WATERBURY PUBLICATIONS, INC.
Editorial Director: Lisa Kingsley
Creative Director: Ken Carlson
Associate Design Director: Doug Samuelson
Contributing Copy Editor: Russell Santana, E4 Editorial Services
Contributing Proofreader: Carrie Truesdell
Contributing Indexer: Mary Williams

Recipe Developers and Testers: People Inc. Food Studios

Library of Congress Control Number: A Library of Congress Control Number has been applied for.

ISBN: 978-1-4197-8812-3

First Edition 2025
Printed in Canada.
10 9 8 7 6 5 4 3 2 1
Call 1-800-826-4707 for more information.

Distributed in 2025 by Abrams, an imprint of ABRAMS.
Abrams® is a registered trademark of Harry N. Abrams, Inc.

Pictured on front cover:
Holiday Mahogany Cake, page 291

Southern Living
DESSERT
OVER 200 OF OUR BEST RECIPES FOR CAKES, PIES, COOKIES, AND MORE
Southern Living
ONE-POT
RECIPES
2025
CHRISTMAS
with Southern Living
INSPIRED IDEAS
FOR HOLIDAY
COOKING AND
DECORATING